THE

SAGA

OF

WALTHER OF AQUITAINE

BY

MARION DEXTER LEARNED, Ph.D.

ASSOCIATE IN GERMAN AT THE JOHNS HOPKINS UNIVERSITY.

GREENWOOD PRESS, PUBLISHERS
WESTPORT, CONNECTICUT

Originally published in 1892
by the Modern Language Association of America, Baltimore

First Greenwood Reprinting 1970

Library of Congress Catalogue Card Number 76-98848

SBN 8371-3903-1

Printed in the United States of America

PREFACE.

THE present edition of the Walther Saga is the first attempt to offer in complete form all the surviving episodes of the Saga. The point of view and method of treatment are historical from first to last. The texts of the versions have been arranged in chronological order so as to present the Saga in its transmitted form. The aim of the treatment is to set forth the historical elements and setting of the Saga, and thus rescue it from vague, mythical interpretations. If order is ever to be brought out of chaos in the interpretation of Saga and Myth, it must be done by keeping in view the historical background, and by close adherence to the historical method. Indeed, both myth and saga express in some form actual events,—the one in the realm of natural phenomena, the other in that of historical occurrences.

In reproducing such a great variety of texts it has been necessary, in some cases, to make typographical substitutions, particularly in the Polish texts. The author, therefore, begs the indulgence of those whose eye may be offended by the liberty taken with the customary Polish characters, which could not be obtained at the time (cf. note on page 110). The few cases in which possible confusion might arise are the following: *genitive feminine forms* (including those used adverbially), which readers of Polish will readily recognize.

The author makes grateful acknowledgement to those who have rendered assistance in the preparation of the work: to Dr. Uhler, of the Peabody Library; Dr. Kiernan, of the Harvard Library; Professor Palmer (now of Yale University) and Dr. Warren, of Adelbert College (Scherer Library); Dr. Hench, of the University of Michigan, who copied a part of the Old

PREFACE.

Norse text; Professor Creiznach, of the University of Cracovia, who kindly furnished a copy of the Polish texts; Dr. Shefloe, of the Woman's College of Baltimore, who read the proof-sheets of the Old Swedish texts.

Special thanks are due to Dr. Hermann Schoenfeld, who has carefully read the Polish proof-sheets; to Dr. James W. Bright, who read the Anglo-Saxon proof-sheets, and offered many helpful suggestions; to Professor A. Marshall Elliott for suggestions touching the typography of the work; and to Dr. Henry Wood, whose interest and judgment in this, as in the earlier work of the author, have been an unfailing source of encouragement and help.

MARION DEXTER LEARNED.

JOHNS HOPKINS UNIVERSITY,
    BALTIMORE, MD., *April 1, 1892.*

CONTENTS.

		PAGE.
PREFACE		iii–iv
VERSIONS OF THE SAGA		1–129
i.	Waldere Fragments (WF)	3–4
ii.	Waltharius (W)	5–43
iii.	Chronicon Novaliciense (NC)	44–61
iv.	Walther und Hildegunde	62–63
v.	Nibelungenlied (Nl)	64
vi.	Graz Fragment (GF)	65–66
vii.	Vienna Fragment (VF)	67–72
viii.	Biterolf und Dietleib (BD)	73–82
ix.	Alpharts Tod (AT)	83–84
x.	Rosengarten	85–88
	Der Grôse Rôsengarte (R)	85–87
	Rosengarten Fragments (RF 1. 2)	87–88
xi.	Dietrichs Flucht (DF)	89–90
xii.	Rabenschlacht (Rs)	91–92
xii.	Thidrekssaga	93–104
	Old Norse Version (Ths)	93–100
	Old Swedish Version (OS)	100–104
	(Hlod and Angantheow's Lay	104)
xiv.	Boguphali Chronicon (BC)	105–109
xv.	Paprocki (P)	110–113
xvi.	Bielski (B)	114–115
xvii.	Niesiecki (N)	116–117
xviii.	Procosius	118
xix.	Wójcicki (Woj)	119–122
Appendix	i (Von dem übelen wîbe)	123
"	ii (Chanson de Roland)	124–126
"	iii (Rolandslied)	127–129

vi CONTENTS.

PAGE.

ORIGIN AND DEVELOPMENT OF THE WALTHER SAGA........ 131–195

1. Elements of the Saga........................131–175

    1. Analysis of the Saga....................131–156

    2. Historical Elements of the Saga............157–165

    3. Legendary Elements of the Saga...........166–175

2. Relation of the Versions............................ 176–195

    1. Original Form of the Saga............... 176–181

    2. Later Versions of the Saga................182–187

3. Walther of Aquitaine................................ 188–195

BIBLIOGRAPHY...................................... 198–201

INDEX... 203–205

ERRATA... 207–208

VERSIONS OF THE WALTHER SAGA.

The Saga of Walther of Aquitaine, or of Walther and Hildegunde, is preserved in a variety of versions: Anglo-Saxon,
Latin, Middle High German, Old Norse, Polish, all but one of
which (Waltharius) are brief or fragmentary in their present
form. The original texts of these various versons are repro-
duced in the following pages in chronological order, so as to
present the Saga in its transmitted form which may serve as a
basis for historical treatment.

In reprinting the original texts of the Saga the best established texts have been selected, and only such variant readings
given as were deemed necessary for the purpose in hand.
Other variants affecting the form of the Saga are referred to in
the discussions which follow the texts.

The probable chronological order of the versions is the following:

1. *Waldere*, or the Anglo-Saxon Waldere Fragments, consisting of
two leaves, the MS. of which belongs to the ninth century.

2. *Waltharius*, a Latin poem in hexameters composed, in its original
form, by Ekkehard I, of St. Gall, about 920–930.

3. *Chronicon Novaliciense*, chapters vii–xiii, of the eleventh century.

4. *Walther und Hildegunde*, a poem by Walther von der Vogelweide, containing an evident reference to the Walther Saga, of the
end of the twelfth century.

5. *Nibelungen Lied* (Zarncke 268, 3; 274, 4; 358, 2) of the end of
the twelfth, or beginning of the thirteenth century.

6. The *Graz Fragment* of Walther, the remains of a Middle High German poem of the thirteenth century.

7. The *Vienna Fragment* of Walther und Hildegunde, the remains of a Middle High German poem, written in a variation of the Nibelungen strophe, in the thirteenth century.

8. *Biterolf und Dietleib*, a Middle High German Epic of the first half of the thirteenth century.

9. *Alpharts Tod*, a Middle High German epic, of about the middle of the thirteenth century,

10. *Rosengarten*, a Middle High German poem belonging, probably, to the second half of the thirteenth century.

11. *Dietrichs Flucht*, a Middle High German Epic of the second half of the thirteenth century.

12. *Rabenschlacht*, of about the same time. Both of the last-named poems were written, according to Martin, by Heinrich der Vogler, not long after 1282.

13. *Thidrekssaga*, or *Wilkinasaga*, an Old Norse prose Saga of the end of the thirteenth century. This Saga was later translated into Swedish and Latin ; compare Peringskiold's edition of 1715, where the three texts, Old Norse, Swedish and Latin, are printed together.[1]

14. *Boguphali Chronicon*, the Latin Chronicle attributed to Bishop Boguphalus († 1253) of Posen. In its revised form it constitutes the Great Polish Chronicle of the fourteenth century. Bielowski, 2, 510ff.

15. *B. Paprocki*, Herby Rycerstwa Polskiego. Krakau, 1584. p. 8 ff.

16. *Joachim Bielski*, Kronika of 1597 (cf. Heinzel s. 52). An edition of this chronicle appeared, doubtless, as early as 1550, possibly in 1534 (cf. Heinzel s. 53 An,) Turowski's Edition (1856) 1, 175 ff.

17. *K. Niesiecki* († 1744)). Korona Polska. 1743. 4, 365 f.

18. *Procosius*, Chronicon Slavo-Sarmaticum, belonging to the eighteenth century. Edition of 1827, p. 109, 128 f.

19. *Wojcicki*, Klechdy Starożytne Podania i Powiesci Ludowe. I, 32–42, 1851.

---

[1] For possible further reminiscence of the Walther Saga in Old Norse, compare Hlod and Angantheow Lay and the Gunlaug Saga. ('Corpus Poeticum Boreale,' i, 348 ff ; 565 ff. ii 505 ff.)

I.

WALDERE.*

A.

(1ª) . . . . hyrde hyne georne.
   huru Welandes   geworc ne geswiceð
   monna ænigum   þara ðe Mimming can
   hearne gehealdan.   oft æt hilde gedreas
5 swatfag and sweordwund   sec æfter oðrum.
   Ætlan ordwyga,   ne læt þin ellen nu gyt
   gedreosan to dæge,   dryhtscipe (feallan)!
   . . . .   nu is se dæg cumen,
   þæt ðu scealt aninga   oðer twega,
10 lif forleosan   oððe lange dom
   agan mid eldum,   Ælfheres sunu.
   nalles ic ðe, wine min,   wordum cide,
   ðy ic ðe gesawe   æt ðæm sweordplegan
   ðurh edwitscype   æniges monnes
15 wig forbugan   oððe on weal fleon,
   lice beorgan,   ðeah þe laðra fela
   dinne byrn (1ᵇ) homon   billum heowun.
   ac ðu symle furðor   feohtan sohtest
   mæl ofer mearce: ðy ic ðe metod ondred,
20 þæt ðu fyrenlice   feohtan sohtest
   æt ðam ætstealle,   oðres monnes
   wigrædenne.   weorða ðe selfne
   godum dædum,   ðenden ðin god recce.
   ne murn ðu for ði mece: ðe wearð maðma cyst
25 gifede to eoce unc.   ðy ðu Guðhere scealt
   beot forbigan,   ðæs ðe he ðas beaduwe ongan
   mid unryhte   ærest secan.
   forsoc he ðam swurde   and ðam syncfatum,
   beaga menigo: nu sceal beaga leas

---

6 Ætla *with traces of an* n *in MS.* K.—8 nu B., K., Ac Gr. W.—
14 eð wit K.—19 mæles B.—21 ætðam K.—25 guð here K.

* The text is reprinted from Wülcker's critical edition of Grein, with emendations and additions from the new collation of Kölbing (*Englische Studien* v, 240 f.; 292 f.). Cf. variants noted below the text.

30   hworfan from ðisse hilde,   hlafurd secan
     ealdne eðel,   oððe her ær swefan,
     gif he ða . . . .

B.

(2ᵃ)   ce bæteran
     buton ðam anum,   ðe ic eac hafa,
     on stanfate   stille gehided.
     ic wat þæt hit ðohte   Ðeodric Widian
5   selfum onsendon   and eac sinc micel
     maðma mid ði mece,   monig oðres mid him
     golde gegirwan,   iulean genam,
     þæs ðe hine of nearwum   Niðhades mæg,
     Welandes bearn,   Widia ut forlet:
10   ðurh fifela gefeald   forð onette.
     Waldere maðelode,   wiga ellenrof
     hæfde him on handa   hildefromre
     guðbilla gripe,   gyddode wordum :
     hwæt, ðu huru wendest,   wine Burgenda,
15   þæt me Hagenan hand   hilde gefremede
     and getwæmde feðewigges : feta, gyf ðu dyrre,
     aet ðus heaðuwerigan   hare byrnan.
     standeð me her on eaxelum   Ælfheres laf,
     god and geapneb,   golde geweorðod,
20   ealles unscende   æðelinges reaf
     to habbanne,   ðonne hand wereð
     feorhhord feondum.   he bið fah wið me,
     þonne . . . unmægas   eft ongynnað,
     mecum gemetað   swa ge me dydon.
25   ðeah mæg sige syllan   se ðe symle byð
     recen and rædfest   ryhta gehwilces :
     se ðe him to ðam halgan   helpe gelifeð,
     to gode gioce,   he þær gearo findeð,
     gif ða earnunga   ær geðenceð ;
30   þonne moten wlanc   welan britnian,
     æhtum wealdan,   þæt is . . . . . .

---

1 me *before* ce St.—7 iu lean genam K.—10 *not certain whether*
feald *or* stealg K.—12 B, *K. reads a stroke over* o; hildefrofre D., R.,
Gr. W. hilde frore MS.— 19 ge weorðod K.—21 had MS. (Heinzel).—
22 he St., K.; ne Gr. W.; heo Heinzel.—24 ge metað K.;—26 recon
St.; recen R.; reccend D. Gr.—27 Seðe K.; ge lifeð K.

II.

WALTHARIUS.*

POESIS GERALDI DE GUALTARIO.†

OMNIPOTENS genitor, summae uirtutis amator,
Iure pari natusque amborum spiritus almus,
Personis trinus, uera deitate sed unus,
Qui uita uiuens cuncta et sine fine tenebis,
5 Pontificem summum tu salua nunc et in aeuum
Claro Erchamboldum fulgentem nomine dignum,
Crescat ut interius sancto spiramine plenus,
Multis infictum quo sit medicamen in aeuum.
Praesul sancte dei nunc accipe munera serui,
10 Quae tibi decreuit de larga promere cura
Peccator fragilis Geraldus nomine uilis,
Qui tibi nam certus corde estque fidelis alumnus.
Quod precibus dominum iugiter precor omnitonantem,
Ut nanciscaris factis, quae promo loquelis,
15 Det pater ex summis caelum terramque gubernans.
Serue dei summi, ne despice uerba libelli,
Non canit alma dei, resonat sed mira tyronis,
Nomine Waltharii, per proelia multa resecti.
Ludendum magis est, dominum quam sit rogitandum;
20 Perlectus longe uim stringit in ampla diei.
Sis felix sanctus per tempora plura sacerdos,
Sit tibi mente tua Geraldus carus adelphus.

---

*A thoroughly satisfactory edition of the 'Waltharius' is yet a desideratum. The text
given here is that of Scheffel-Holder (1874), and the only liberty taken with it is the printing
of *u* for *v* and the introduction of slight changes in punctuation. Variants of Peiper's
readings compared with those of Scheffel-Holder, are found below the text here presented.

† Icipit poesis geraldi de gualtario B.

TERTIA pars orbis, fratres, Europa uocatur
    Moribus ac linguis uarias et nomine gentes
Distinguens cultu, tum relligione sequestrans.
Inter quas gens Pannoniae residere probatur
5 Quam tamen et Hunos plerumque uocare solemus.
Hic populus fortis uirtute uigebat et armis
Non circum positas solum domitans regiones,
Litoris oceani sed pertransiuerat oras
Foedera supplicibus donans sternensque rebelles :
10 Ultra millenos fertur dominarier annos.
Attila rex quodam tulit illud tempore regnum
Impiger antiquos sibimet renouare triumphos.
Qui sua castra mouens mandauit uisere Francos,
Quorum rex Gibicho solio pollebat in alto
15 Prole recens orta gaudens quam postea narro :
Namque marem genuit quem Guntharium uocitauit.
Fama uolans pauidi regis transuerberat aures
Dicens hostilem cuneum transire per Histrum,
Uincentem numero stellas atque amnis harenas.
20 Qui non confidens, armis uel robore plebis
Concilium cogit, quae sint facienda requirit.
Consensere omnes : foedus debere precari
Et dextras, si forte darent, coniungere dextris
Obsidibusque datis censum persoluere iussum.
25 Hoc melius fore quam uitam simul ac regionem
Perdiderint natosque suos pariterque maritas.
Nobilis hoc Hagano fuerat sub tempore tyro
Indolis egregiae ueniens de germine Troiae.
Hunc, quia Guntharius nondum peruenit ad aeuum,
30 Ut sine matre queat uitam retinere tenellam,
Cum gaza ingenti decernunt mittere regi.
Nec mora, legati censum iuuenemque ferentes
Deueniunt pacemque rogant ac foedera firmant.
Tempore quo ualidis steterat Burgundia sceptris
35 Cuius primatum Heriricus forte gerebat.
Filia huic tantum fuit unica nomine Hiltgunt
Nobilitate quidem pollens ac stemmate formae.
Debuit haec heres aula residere paterna
Atque diu congesta frui, si forte liceret.

19 arenas P.—20 longaeui P.—37 scemate P.

40   Iamque Auares firma cum Francis pace peracta
     Suspendunt a fine quidem regionis eorum.
     Attila sed celeres mox huc deflectit habenas
     Nec tardant reliqui satrapae uestigia adire.
     Ibant aequati numero, sed et agmine longo,
45   Quadrupedum cursu tellus concussa gemebat,
     Scutorum sonitu pauidus superintonat aether.
     Ferrea silua micat totos rutilando per agros :
     Haud aliter, primo quam pulsans aequora mane
     Pulcher in extremis renitet sol partibus orbis.
50   Iamque Ararim Rodanumque amnes transiuerat altos
     Atque ad praedandum cuneus dispergitur omnis.
     Forte Cauilloni sedit Heriricus, et ecce
     Attollens oculos speculator uociferatur :
     ' Quaenam condenso consurgit puluere nubes ?
55   Uis inimica uenit, portas iam claudite cunctas.'
     Iam tum quid Franci fecissent ipse sciebat
     Princeps et cunctos conpellat sic seniores :
     ' Si gens tam fortis cui nos similare nequimus,
     Cessit Pannoniae, qua nos uirtute putatis
60   Huic conferre manum et patriam defendere dulcem ?
     Est satius, pactum faciant censumque capessant.
     Unica nata mihi quam tradere pro regione
     Non dubito : tantum pergant qui foedera firment.'
     Ibant legati totis gladiis spoliati,
65   Hostibus insinuant quod regis iussio mandat :
     Ut cessent uastare, rogant. quos Attila ductor
     Ut solitus fuerat, blande suscepit et inquit :
     ' Foedera plus cupio quam proelia mittere uulgo.
     Pace quidem Huni malunt regnare, sed armis
70   Inuiti feriunt quos cernunt esse rebelles.
     Rex ad nos ueniens pacem det atque resumat.'
     Exiuit princeps asportans innumeratos
     Thesauros pactumque ferit natamque relinquit.
     Pergit in exilium pulcherrima gemma parentum.
75   Postquam compleuit pactum statuitque tributum,
     Attila in occiduas promouerat agmina partes.
     Namque Aquitanorum tunc Alphere regna tenebat
     Quem sobolem sexus narrant habuisse uirilis

57 compellat P.—62 mihi est P.—71 pacem*que* P.

Nomine Waltharium primeuo flore nitentem.
80 Nam iusiurandum Heriricus et Alphere reges
Inter se dederant, pueros quod consociarent,
Cum primum tempus nubendi uenerit illis.
Hic ubi cognouit gentes has esse domatas,
Coeperat ingenti cordis trepidare pauore.
85 Nec iam spes fuerat saeuis defendier armis.
'Quid cessemus' ait, 'si bella mouere nequimus?
Exemplum nobis Burgundia, Francia donant.
Non incusamur, si talibus aequiperamur.
Legatus mitto foedusque ferire iubebo
90 Obsidis inque uicem dilectum porrigo natum
Et iam nunc Hunis censum persoluo futurum.'
Sed quid plus remorer? dictum compleuerat actis.
Tunc Auares gazis onerati denique multis
Obsidibus sumptis Haganone Hiltgunde puella
95 Nec non Walthario redierunt pectore laeto.
    Attila Pannonias ingressus et urbe receptus
Exulibus pueris magnam exhibuit pietatem
Ac ueluti proprios nutrire iubebat heredes.
[Uirginis et curam reginam mandat habere.]
100 Ast adolescentes propriis conspectibus ambos
Semper adesse iubet, sed et artibus imbuit illos
Praesertimque iocis belli sub tempore habendis.
Qui simul ingenio crescentes mentis et aeuo
Robore uincebant fortes animoque sophistas,
105 Donec iam cunctos superarent fortiter Hunos.
Militiae primos tunc Attila fecerat illos,
Sed haud inmerito, quoniam, si quando moueret
Bella, per insignes isti micuere triumphos.
Idcircoque nimis princeps dilexerat ambos.
110 Uirgo etiam captiua deo praestante supremo
Reginae uultum placauit et auxit amorem
Moribus eximiis operumque industria habundans.
Postremum custos thesauris prouida cunctis
Efficitur modicumque deest, quin regnet et ipsa,
115 Nam quicquid uoluit, de rebus fecit et actis.
    Interea Gibicho defungitur ipseque regno
Guntharius successit et ilico Pannoniarum

---

79 primaeuo P.—109 illos P.

Foedera dissoluit censumque subire negauit.
Hoc ubi iam primum Hagano cognouerat exul,
120 Nocte fugam molitur et ad dominum properauit.
Waltharius tamen ad pugnas praecesserat Hunos
Et quocumque iret. mox prospera sunt comitata.
Ospirin elapsum Haganonem regia coniunx
Attendens domino suggessit talia dicta :
125 ' Prouideat caueatque precor sollertia regis,
Ne uestri imperii labatur forte columna,
Hoc est, Waltharius uester discedat amicus
in quo magne potestatis uis extitit huius :
Nam uereor, ne fors fugiens Haganonem imitetur.
130 Idcircoque meam perpendite nunc rationem :
Cum primum ueniat, haec illi dicite uerba :
"Seruitio in nostro magnos plerumque labores
Passus eras ideoque scias, quod gratia nostra
Prae cunctis temet nimium dilexit amicis.
135 Quod uolo plus factis te quam cognoscere dictis :
Elige de satrapis nuptam tibi Pannoniarum
Et non pauperiem propriam perpendere cures.
Amplificabo quidem * * te rure domique
Nec quisquam, qui dat sponsam, post facta pudebit."
140 Quod si completis, illum stabilire potestis.'
Complacuit sermo regi coepitque parari.
Waltharius uenit : cui princeps talia pandit
Uxorem suadens sibi ducere, sed tamen ipse
Iam tum praemeditans quod post compleuerat actis,
145 Inuestiganti his suggestibus obuius infit :
' Uestra quidem pietas est, quod modici famulatus
Causam conspicitis. sed quod mea sergia, mentis
Intuitu, fertis, numquam meruisse ualerem.
Sed precor, ut serui capiatis uerba fidelis :
150 Si nuptam accipiam domini praecepta secundum,
Uinciar in primis curis et amore puellae
Atque a seruitio regis plerumque retardor.
Aedificare domos cultumque intendere ruris
Cogor et hoc oculis senioris adesse moratur
155 Et solitam regno Hunorum impendere curam.
Namque uoluptatem quisquis gustauerit, exin

123 coniux P.—138 donis P.

Intolerabilius consueuit ferre labores.
Nil tam dulce mihi, quam semper inesse fideli
Obsequio domini : quare precor absque iugali
160 Me uinclo permitte meam iam ducere uitam.
Si sero aut medio noctis mihi tempore mandas,
Ad quaecumque iubes securus et ibo paratus.
In bellis nullae persuadent cedere curae
Nec nati aut coniunx retrahentque fugamque mouebunt.
165 Testor per propriam temet pater optime uitam
Atque per inuictam nunc gentem Pannoniarum,
Ut non ulterius me cogas sumere taedas.'
His precibus uictus suasus rex deserit omnes
Sperans Waltharium fugiendo recedere numquam.
170   Uenerat interea satrapae certissima fama
Quandam quae nuper superata resistere gentem
Ac bellum Hunis confestim inferre paratam.
   Tunc ad Waltharium conuertitur actio rerum :
Qui mox militiam percensuit ordine totam
175 Et bellatorum confortat corda suorum
Hortans praeteritos semper memorare triumphos
Promittensque istos solita uirtute tyrannos
Sternere et externis terrorem imponere terris.
   Nec mora, consurgit sequiturque exercitus omnis.
180 Ecce locum pugnae conspexerat et numeratam
Per latos aciem campos digessit et agros.
Iamque infra iactum teli congressus uterque
Constiterat cuneus : tunc undique clamor ad auras
Tollitur, horrendam confundunt classica uocem
185 Continuoque hastae uolitant hinc indeque densae.
Fraxinus et cornus ludum miscebat in unum
Fulminis inque modum cuspis uibrata micabat.
Ac ueluti boreae sub tempore nix glomerata
Spargitur, haud aliter saeuas iecere sagittas.
190 Postremum cunctis utroque ex agmine pilis
Absumptis manus ad mucronem uertitur omnis :
Fulmineos promunt enses clipeosque reuoluunt,
Concurrunt acies demum pugnamque restaurant.
Pectoribus partim rumpuntur pectora equorum
195 Sternitur et quaedam pars duro umbone uirorum.

_____

164 coniux P.

Waltharius tamen in medio furit agmine bello
Obuia quaeque metens armis ac limite pergens.
Hunc ubi conspiciunt hostes tantas dare strages,
Ac si praesentem metuebant cernere mortem :
200 Et quemcumque locum seu dextra siue sinistra
Waltharius peteret, cuncti mox terga dederunt
Et uersis scutis laxisque feruntur habenis.
Tunc imitata ducem gens maxima Pannoniarum
[Saeuior insurgit caedemque audacior auget,]
205 Deicit obstantes, fugientes proterit, usque
Dum caperet plenum belli sub sorte triumphum.
Tum super occisos ruit et spoliauerat omnes
Et tandem ductor recauo uocat agmina cornu.
Ac primus frontem festa cum fronde reuinxit
210 Uictrici lauro cingens sua tempora uulgo,
Post hunc signiferi sequitur quos cetera pubes.
Iamque triumphali redierunt stemmate compti
Et patriam ingressi propria se quisque locauit
Sede, sed ad solium mox Waltharius properauit.
215 Ecce palatini decurrunt arce ministri
Illius aspectu hilares equitemque tenebant,
Donec uir sella descenderet inclitus alta.
Si bene res uergant, tum demum forte requirunt.
Ille aliquid modicum narrans intrauerat aulam,
220 Lassus enim fuerat regisque cubile petebat.
Illic Hiltgundem solam offendit residentem.
Cui post amplexus atque oscula dulcia dixit:
' Ocius huc potum ferto, quia fessus anhelo.'
Illa mero tallum conpleuit mox pretiosum
225 Porrexitque uiro, qui signans accipiebat
Uirgineamque manum propria constrinxit. at illa
Astitit et uultum reticens intendit herilem
Walthariusque bibens uacuum uas porrigit olli,
Ambo etenim norant de se sponsalia facta.
230 Prouocat et tali caram sermone puellam :
' Exilium pariter patimur iam tempore tanto
Non ignorantes, quid nostri forte parentes
Inter se nostra de re fecere futura.
Quamne diu tacito premimus haec ipsa palato ? '

200 quemcunque P.—210 timpora P.—224 complevit P.

235 Uirgo per hyroniam meditans hec dicere sponsum
Paulum conticuit, sed postea talia reddit:
' Quid lingua simulas quod ab imo pectore damnas
Oreque pursuades toto quod corde refutas?
Sit ueluti talem pudor ingens ducere nuptam.'
240 Uir sapiens contra respondit et intulit ista:
'Absit quod memoras? dextrorsum porrige sensum.
Noris me nihilum simulata mente locutum
Nec quicquam nebulae uel falsi interfore crede.
Nullus adest nobis exceptis namque duobus.
245 Si nossem temet mihi promptam inpendere mentem
Atque fidem uotis seruare per omnia cautis,
Pandere cuncta tibi cordis mysteria uellem.'
Tandem uirgo uiri genibus curuata profatur:
'Ad quaecumque uocas, mi domne, sequar studiose
250 Nec quicquam placitis malim praeponere jussis.'
Ille dehinc: ' piget exillii me denique nostri
Et patriae fines reminiscor saepe relictos:
Idcircoque fugam cupio celerare latentem.
Quod iam prae multis potuissem forte diebus,
255 Si non Hiltgundem solam remanere dolerem.'
Addidit has imo uirguncula corde loquelas:
[' Uestrum uelle meum, solis his aestuo rebus,]
Praecipiat dominus, seu prospera siue sinistra,
Eius amore pati toto sum pectore praesto.'
260 Waltharius tandem sic uirginis inquit in aurem:
' Publica custodem rebus te nempe potestas
Fecerat, idcirco memor haec mea uerba notato:
Inprimis galeam regis tunicamque, trilicem
Assero loricam fabrorum insigne ferentem,
265 Diripe, bina dehinc mediocria scrinia tolle.
His armillarum tantum da pannonicarum,
Donec uix unum releues ad pectoris imum.
Inde quater binum mihi fac de more coturnum
Tantundemque tibi patrans inponito uasis:
270 Sic fors ad summum conplentur scrinia labrum.
Insuper a fabris hamos clam posce retortos.
Nostra uiatica sint pisces simul atque uolucres,
Ipse ego piscator, sed et auceps esse coartor.

---

235 haec P.; hec S.-H.; hoc BT.—245 impendere P.—270 complen-
tur P.

Haec intra ebdomadem caute per singula comple.
275 Audisti, quid habere uianti forte necesse est.
Nunc quo more fugam ualeamus inire recludo:
Postquam septenos Phoebus remeauerit orbes,
Regi ac reginae satrapis ducibus famulisque
Sumptu permagno conuiuia laeta parabo
280 Atque omni ingenio potu sepelire studebo,
Donec nullus erit qui sentiat hoc quod agendum est.
Tu tamen interea mediocriter utere uino,
Atque sitim uix ad mensam restinguere cura.
Cum reliqui surgant, ad opuscula nota recurre.
285 Ast ubi iam cunctos superat uiolentia potus,
Tum simul occiduas properemus quaerere partes.'
Uirgo memor praecepta uiri compleuit. et ecce
Praefinita dies epularum uenit et ipse
Waltharius magnis instruxit sumptibus escas.
290 Luxuria in media residebat denique mensa
Ingrediturque aulam uelis rex undique septam.
Heros magnanimus solito quem corde salutans
Duxerat ad solium. quod compsit bissus et ostrum.
Consedit laterique duces hinc indeque binos
295 Assedisse iubet. reliquos locat ipse minister.
Centenos simul accubitus iniere sodales
Diuersasque dapes libans conuiua resudat:
His et sublatis aliae referuntur edendae
Atque exquisitum feruebat migma per aurum.
300 Aurea bissino tantum stant gausape uasa
Et pigmentatus crateres Bacchus adornat:
Illicit ad haustum species dulcedoque potus,
Waltharius cunctos ad uinum hortatur et escas.
    Postque epulis absumpta quies mensaeque remotae,
305 Heros iam dictus dominum laetanter adorsus
Inquit: 'in hoc rogito clarescat gratia uestra,
Ut uos inprimis reliquos nunc laetificetis.'
Et simul in uerbo nappam dedit arte peractam
Ordine sculpturae referentem gesta priorum,
310 Quam rex accipiens haustu uacuauerat uno
Confestimque iubet reliquos imitarier omnes.
Ocius accurrunt pincernae moxque recurrunt,

---

293 quem P.—300 bis seno P.—304 postquam P.

Pocula plena dabant et inania suscipiebant,
Hospitis ac regis certant hortatibus omnes.
315 Ebrietas feruens tota dominatur in aula,
Balbuttit madido facundia fusa palato,
Heroas ualidos plantis titubare uideres.
Taliter in seram produxit bachica noctem
Munera Waltharius retrahitque redire uolentes ;
320 Donec ui potus pressi somnoque grauati
Passim porticibus sternuntur humotenus omnes.
Et licet ignicremis uellet dare moenia flammis,
Nullus qui causam potuisset scire remansit.
Tandem dilectam uocat ad semet mulierem
325 Praecipiens causas citius deferre paratas.
Ipseque de stabulis uictorem duxit equorum :
Hunc ob uirtutem uocitauerat ille leonem.
Stat sonipes ac frena ferox spumantia mandit.
Hunc postquam faleris solito circumdedit, ecce
330 Scrinia plena gazae lateri suspendit utrique
Atque iteri longo modicella cibaria ponit
Loraque uirgineae mandat fluitantia dextrae.
Ipseque lorica uestitus more gigantis
Inposuit capiti rubras cum casside cristas
335 Ingentesque ocreis suras conplectitur aureis,
Et laeuum femur ancipiti praecinxerat ense
Atque alio dextrum pro ritu Pannoniarum :
Is tamen ex una tantum dat uulnera parte.
Tunc hastam dextra rapiens clipeumque sinistra
340 Coeperat inuisa trepidus decedere terra.
Femina duxit equum non nulla talenta gerentem
In manibusque simul uirgam tenet ipsa colurnam,
In qua piscator hamum transponit in undam,
Ut cupiens pastum piscis deglutiat uncum.
345 Namque gravatus erat uir maximus undique telis
Suspectamque habuit cuncto sibi tempore pugnam.
Omni nocte quidem properabant currere, sed cum
Prima rubens terris ostendit lumina Phoebus,
In siluis latitare student et opaca requirunt
350 Sollicitatque metus uel per loca tuta fatigans.
In tantumque timor muliebria pectora pulsat,

---

324 indeque P.—331 Atque iterilongo P. ; Atq e iteriluongo S.-H.—
335 complectitur P.—341 nonnulla P.

Horreat ut cunctos aurae uentique susurros
Formidans uolucres collisos siue racemos.
Hinc odium exilii patriaeque amor incubat inde ;
355 Uicis defugiunt, speciosa noualia linquunt
Montibus intonsis cursus ambage recuruos
Sectantes : tremulos uariant per deuia gressus.
Ast urbis populus somno uinoque solutus
Ad medium lucis siluit recubando sequentis.
360 Sed postquam surgunt, ductorem quique requirunt,
Ut grates faciant ac festa laude salutent.
Attila nempe manu caput amplexatus utraque
Egreditur thalamo rex, Walthariumque dolendo
Aduocat, ut proprium quereretur forte dolorem.
365 Respondent ipsi se non potuisse ministri
Inuenisse uirum, sed princeps sperat eundem
Hactenus in somno tentum recubare quietum
Occultumque locum sibi delegisse sopori.
Ospirin Hiltgundem postquam cognouit abesse
370 Nec iuxta morem uestes deferre suetum,
Tristior inmensis satrapae clamoribus inquit :
' O detestandas quas heri sumpsimus escas !
O uinum quod Pannonias destruxerat omnes !
Quod domino regi iam dudum praescia dixi,
375 Approbat iste dies quem nos superare nequimus.
En hodie imperii uestri cecidisse columna
Noscitur, en robur procul inuit et inclita uirtus :
Waltharius lux Pannoniae discesserat inde,
Hiltgundem quoque mi caram deduxit alumnam.'
380 Iam princeps nimia succenditur efferus ira,
Mutant laetitiam maerentia corda priorem.
Ex humeris trabeam discindit ad infima totam
Et nunc huc animum tristem, nunc diuidit illuc.
Ac uelut aeolicis turbatur arena procellis,
385 Sic intestinis rex fluctuat undique curis
Et uarium pectus uario simul ore imitatus
Prodidit exterius quicquid tolerauerat intus
Iraque sermonem permisit promere nullum.
Ipso quippe die potum fastidit et escam
390 Nec placidam menbris potuit dare cura quietem.

372 sero P.—390 membris.

Namque ubi nox rebus jam dempserat atra colores,
Decidit in lectum, uerum nec lumina clausit
Nunc latus in dextrum fultus nunc inque sinistrum
Et ueluti iaculo pectus transfixus acuto
395 Palpitat atque caput huc et mox iactitat illuc
Et modo subrectus fulcro consederat amens.
Nec iuuat hoc, demum surgens discurrit in urbem
Atque thorum ueniens simul attigit atque reliquit.
Taliter insomnem consumpserat Attila noctem.
400 At profugi comites per amica silentia euntes
Suspectam properant post terga relinquere terram.
Uix tamen erupit cras, rex patribusque uocatis
Dixerat : ' o si quis mihi Waltharium fugientem
Afferat euinctum ceu nequam forte liciscam !
405 Hunc ego mox auro uestirem saepe recocto
Et tellure quidem stantem hinc inde onerarem
Atque uiam penitus clausissem uiuo talentis.'
Sed nullus fuit in tanta regione tyrannus
Uel dux siue comes seu miles siue minister,
410 Qui, quamuis cuperet proprias ostendere uires
Ac uirtute sua laudem captare perennem
Ambiretque simul gazam infarcire crumenis,
Waltharium tamen iratum praesumpserit armis
Insequier strictoque uirum mucrone uidere.
415 Nota equidem uirtus, experti sunt quoque quantas
Incolumis dederit stranges sine uulnere uictor.
Nec potis est ullum rex persuadere uirorum
Qui promissa uelit hac condicione talenta.
Waltharius fugiens, ut dixi, noctibus iuit
420 Atque die saltus arbustaque densa requirens
Arte, accersita pariter capit arte uolucres
Nunc fallens uisco, nunc fisso denique ligno.
Ast ubi peruenit qua flumina curua fluebant,
Inmittens hamum rapuit sub gurgite praedam
425 Atque famis pestem pepulit tolerando laborem :
Namque fugae toto se tempore uirginis usu
Continuit uir Waltharius laudabilis heros.
Ecce quater denos sol circumflexerat orbes
Ex quo pannonica fuerat digressus ab urbe.
430 Ipso quippe die numerum qui clauserat istum,

416 incolomes P.

Uenerat ad fluuium iam uespere tum mediante
Scilicet ad Rhenum, qua cursus tendit ad urbem
Nomine Wormatiam regali sede nitentem.
Illic pro naulo pisces dedit antea captos.
435 Et mox transpositus graditur properanter anhelus.
Orta dies postquam tenebras discusserat atras,
Port.tor exsurgens praefatam uenit in urbem
Regalique coco reliquorum quippe magistro
Detulerat pisces quos uir dedit ille uiator.
440 Hos cum pigmentis condisset et apposuisset
Regi Gunthario, miratus fatur ab alto :
' Istius ergo modi pisces mihi Francia numquam
Ostendit : reor externis a finibus illos.
Dic mihi quantocius : cuias homo detulit illos ? '
445 Ipseque respondens narrat, quod nauta dedisset.
Accersire hominem princeps praecepit eundem.
Et, cum uenisset, de re quaesitus eadem
Talia dicta dedit causamque ex ordine pandit :
' Uespere praeterito residebam litore Rheni
450 Conspexique uiatorem propere uenientem
Et ueluti pugnae certum per membra paratum :
Aere etenim penitus fuerat rex inclite cinctus
Gesserat et scutum gradiens hastamque coruscam.
Namque uiro forti similis fuit et licet ingens
455 Asportaret onus, gressum tamen extulit acrem.
Hunc incredibili formae decorata nitore
Assequitur calcemque terit iam calce puella.
Ipsaque robustum rexit per lora caballum
Scrinia bina quidem dorso non parua ferentem,
460 Quae, dum ceruicem sonipes discusserit altam,
Atque superba cupit glomerare uolumina crurum,
Dant sonitum, ceu quis gemmis illiserit aurum.
Hic mihi praesentes dederat pro munere pisces.'
His Hagano auditis, ad mensam quippe resedit,
465 Laetior in medium prompsit de pectore uerbum :
' Congaudete mihi quaeso, quia talia noui :
Waltharius collega meus remeauit ab Hunis.'
Uociferatur et omnis ei mox aula reclamat.
Guntharius princeps ex hac ratione superbus :
470 ' Congaudete mihi iubeo, quia talia uixi.

458 cauallum P.

Gazam quam Gibicho regi transmisit eoo,
Hanc nunc cunctipotens huc in mea regna remisit.'
Haec ait et mensam pede perculit exiliensque
Ducere equum iubet et sella conponere sculpta
475 Atque omni de plebe uiros secum duodenos
Uiribus insignes, animis plerumque probatos
Legerat.   inter quos simul ire Haganona iubebat.
Qui memor antiquae fidei sociique prioris
Nititur a coeptis dominum transuertere rebus.
480 Rex tamen e contra nihilominus instat et infit :
' Ne tardata uiri, praecingite corpora ferro
Fortia, squamosus thorax iam terga recondat.
Hic tantum gazae Francis deducat ab oris ? '
Instructi telis, nam iussio regis adurget,
485 Exibant portis te Waltharium cupientes
Sternere et inbellem lucris fraudare putantes.
Sed tamen omnimodis Hagano prohibere studebat :
At rex infelix coeptis resipiscere non uult.
Interea uir magnanimus de flumine pergens
490 Uenerat in saltum iam tunc Vosagum uocitatum.
Nam nemus est ingens spatiosum, lustra ferarum
Plurima habens, suetem canibus resonare tubisque.
Sunt in secessu bini montesque propinqui,
Inter quos licet angustum specus extat amenum
495 Non tellure caua factum sed uertice rupum :
Apta quidem statio latronibus illa cruentis.
Angulus hic uirides ac uescas gesserat herbas.
Hunc mox ut uidit iuuenis : ' huc ' inquit ' eamus,
His iuuat in castris fessum conponere corpus.
500 Nam postquam fugiens Auarum discesserat oris,
Non aliter somni requiem gustauerat idem
Quam super innixus clipeo : uix clauserat orbes.
Bellica tum demum deponens pondera dixit
Uirginis in gremium fusus : ' circumspice caute
505 Hiltgunt et nebulam si tolli uideris atram,
Attactu blando me surgere conmonitato;
Et licet ingentem conspexeris ire cateruam,
Ne subito excutias somno mi cara caueto,
Nam procul hinc acies potis es transmittere puras.

486 cernere P.—494 amoenum P.

510 Instanter cunctam circa explora regionem.'
Haec ait atque oculos concluserat ipse nitentes
Iamque diu satis optata fruitur requiete.
Ast ubi Guntharius uestigia puluere uidit,
Cornipedem rapidum saeuis calcaribus urget
515 Exultansque animis frustra sic fatur ad auras :
'Accelerate uiri, iam nunc capietis eundem :
Numquam hodie effugiet, furata talenta relinquet.'
Inclitus at Hagano contra mox reddidit ista :
' Unum dico tibi regum fortissime tantum :
520 Si totiens tu Waltharium pugnasse uideres
Atque noua totiens quotiens ego caede furentem,
Numquam tam facile spoliandum forte putares.
Uidi Pannonias, acies cum bella cierent
Contra aquilonares siue australes regiones :
525 Illic Waltharius propria uirtute coruscus
Hostibus inuisus sociis mirandus obibat :
Quisquis ei congressus erat, mox tartara uidit.
O rex et comites experto credite, quantus
In clipeum surgat, quanta ui torqueat hastam.'
530 Sed dum Guntharius male sana mente grauatus
Nequaquam flecti posset, castris propiabant.
At procul aspiciens Hiltgunt de uertice montis
Puluere sublato uenientes sensit et ipsum
Waltharium placido tactu uigilare monebat.
535 Qui caput attollens scrutatur, si quis adiret.
Eminus illa refert quandam uolitare phalangem.
Ipse oculos tersos somni glaucomate purgans
Paulatim rigidos ferro uestiuerat artus
Atque grauem rursus parmam collegit et hastam
540 Et saliens uacuas ferro transuerberat auras
Et celer ad pugnam telis prolusit amaram.
Cominus ecce coruscantes mulier uidet hastas
Ac stupefacta nimis : ' Hunos hic' inquit 'habemus.'
In terramque cadens effatur talia tristis :
545 ' Obsecro, mi senior, gladio mea colla recide
Ut, quae non merui pacto thalamo sociari,
Nullius ulterius patiar consortia carnis.'
Tum iuuenis : ' cruor innocuus me tinxerit ? ' inquit

532 Et P.—534 iubebat P.—545 secentur P.—548 an nocuus P.

'Aut quo forte modo gladius potis est inimicos
550 Sternere, tam fidae si nunc non parcit amicae ?
Absit quod rogitas, mentis depone pauorem.
Qui me de uariis eduxit saepe periclis,
Hic ualet hic hostes credo confundere nostros.'
Haec ait atque oculos tollens effatur ad ipsam :
555 ' Non assunt Auares hic sed Franci nebulones
Cultores regionis,' et en galeam Haganonis
Aspicit et noscens iniunxit talia ridens :
' Et meus hic socius Hagano collega ueternus.
Hoc heros dicto introitum stationis adibat
560 Inferius stanti praedicens sic mulieri :
' Hac coram porta uerbum modo iacto superbum :
Hinc nullus rediens uxori dicere Francus
Praesumet se inpune gazae quid tollere tantae.'
Nec dum sermonem conpleuit, humotenus ecce
565 Corruit et ueniam petiit, quia talia dixit.
Postquam surrexit contemplans cautius omnes :
' Horum quos uideo nullum Haganone remoto
Suspicio : namque ille meos per proelia mores
Iam didicit, tenet hic etiam sat callidus artem.
570 Quam si forte uolente deo intercepero solam,
Tunc' ait ' ex pugna tibi Hiltgunt sponsa reseruor.'
Ast ubi Waltharium tali statione receptum
Conspexit Hagano, satrapae mox ista superbo
Suggerit : ' o senior desiste lacessere bello
575 Hunc hominem.   pergant primum qui cuncta requirant
Et genus et patriam nomenque locumque relictum.
Uel, si forte petat pacem sine sanguine praebens
Thesaurum, per responsum cognoscere homonem
Possumus, et si Waltharius remoratur ibidem,
580 Est sapiens, forsan uestro concedet honori.'
Praecipit ire uirum cognomine rex Camelonem,
Inclita metensi quem Francia miserat urbi
Praefectum, qui dona ferens deuenerat illo
Anteriore die quam princeps nouerat ista.
585 Qui dans frena uola trapidoque simillimus Euro
Transcurrit spatium campi iuuenique propinquat
Ac sic obstantem conpellat : ' dic homo quisnam

---

564 compleuit P.—587 compellat P.

Sis? aut unde uenis * * * quo pergere tendis?'
Heros magnanimus respondit talia dicens :
590 ' Sponte tua uenias an huc te miserit ullus,
Scire uelim.' Camelo tunc reddidit ore superbo :
' Noris Guntharium regem tellure potentem
Me misisse tuas quaesitum pergere causas.'
His auscultatis suggesserat hoc adolescens :
595 ' Ignoro penitus, quid opus sit forte uiantis
Scrutari causas : sed promere non trepidamus.
Waltharius uocor, ex Aquitanis sum generatus.
A genitore meo modicus puer obsidis ergo
Sum datus ad Hunos, ibi uixi nuncque recessi
600 Concupiens patriam dulcemque reuisere gentem.'
Missus ad haec ' tibi iam dictus per me iubet heros,
Ut cum scriniolis equitem des atque puellam :
Quod si promptus agis, uitam concedet et artus.'
Waltharius contra fidenter protulit ista
605 ' Stultius effatum me non audisse sophistam
Arbitror. en memoras, quod princeps nescio uel quis
Promittat, quod non retinet nec fors retinebit.
An deus est, ut iure mihi concedere uitam
Possit? num manibus tetigit? num carcere trusit
610 Uel post terga meas torsit per uincula palmas?
Attamen ausculta : si me certamine laxat,—
Aspicio, ferratus adest, ad proelia uenit—
Armillas centum de rubro quippe metallo
Factas transmittam, quo nomen regis honorem.'
615 Tali responso discesserat ille rccepto.
Principibus narrat quod protulit atque resumpsit.
Tunc Hagano ad regem : ' porrectam suscipe gazam,
Hac potis es decorare, pater, tecum comitantes ;
Et modo de pugna palmam reuocare memento.
620 Ignotus tibi Waltharius et maxima uirtus.
Ut mihi praeterita portendit uisio nocte,
Non, si conserimus, nos prospera cuncta sequentur.
Uisum quippe mihi te colluctarier urso,
Qui post conflictus longos tibi mordicus unum
625 Crus cum poblite ad usque femur decerpserat omne

---

588 inuenis P.—590 huc an P.—618 te concomitantes P.

Et mox auxilio subeuntem ac tela ferentem
Me petit atque oculum cum dentibus eruit unum.'
His animaduersis clamat rex ille superbus :
' Ut uideo, genitorem imitaris Hagathien ipse.
630 Hic quoque perpauidam gelido sub pectore mentem
Gesserat et multis fastidit proelia uerbis.'
Tunc heros magnam iuste conceperat iram,—
Si tamen in dominum licitum est irascier ullum.
' Haec ' ait ' in uestris consistat omnia telis.
635 Est in conspectu quem uultis. dimicet omnis.
Cominus astatis nec iam timor inpedit ullum ;
Euentum uideam nec consors sim spoliorum ;
Dixerat et collem petiit mox ipse propinquum
Descendensque ab equo consedit et aspicit illo.
640 Post haec Guntharius Cameloni praecipit aiens :
' Perge et thesaurum reddi mihi praecipe totum.
Quodsi cunctetur, scio tu uir fortis et audax,
Congredere et bello deuictum mox spoliato.'
Ibat metensis Camelo metropolitanus,
645 Uertice fulua micat cassis, de pectore torax,
Et procul acclamans : ' heus audi ' dixit ' amice !
Regi Francorum totum transmitte metallum,
Si uis ulterius uitam uel habere salutem.'
Conticuit paulum uerbo fortissimus heros,
650 Opperiens propius hostem aduentare ferocem.
Aduolitans missus uocem repetiuerat istam.
[' Regi Francorum totum transmitte metallum ! ']
Tum iuuenis constans responsum protulit istud :
' Quid quaeris ? uel quid reddi, inportune coartas ?
655 Numquid Gunthario furabar talia regi ?
Aut mihi pro lucro quicquam donauerat ille,
Ut merito usuram me cogat soluere tantam ?
Num pergens ego dampna tuli uestrae regioni,
Ut uel hinc iuste uidear spoliarier a te ?
660 Si tantam inuidiam cuntis gens exhibet ista,
[Ut calcare solum nulli concedat eunti,]
Ecce uiam mercor, regi transmitto ducentas
Armillas. pacem donet modo bella remittens.
Haec postquam Camelo percepit corde ferino :

---

634 haec P., hec S.-H.—636 impedit P,—654 importune P.

665 'Amplificabis' ait 'donum, dum scrinia pandis.
Consummare etenim sermones nunc uolo cunctos :
Aut quaesita dabis, aut uitam sanguine fundes.'
Sic ait et triplicem clipeum collegit in ulnam
Et crispans hastile micans ui nititur omni.
670 Ac iacit. at iuuenis deuitat cautior ictum.
Hasta uolans casso tellurem uulnere mordit.
Waltharius tandem : 'si sic placet,' inquit 'agamus.'
Et simul in dictis hastam transmisit. at illa
Per laeuum latus umbonis transiuit et ecce
675 Palmam qua Camelo mucronem educere cepit
Confixit femori transpungens terga caballi.
Nec mora, dum uulnus sensit sonipes, furit atque
Excutiens dorsum sessorem sternere temptat
Et forsan faceret, ni lancea fixa teneret.
680 Interea parmam Camelo dimisit et hastam
Conplexus leua satagit diuellere dextram.
Quod mox perspiciens currit celeberrimus heros
Et pede conpresso capulo tenus ingerit ensem,
Quem simul educens hastam de uulnere traxit.
685 Tunc equus et dominus hora cecidere sub una.
At dum forte nepos conspexerat hoc Camelonis,
Filius ipsius Kimo cognomine fratris,
Quem referunt quidam Scaramundum nomine dictum,
Ingemit et lacrimis conpellat tristior omnes :
690 'Haec me prae cunctis heu respicit actio rerum.
Nunc aut conmoriar uel carum ulciscar amicum.'
Namque angusta loci solum concurrere soli
Cogebant nec quisquam alii succurrere quiuit.
Aduolat infelix Scaramundus iam moriturus
695 Bina manu lato crispans hastilia ferro.
Qui dum Waltharium nullo terrore uideret
Permotum fixumque loco consistere in ipso,
Sic ait infrendens et equinam uertice caudam
Concutiens : 'in quo fidis? uel quae tua spes est?
700 Non ego iam gazam uel rerum quidque tuarum
Appeto, sed uitam cognati quaero perempti.'
Ille dehinc : 'si conuincar, quod prelia primus

675 coepit P.—676 caualli P.—681 complexus P., laeua P., dextra P.
682 tum P.—683 compresso P.—687 Kuno P.—689 compellat P.—691
commoriar P.—700 quicque P.—702 proelia P.

Temptarim seu quid merui, quod talia possim
Jure pati, absque mora tua me transuerberet hasta.
705 Necdum sermonem concluserat, en Scaramundus
Unum de binis hastile retorsit in illum
Confestimque aliud.   quorum celeberrimus heros
Unum deuitat, quatit ex umbone secundum.
Tunc aciem gladii promens Scaramundus acuti
710 Proruit in iuuenem cupiens praescindere frontem,
Effrenique in equo propius deuectus ad illum
Non ualuit capiti libratum infindere uulnus.
Sed capulum galeae inpegit: dedit illa resultans
Tinnitus ignemque simul transfudit ad auras.
715 Sed non cornipedem potuit girare superbum,
Donec Waltharius sub mentum cuspidis ictum
Fixerat et sella moribundum sustulit alta.
Qui caput orantis proprio mucrone recidens
Fecit cognatum pariter fluitare cruorem.
720   Hunc ubi Guntharius conspexit obire superbus,
Hortatur socios pugnam renouare furentes:
'Aggrediamur eum nec respirare sinamus,
Donec deficiens lassescat et inde reuinctus
Thesauros reddet luet et pro sanguine penas.
725   Tertias en Wurhardus abit bellumque lacessit,
Quamlibet ex longa generatus stirpe nepotum
O uir clare tuus cognatus et artis amator,
Pandare, qui quondam iussus confundere foedus
In medios telum torsisti primos Achiuos.
730 Hic spernens hastam pharetram gestauit et arcum,
Eminus emissis haut aequo Marte sagittis
Waltharium turbans.   contra tamen ille uirilis
Constitit opponens clipei septemplicis orbem,
Saepius eludens uenientes prouidus ictus.
735 Nam modo dissiluit, parmam modo uergit in austrum
Telaque discussit, nullum tamen attigit illum.
Postquam Pandarides se consumpsisse sagittas
Incassum uidet, iratus mox exerit ensem
Et demum aduolitans has iactitat ore loquelas:
740 ' O si uentosos lusisti callide iactus,
Forsan uibrantis dextrae iam percipis ictum.'

---

724 poenas P. (cf. pęnam B).—725 Ewurhardus P.—731 haud P.

Olli Waltharius ridenti pectore adorsus :
' Iamque diu satis expecto certamina iusto
Pondere agi. festina, in me mora non erit ulla.'
745 Dixerat et toto conixus corpore ferrum
Conicit. hasta uolans pectus reserauit equinum :
Tollit se arrectum quadrupes et calcibus auras
Uerberat effundensque equitem cecidit super illum.
Accurrit iuuenis et ei ui diripit ensem.
750 Casside discussa crines conplectitur albos
Multiplicesque preces nectenti dixerat heros :
' Talia non dudum iactabas dicta per auras.'
Haec ait et truncum secta ceruice reliquit.
Sed non dementem tria uisa cadauera terrent
755 Guntharium : iubet ad mortem properare uicissim.
En a saxonicis oris Ekeurid generatus
Quartus temptauit bellum, qui pro nece facta
Cuiusdam primatis eo diffugerat exul.
Quem spadix gestabat equus maculis uariatus.
760 Hic ubi Waltharium promptum uidet esse duello :
' Dic,' ait ' an corpus uegetet tractabile temet
Siue per aerias fallas maledicte figuras ?
Saltibus assuetus faunis mihi quippe uideris.'
Illeque sublato dedit haec responsa cachino :
765 ' Celtica lingua probat te ex illa gente creatum
Cui natura dedit reliquas ludendo praeire.
At si te propius uenientem dextera nostra
Attingat, post Saxonibus memorare ualebis,
Te nunc in Vosago fauni fantasma uidere.'
770 'Attemptabo quidem, quid sis,' Ekeurid ait, ac mox
Ferratam cornum grauiter iacit. illa retorto
Emicat ammento : quam duras fregerat umbo.
Waltharius contra respondit cuspide missa :
' Haec tibi siluanus transpondet munera faunus.
775 Aspice, num mage sit telum penetrabile nostrum.'
Lancea taurino contextum tergore lignum
Diffidit ac tunicam scindens pulmone resedit.
Uoluitur infelix Ekeurid riuumque cruoris
Euomit : en mortem fugiens incurrit eandem.
780 Cuius equum iuuenis post tergum in gramen abegit.

742 Illi P.—765 me P.—774 transponit P.

Tunc a Gunthario clipeum sibi postulat ipsum
Quintus ab inflato Hadawartus pectore lusus.
Qui pergens hastam sociis dimisit habendam
Audax in solum confisus inaniter ensem.
785 Et dum conspiceret deiecta cadauera totam
Conclusisse uiam nec equum transire ualere,
Dissiliens parat ire pedes. stetit acer in armis
Waltharius laudatque uirum, qui praebuit aequam
Pugnandi sortem. Hadawart tum dixit ad illum :
790 ' O uersute dolis et fraudis conscie serpens !
Occultare artus squamoso tegmine suetus
Ac ueluti coluber girum collectus in unum,
Tela tot euitas tenui sine uulneris ictu
Atque uenenatas ludis sine more sagittas ?
795 Nunquid et iste putas astu uitabitur ictus
Quem propius stantis certo libramine mittit
Dextra manus?   neque enim is teli seu uulneris auctor.
Audi consilium, parmam deponito pictam :
Hanc mea sors quaerit, regis quoque sponsio praestat,
800 Nolo quidem laedas, oculis quia conplacet istis.
Sin alias, licet et lucem mihi dempseris almam,
Assunt hic plures socii carnisque propinqui,
Qui, quamuis uolucrem similes pennasque capessas.
Te tamen inmunem nunquam patiantur abire.
805   Belliger at contra nil territus intulit ista :
' De reliquis taceo, clipeum defendere curo.
Pro meritis mihi crede bonis sum debitor illi.
Hostibus ipse meis se opponere saepe solebat
Et pro uulneribus suscepit uulnera nostris.
810 Quam sit oportunus hodie mihi cernis, et ipse
Non cum Walthario loquereris forsan, abesset.
Uiribus o summis hostem depellere cures,
Dextera ne rapiat tibi propugnacula muri.
Tu clauum umbonis studeas retinere sinistra,
815 Atque ebori digitos circumfer glutine fixos.'
Istic deponas pondus, quod tanta uiarum
Portasti spatia ex Auarum nam sedibus altis?
Ille dehinc: ' inuitus agis, si sponte recusas.
Nec solum parmam, sed equum cum uirgine et auro

787 petit P.—789 Pugnandi sortem Hadawartum. dixit at ille P.—
795 Numquid P.—800 complacet P., ista P.—808 iste P.

820 Reddes: tum demum scelerum cruciamina pendes.'
Haec ait et notum uagina diripit ensem.
Inter se uariis terrarum partibus orti
Concurrunt. stupuit Vosagus haec fulmina et ecce
Ambo sublimes animis ac grandibus armis,
825 Hic gladio fidens hic acer et arduus hasta
Inter se multa et ualida ui praelia miscent.
Non sic nigra sonat percussa securibus ilex,
Ut dant tinnitus galeae clipeique resultant.
Mirantur Franci, quod non lassesceret heros
830 Waltharius cui nulla quies spatiumue dabatur.
Emicat hic inpune putans iam Wormaciensis
Alte et sublato consurgit feruidus ense
Hoc ictu memorans semet finire duellum :
Prouidus at iuuenis ferientem cuspide adacta
835 Intercepit et ignauum dimmitere ferrum
Cogebat. procul in dumis resplenduit ensis.
Hic ubi se gladio spoliatum uidit amico,
Accelerare fugam fruticesque uolebat adire.
Alpharides fretus pedibus uiridique iuuenta
840 Insequitur dicens: 'quonam fugis? accipe scutum.'
Sic ait atque hastam manibus leuat ocius ambis
Et ferit. Ille cadit, clipeus superintonat ingens.
Nec tardat iuuenis: pede collum pressit et hasta
Diuellens parmam telluri infixerat illum.
845 Ipse oculos uertens animam sufflauit in auram.
    Sextus erat Pataurid. soror hunc germana Haganonis
Protulit ad lucem. quem dum procedere uidit,
Uocibus et precibus conatur auunculus inde
Flectere proclamans : 'quonam ruis? aspice mortem,
850 Qualiter aridet. desiste ! en ultima Parcae
Fila legunt. o care nepos te mens tua fallit.
Desine. Waltharii tu denique uiribus inpar.'
Infelix tamen ille means haec omnia spreuit.
Arsit enim iuuenis laudem captare cupiscens.
855 Tristatusque Hagano suspiria pectore longa
Traxit et has imo fudit de corde loquelas :
'O uortex mundi fames insatiatus habendi,
Gurges auaritiae, cunctorum fibra malorum !

826 proelia P.—831 Wormatiensis P.—835 ignarum P.—854 uenis P.

    O utinam solum glutires dira metallum
860 Diuitiasque alias homines inpune remittens.
    Sed tu nunc homines peruerso numine perflans
    Incendis nullique suum iam sufficit. ecce
    Non trepidant mortem pro lucro incurrere turpem.
    Quanto plus retinent, tanto sitis ardet habendi.
865 Externis modo ui modo furtiue potiuntur
    Et quod plus renouat gemitus lacrimasque ciebit,
    Caeligenas animas Erebi fornace retrudunt.
    Ecce ego dilectum nequeo reuocare nepotem,
    Instimulatus enim de te est o saeua cupido.
870 En caecus mortem properat gustare nefandam
    Et uili pro laude cupit descendere ad umbras.
    Heu mihi care nepos matri quid perdite mandas?
    Quis nuper ductam refouebit care maritam,
    Cui nec rapta spei pueri ludicra dedisti?
875 Quis tibi nam furor est? unde haec dementia uenit'?
    Sic ait et gremium lacrimis consparsit obortis,
    Et 'longum formose uale' singultibus edit.
      Waltharius licet a longe socium fore maestum
    Attendit clamorque simul peruenit ad aures.
880 Unde incursantem sic est affatus equestrem:
    'Accipe consilium iuuenis fortissime nostrum
    Et te conseruans melioribus utere fatis.
    Desine, nam tua te feruens fiducia fallit.
    Heroum tot cerne neces et cede duello,
885 Ne suprema uidens hostes facias mihi plures.'
    ' Quid de morte mea curas' ait ille 'tyranne?
    Est modo pugnandum tibimet, non sermocinandum.'
    Dixit et in uerbo nodosam destinat hastam,
    Cuspide quam propria diuertens transtulit heros,
890 Quae subuecta choris ac uiribus acta furentis
    In castrum uenit atque pedes stetit ante puellae.
    Ipsa metu perculsa sonum prompsit muliebrem.
    At postquam tenuis redit in praecordia uirtus,
    Paulum suspiciens spectat, num uiueret heros.
895   Tum quoque uir fortis Francum discedere bello
    Iussit. at ille furens gladium nudauit et ipsum
    Incurrens petiit uulnusque a uertice librat.

874 rapte P.

Alpharides parmam demum concusserat aptam
Et spumantis apri frendens de more tacebat.
900 Ille ferire uolens se pronior omnis ad ictum
Exposuit, sed Waltharius sub tegmine flexus
Delituit corpusque suum contraxit et ecce
Uulnere delusus iuuenis recidebat ineptus.
Finis erat, nisi quod genibus tellure refixis
905 Belliger accubuit calibemque sub orbe cauebat.
Hic dum consurgit, pariter se subrigit ille
Ac citius scutum trepidus sibi praetulit atque
Frustra certamen renouare parabat. at illum
Alpharides fixa gladio petit ocius hasta
910 Et mediam clipei dempsit uasto inpete partem
Amatam resecans loricam atque ilia nudans.
Labitur infelix Pataurid sua uiscera cernens
Siluestrique ferae corpus, animam dedit Orco.
Hunc sese ulturum spondens Gerwicus adiuit,
915 Qui forti subuectus equo suprauolat omnem
Stragem quae angustam concluserat obuia callem.
Et dum bellipotens resecaret colla iacentis,
Uenit et ancipitem uibrauit in ora bipennem.
Istius ergo modi Francis tunc arma fuere.
920 Uir celer obiecit peltam frustrauit et ictum
Ac retro saliens hastam rapiebat amicam
Sanguineumque ulua uiridi dimiserat ensem.
Hic uero metuenda uirum tum bella uideres.
Sermo quidem nullus fuit inter martia tella :
925 Sic erat aduerso mens horum intenta duello
Is furit, ut caesos mundet uindicta sodales,
Ille studet uitam toto defendere nisu
Et, sifors dederit, palmam retinere triumphi.
Hic ferit, ille cauet, petit ille, reflectitur iste :
930 Ad studium fors et uirtus miscentur in unum.
Longa tamen cuspes breuiori depulit hostem
Armatum telo, girat sed et ille caballo
Atque fatigatum cupiebat fallere homonem.
Iam magis atque magis irarum mole grauatus
935 Waltharius clipeum Gerwici sustulit imum
Transmissoque femur penetrauerat inguine ferrum.

910 impete P.—914 Gewitus P.—922 demerserat P.—932 cauallo P.—
935 Gerwiti P.

Qui post terga ruens clamorem prodidit atrum
Exiciumque dolens pulsabat calcibus aruum.
Hunc etiam truncum caesa ceruice reliquit.
940 Hic in Wormatiae campis comes extitit ante.
Tunc primum Franci ceperunt forte morari
Et magnis precibus dominum decedere pugna
Deposcunt. furit ille miser caecusque profatur :
' Quaeso uiri fortes et pectora saepe probata,
945 Ne fors haec cuicumque metum sed conferat iram.
Quid mihi, si Vosago sic sic inglorius ibo ?
Mentem quisque meam sibi uindicet. en ego partus
Ante mori sum, Wormatiam quam talibus actis
Ingrediar. petat hic patriam sine sanguine uictor ?
950 Hactenus arsistis hominem spoliare metallis,
Nunc ardete uiri fusum mundare cruorem,
Ut mors abstergat mortem, sanguis quoque sanguem
Soleturque necem sociorum plaga necantis.'
His animum dictis demens incendit et omnes
955 Fecerat inmemores uitae simul atque salutis.
Ac uelut in ludis alium praecurrere quisque
Ad mortem studuit, sed semita, ut antea dixi,
Cogebat binos bello decidere solos.
Uir tamen illustris dum cunctari uidet illos,
960 Uertice distractas suspendit in arbore cristas
Et uentum captans sudorem tersit anhelus.
Ecce repentino Randolf athleta caballo
Praeuertens reliquos hunc inportunus adiuit
Ac mox ferrato petiit sub pectore conto.
965 Et nisi duratis Welandia fabrica giris
Obstaret, spisso penetrauerit ilia ligno.
Ille tamen subito stupefactus corda pauore
Munimen clipei obiecit mentemque recepit :
Nec tamen et galeam fuerat sumpsisse facultas.
970 Francus at emissa gladium nudauerat hasta
Et feriens binos Aquitani uertice crines
Abrasit, sed forte cutem praestringere summam
Non licuit rursumque alium uibrauerat ictum
Et praeceps animi directo obstamine scuti

---

937 acrum P.—938 Exitiumque P.—941 coeperunt P.—955 imme-
mores P.—962 cauallo P.—966 penetrauerat P.

975 Inpegit chalibem nec quiuit uiribus ullis
     Elicere. Alpharides retro se fulminis instar
     Excutiens Francum ualida ui fudit ad aruum
     Et super assistens pectus conculcat et inquit:
     'En pro caluitio capitis te uertice fraudo,
980 Ne fiat ista tuae de me iactantia sponsae.'
     Uix haec effatus truncauit colla precantis.
     At nonus pugnae Helmnod successit et ipse
     Insertum triplici gestabat fune tridentem,
     Quem post terga quidem socii stantes tenuerunt.
985 Consiliumque fuit, dum cuspis missa sederet
     In clipeo, cuncti pariter traxisse studerent,
     Ut uel sic hominem deiecissent furibundum:
     Atque sub hac certum sibi spe posuere triumphum.
     Nec mora, dux totas fundens in brachia uires
990 Misit in aduersum magna cum uoce tridentem
     Edicens: 'ferro tibi finis calue sub isto!'
     Qui uentos penetrat iaculorum more coruscans:
     Quod genus aspidis exalta sese arbore tanto
     Turbine demittit, quo cuncta obstantia uincat.
995 Quid moror? umbonem sciderat peltaque resedit.
     Clamorem Franci tollunt saltusque resultat
     Obnixique trahunt restim simul atque uicissim
     Nec dubitat princeps tali se aptare labori.
     Manarunt cunctis sudoris flumina menbris.
1000 Sed tamen haec inter uelut aesculus astitit heros
     Quae non plus petit astra comis quam tartara fibris
     Contempnens omnes uentorum inmota fragores.
     Certabant hostes hortabanturque uiritim,
     Ut si non quirent ipsum detrudere ad aruum,
1005 Munimen clipei saltem extorquere studerent,
     Quo dempto uiuus facile caperetur ab ipsis.
        Nomina quae restant edicam iamque trahentum:
     Nonus Eleuter erat Helmnod cognomine dictus.
     Argentina quidem decimum dant oppida Trogum,
1010 Extulit undecimum pollens urbs Spira Tanastum
     Absque Haganone locum rex suppleuit duodenum.

---

975 calibem P.—982 Et P., Heimnod P.—985 cuspes dum P.—992
penetrans P., coruscat P.—994 dimittit P.—995 scidit P.—999 membris
P.—1000 aesculus P.—1002 immota P.—1006 facile uiuus P.—1008
Heimnod P.—1009 Trogunt P.—1011 supplevit rex P.

Quatuor hi aduersum summis conatibus unum
Contendunt pariter multo uarioque tumultu.
Interea Alpharidi uanus labor incutit iram.
1015 Et qui iam pridem nudarat casside frontem
In framea tunicaque simul confisus aena
Omisit parmam primumque inuasit Eleutrim.
Huic galeam findens cerebrum diffudit et ipsam
Ceruicem resecans pectus patefecit, at aegrum
1020 Cor pulsans animam liquit mox atque calorem.
Inde petit Trogum haerentem in fune nefando.
Qui subito attonitus recidentis morte sodalis
Horribilique hostis conspectu ceperat acrem
Necquicquam temptare fugam uoluitque relicta
1025 Arma recolligere, ut rursum repararet agonem.
Nam cuncti funem tracturi deposuerunt
Hastas cum clipeis, sed quanto maximus heros
Fortior extiterat, tanto fuit ocior olli
Et cursu capto suras mucrone recidit
1030 Ac sic tardatum praeuenit et abstulit ejus
Scutum. sed Trogus quamuis de uulnere laesus
Mente tamen feruens saxum circumspicit ingens,
Quod rapiens subito obnixum contorsit in hostem
Et proprium a summo clipeum fidit usque deorsum,
1035 Sed retinet fractum pellis superaddita lignum.
Moxque genu posito uiridem uacuauerat aedem
Atque ardens animis uibratu terruit auras
Et si non quiuit uirtutem ostendere factis,
Corde tamen habitum patefecit et ore uirilem.
1040 Nec manes ridere uidens audaciter infit:
'O mihi si clipeus uel si modo adesset amicus!
Fors tibi uictoriam de me, non inclita uirtus
Contulit. ad scutum mucronem tollito nostrum!'
Tum quoque subridens: 'uenio iam,' dixerat heros
1045 Et cursu aduolitans dextram ferientis ademit.
Sed cum athleta ictum libraret ab aure secundum
Pergentique animae ualuas aperire studeret,
Ecce Tanastus adest telis cum rege resumptis
Et socium obiecta protexit uulnere pelta.

1020 mox liquerat P.—1021 Trogunt P.—1023 coeperat P.—1024 ne-
quiquam P.—1031 Trogunt P.—1035 scissum P.—1036 ensem P.

1050 Hinc indignatus iram conuertit ad ipsum
Waltharius humerumque eius de cardine uellit,
Perque latus ducto suffudit uiscera ferro.
Aue! procumbens submurmurat ore Tanastus.
Quo recidente preces contempsit promere Trogus
1055 Conuiciisque sui uictorem incendit amaris,
Seu uirtute animi, seu desperauerat. exin
Alpharides : ' morere' inquit 'et haec sub tartara transfer
Enarrans sociis, quod tu sis ultus eosdem.'
His dictis torquem collo circumdedit aureum.
1060 Ecce simul caesi uoluuntur puluere amici
Crebris foedatum ferientes calcibus aruum.
His rex infelix uisis suspirat et omni
Aufugiens studio falerati terga caballi
Scandit et ad mestum citius Haganona uolauit
1065 Omnimodisque illum precibus flexisse sategit,
Ut secum pergens pugnam repararet; at ille :
' Me genus infandum prohibet bellare parentum
Et gelidus sanguis mentem mihi dempsit in armis.
Tabescebat enim genitor, dum tela uideret
1070 Et timidus multis renuebat proelia uerbis :
Haec dum iactasses rex inter te comitantes,
Extitit indignum nostri tibi quippe iuuamen.'
Ille recusanti precibus nihilominus instans
Talibus auersum satagit reuocare loquelis
1075 ' Deprecor ob superos, conceptum pone furorem.
Iram de nostra contractam decute culpa,
Quam uita comitante, domum si uenero tecum,
Impensis tibimet benefactis diluo multis.
Nonne pudet sociis tot cognatisque peremptis
1080 Dissimulare uirum ? magis, ut mihi quippe uidetur,
Uerba ualent animum quam facta nefanda mouere.
Iustius in saeuum tumuisses mente tyrannum
Qui solus hodie caput infamauerat orbis.
Non modicum patimur dampnum de caede uirorum,
1085 Dedecus at tantum superabit Francia numquam.
Antea quis fuimus sublati sibila dantes :

1053 Salue P.—1054 Trogunt P.—1063 caualli P.—1064 maestum P.
—1075 Obsecro P., per P.—1078 Impensis P.—1085 a P.—1086 subjecti
P.

" Francorum " dicent " exercitus omnis ab uno,
Pro pudor ignotum vel quo, est inpune necatus !"
Cunctabatur adhuc Haganon et pectore sponsam
1090 Waltario plerumque fidem uoluebat et ipsum
Euentum gestae recolebat in ordine causae.
Supplicius tamen infelix rex institit illi.
Cuius subnixe rogitantis acumine motus
Erubuit, domini uultum replicabat honorem
1095 Uirtutis propriae qui fors uilesceret inde,
Si quocumque modo in rebus sibi parceret istis.
Erupit tandem et clara sic uoce respondit :
' Quo me domne uocas ? quo te sequar inclite princeps ?
Quae nequeunt fieri, spondet fiducia cordi :
1100 Quis tam desipiens quandoque fuisse probatur,
Qui saltu baratrum sponte attemptarit apertum ?
Nam scio Waltharium per campos sic fore acerbum,
Ut tali castro nec non statione locatus
Ingentem cuneum uelut unum tempnat homullum.
1105 Et licet huc cunctos equites simul atque pedestres
Francia misisset, sic his ceu fecerat istis.
Sed quia conspicio te plus doluisse pudore
Quam caedis dampno nec sic discedere uelle,
Conpatior propriusque dolor succumbit honori
1110 Regis : et ecce uiam conor reperire salutis,
Quae tamen aut numquam ostendet se siue coacte.
Nam propter carum fateor tibi domne nepotem
Promissam fidei normam corrumpere nollem.
Ecce in non dubium pro te rex ibo periclum,
1115 Ast hic me penitus conflictu cedere noris.
Secedamus eique locum praestemus eundi
Et positi in speculis tondamus prata caballis,
Donec iam castrum securus deserat artum
Nos abiisse ratus. campos ubi calcet apertos,
1120 Insurgamus et attonitum post terga sequamur :
Sic aliquod uirtutis opus temptare ualemus.
Haec mihi in abiguis spes est certissima rebus.
Tum bellare potes, belli rex si tibi mens est :
Quippe fugam nobis numquam dabit ille duobus,

1125 At nos aut fugere aut acrum bellare necesse est.'
      Laudat consilium satrapa et complectitur illum
      Oscilloque uirum demulcet. Et ecce recedunt.
      Insidiisque locum circumspexere sat aptum
      Demissique ligant animalia gramine laeto.
1130 Interea occiduas uergebat Phoebus in oras
      Ultima per notam signans uestigia Thilen
      Et cum Scotigenis post terga reliquit Hiberos.
      Hic postquam oceanas sensim calefecerat undas
      Hespera et ausoniis obuertit cornua terris,
1135 Tum secum sapiens cepit tractare satelles,
      Utrum sub tuto per densa silentia castro
      Sisteret, an uastis heremi conmitteret aruis.
      Aestuat inmensis curarum fluctibus et quid
      Iam faceret, sollers arguta indagine quaerit.
1140 Solus enim Hagano fuerat suspectus et illud
      Oscillum regis subter copnlexibus actum.
      Ambigerat prorsus, quae sit sententia menti
      Hostis et an urbem uellent remeare relictam,
      Pluribus ut sociis per noctem forte coactis
1145 Primo mane parent bellum renouare nefandum
      An soli insidias facerent propiusque laterent ?
      Terret ad haec triuiis ignoti silua meatus,
      Ne loca fortassis incurreret aspera spinis,
      Immo quippe feris, sponsamque amitteret illis.
1150 His ita prouisis exploratisque profatur :
      ' En quocumque modo res pergant, hic recubabo,
      Donec circuiens lumen spera reddat amatum !
      Ne patriae fines dicat rex ille superbus
      Euasisse fuga furis de more per umbras.'
1155 Dixit et ecce uiam uallo praemuniit artam
      Undique praecisis spinis simul et paliuris.
      Quo facto ad truncos sese conuertit amaro
      Cum gemitu et cuicumque suum caput applicat atque
      Contra orientalem prostratus corpore partem
1160 Ac nudum retinens ensem has uoce precatur :
      ' Rerum factori, sed et omnia facta regenti,

1135 coepit P.—1136 uasta P.—1137 committeret P.—1138 immensis
P.—1141 complexebus P.—1043 velīent urbem P.—1158 genitu P.—1160
Hac ensem nudum retinens cum uoce precatur P.

Nil sine permissu cuius uel denique iussu
Constat, ago grates quod me defendit iniquis
Hostilis turmae telis nec non quoque probris.
1165 Deprecor at dominum contrita mente benignum,
Ut qui peccantes non uult sed perdere culpas,
Hos in caelesti praestet mihi sede uideri.'
Qui postquam orandi finem dedit, ilico surgens
Sex girauit equos et uirgis rite retortis
1170 Vinciit: hi tantum remanebant, nempe duobus
Per tela absumptis ternos rex Gunthere abegit.
His ita conpositis procinctum soluit et alte
Ingenti fumans leuiabat pondere corpus.
Tum maestam laeto solans affamine sponsam
1175 Moxque cibum capiens aegros recreauerat artus,
Oppido enim lassus fuerat, clipeoque recumbens
Primi custodem somni iubet esse puellam,
Ipse matutinam disponens tollere curam
Quae fuerat suspecta magis, tandemque quieuit.
1180 Ad cuius caput illa sedens solito uigilauit
Et dormitantes cantu patefecit ocellos.
Ast ubi uir primum iam expergiscendo soporem
Ruperat, absque mora surgens dormire puellam
Iussit et arrecta se fulciit impiger hasta.
1185 Sic reliquum noctis duxit, modo quippe caballos
Circuit, interdum auscultans uallo propiauit
Exoptans orbi species ac lumina reddi.
Lucifer interea praeco scandebat Olympo
Lucens: Thaprobane clarum uidet insula solem.
1190 Hora fuit gelidus qua terram irrorat eous.
Aggreditur iuuenis caesos spoliarier armis
Armorumque habitu tunicas et cetera linquens:
Armillas tantum cum bullis, baltea et enses,
Loricas quoque cum galeis detraxerat ollis.
1195 Quatuor his onerauit equos sponsamque uocatam
Inposuit quinto, sextum conscenderat ipse
Et primus uallo perrexerat ipse reuulso.
At dum constricti penetratur semita callis,
Circumquaque oculis explorans omnia puris
1200 Auribus arrectis uentos captauit et auras,

1163 qui P.—1170 Uinxit P.—1172 compositis P.—1189 Taprobane P.

Si uel mussantes sentiret uel gradientes
Siue superborum crepitantia frena uirorum,
Seu saltem ferrata sonum daret ungula equorum.
Postquam cuncta silere uidet, praeuortit onustas
1205 Quadrupedes, mulierem etiam praecedere iussit.
Scrinia gestantem conprendens ipse caballum
Audet inire uiam consueto cinctus amictu.
Mille fere passus transcendit et ecce puella —
Sexus enim fragilis animo trepidare coegit —
1210 Respiciens post terga uidet descendere binos
Quodam colle uiros raptim et sine more meantes
Exanguisque uirum conpellat uoce sequentem :
' Dilatus iam finis adest : fuge, domne, propinquant!'
Qui mox conuersus uisos cognouit et inquit :
1215 ' Incassum multos mea dextera fuderat hostes.
Si modo supremis laus desit, dedecus assit.
Est satius pulchram per uulnera quaerere mortem
Quam solum amissis palando euadere rebus.
Uerum non adeo sunt desperanda salutis
1220 Commoda cernenti quondam maiora pericla.
Aurum gestantis tute accipe lora leonis
Et citius pergens luco succede propinquo.
Ast ego in ascensu montis subsistere malo
Euentum operiens aduentantesque salutans.'
1225 Obsequitur dictis uirguncula clara iubentis.
Ille celer scutum collegit et excutit hastam
Ignoti mores equitis temptando sub armis.
    Hunc rex incursans comitante satellite demens
Eminus affatu conpellat ualde superbo :
1230 ' Hostis atrox nisu deluderis! ecce latebrae
Protenus absistunt, ex quis de more liciscae
Dentibus infrendens rabidis latrare solebas.
En in propatulo si vis confligito campo
Experiens, finis si fors queat aequiperari
1235 Principio. scio fortunam mercede vocasti
Idcircoque fugam tempnis seu deditionem.'
    Alpharides contra regi non reddidit ulla,

1203 saltim P.—1204 praeuertit P.—1206 comprendens P., cauallum
P.—1212 compellat P.—1217 pulcram P.—1223 subsidere P.—1229
compellat P.—1236 Iccircoque P.

Sed velut hinc surdus aliô convertitur aiens:
'Ad te sermo mihi Hagano, subsiste parumper.
1240 Quid rogo tam fidum subito mutauit amicum,
Ut, discessurus nuper uix posse reuelli
Qui nostris uisus fuerat conplexibus ultro,
Nullis nempe malis laesus nos appetat armis?
Sperabam fateor de te, sed denique fallor.
1245 Quod si de exilio redeuntem nosse ualeres,
Ipse salutatum mihimet mox obuius ires
Et licet inuitum hospitii requiete foueres
Pacificeque in regna patris deducere uelles.
Sollicitusque fui, quorsum tua munera ferrem:
1250 Namque per ignotas dixi pergens regiones:
" Francorum uereor Haganone superstite nullum."
Obsecro per ludos resipiscito iam pueriles,
Unanimes quibus assueti fuimusque periti
Et quorum cultu primos attriuimus annos.
1255 Inclita quonam migrauit concordia nobis
Semper in hoste domique manens nec scandala noscens?
Quppe tui facies patris obliuiscier egit,
Tecum degenti mihi patria uiluit ampla.
Numquid mente fidem abradis saepissime pactam?
1260 Deprecor hoc abscide nefas neu bella lacessas
Sitque inconuulsum nobis per tempora foedus.
Quod si consentis, iam nunc ditatus abibis
Eulogiis, rutilo umbonem conplebo metallo.'
Contra quae Hagano uultu haec affamina toruo
1265 Edidit, atque iram sic insinuauit apertam:
1266ª ['Ne nos incuses, mihi uim quia tu prior infers.]
Uim prius exerces Walthari postque sopharis.
Tute fidem abscideras, cum memet adesse uideres
Et tot strauisses socios immoque propinquos:
Excusare nequis, quin me tunc affore nosses.
1270 Cuius si facies latuit, tamen arma uidebas
Nota satis habituque uirum rescire ualeres.
Cetera fors tulerim, si uel dolor unus abesset:
Unice enim carum, rutilum, blandum, pretiosum
Carpsisti florem mucronis falce tenellum.

1238 alio P.—1242 complexibus P.—1263 complebo P.—1266ª omitted by S. H.

1275 Haec res est pactum qua irritasti prior almum,
Idcircoque gazam cupio pro foedere nullam.
Sitne tibi soli uirtus uolo discere in armis,
Deque tuis manibus caedem perquiro nepotis,
En aut oppeto, siue aliquid memorabile faxo.'
1280 Dixit et a tergo saltu se iecit equino,
Hoc et Guntharius nec segnior egerat heros
Waltharius, cuncti pedites bellare parati.
Stabat quisque ac uenturo se prouidus ictu
Praestruxit: trepidant sub peltis martia menbra:
1285 Hora secunda fuit qua tres hi congrediuntur,
Aduersum solum conspirant arma duorum.
Primus maligenam collectis uiribus hastam
Direxit Hagano dirupta pace. sed illam
Turbine terribilem tanto et stridore uolantem
1290 Alpharides semet cernens tolerare nequire
Sollers obliqui delusit tegmine scuti:
Nam ueniens clipeo sic est ceu marmore laeui
Excussa et collem uehementer sauciat usque
Ad clauos infixa solo. Tunc pectore magno
1295 Sed modica ui fraxineum hastile superbus
Iecit Guntharius, uolitans quod adhaesit in ima
Waltharii parma, quam mox dum concutit ipse,
Excidit ignauum ligni de uulnere ferrum.
Omine quo maesti confuso pectore Franci
1300 Mox stringunt acies: dolor est conuersus ad iras
Et tecti clipeis Aquitanum inuadere certant.
Strennuus ille tamen ui cuspidis expulit illos
Atque incursantes uultu terrebat et armis.
Hic rex Guntharius ceptum meditatur ineptum,
1305 Scilicet ut iactam subito terraeque relapsam
Ante pedes herois enim diuulsa iacebat —
Accedens tacite furtim sustolleret hastam:
Quandoquidem breuibus gladiorum denique telis
Armati nequeunt accedere cominus illi,
1310 Qui tam porrectum torquebat cuspidis ictum.
Innuit ergo oculis uassum praecedere suadens
Cuius defensu causam supplere ualeret.

1276 Iccircoque P.—1284 membra P.—1300 iramP.—1304 coeptum P.

Nec mora, progreditur Haganon ac provocat hostem.
Rex quoque gemmatum vaginae condidit ensem
1315 Expediens dextram furto tutum faciendo.
Sed quid plura? manum pronus transmisit in hastam
Et iam conprensam sensim subtraxerat ipsam
Fortunae maiora petens. sed maximus heros,
Utpote qui bello semper sat prouidus esset,
1320 Praeter et unius punctum cautissimus horae,
Hunc inclinari cernens persenserat actum,
Nec tulit obstantem, sed mox Haganona reuellens,
Denique sublato qui diuertebat ab ictu,
Insilit et planta direptum hastile retentat
1325 Ac regem furto captum sic increpitauit,
Ut iam perculso sub cuspide genua labarent:
Quem quoque continuo esurienti porgeret Orco,
Ni Hagano armipotens citus succuret atque
Obiecto dominum scuto muniret et hosti
1330 Nudam aciem saevi mucronis in ora tulisset.
Sic dum Waltharius uulnus cauet, ille resurgit
Atque tremens trepidusque stetit uix morte reuersus.
Nec mora nec requies: bellum instauratur amarum,
Incurrunt hominem nunc ambo nuncque uicissim;
1335 Et dum progresso se inpenderet acrius uni,
En de parte alia subit alter et impedit ictum:
Haud aliter numidus quam dum uenabitur ursus
Et canibus circumdatus astat et artubus horret
Et caput occultans submurmurat ac propiantes
1340 Amplexans umbros miserum mutire coartat:
Tum rabidi circum latrant hinc inde molossi
Cominus ac dirae metuunt accedere beluae.
Taliter in nonam conflictus fluxerat horam
Et triplex inerat cunctis maceratio leti:
1345 Terror et ipse labor bellandi solis et ardor.
Interea herois cepit subrepere menti
Quiddam, qui tacito premit has sub corde loquelas:
'Si fortuna uiam non commutauerit, isti
Uana fatigatum memet per ludicra fallent.'
1350 Iilico et elata Haganoni uoce profatur:
'O paliure uires foliis, ut pungere possis,

1317 comprensam P.—1344 Atque P.—1346 coepit P.—1351 uirens P.

Tu saltando iocans astu me ludere temptas,
Sed iam faxo, locum propius ne accedere tardes :
Ecce tuas scio praegrandes ostendito uires.
1355 Me piget incassum tantos sufferre labores.
Dixit et exiliens contum contorsit in illum
Qui pergens onerat clipeum dirimitque aliquantum
Loricae ac magno modicum de corpore stringit :
Denique praecipuis praecinctus fulserat armis.
1360 At uir Waltharius missa cum cuspide currens
Euaginato regem inportunior ense
Inpetit et scuto dextra de parte reuulso
Ictum praeualidum ac mirandum fecit eique
Crus cum poblite ad usque femur decerpserat omne.
1365 Ille super parmam ante pedes mox concidit huius.
Palluit exanguis domino recidente satelles.
Alpharides spatam tollens iterato cruentam
Ardebat lapso postremum infligere uulnus.
Inmemor at proprii Hagano uir forte doloris
1370 Aeratum caput inclinans obiecit ad ictum.
Extensam cohibere manum non quiuerat heros,
Sed cassis fabrefacta diu meliusque peracta
Excipit assultum mox et scintillat in altum,
Cuius duritia stupefactus dissilit ensis
1375 Proh dolor et crepitans partim micat aere et herbis.
Belliger ut frameae murcatae fragmina uidit,
Indigne tulit ac nimia furit efferus ira
Inpatiensque sui capulum sine pondere ferri,
Quamlibet eximio praestaret et arte metallo,
1380 Protinus abiecit monimentaque tristia spreuit :
Qui dum forte manum iam enormiter exeruisset,
Abstulit hanc Hagano sat laetus uulnere prompto.
In medio iactus recidebat dextera fortis
Gentibus ac populis multis suspecta tyrannis,
1385 Innumerabilibus quae fulserat ante tropheis.
Sed uir praecipuus nec laeuis cedere gnarus,
Sana mente potens carnis superare dolores
Non desperauit neque uultus concidit eius,
Uerum uulnigeram clipeo insertauerat ulnam

1354 in corpore P.   1359 procinctus P.—1378 impatiensque P.—1385
trophaeis P.

1390   Incolumique manu mox eripuit semispatam,
        Qua dextrum cinxisse latus memorauimus illum,
        Ilico uindictam capiens ex hoste seueram.
        Nam feriens dextrum Haganoni effodit ocellum
        Ac timpus resecans pariterque labella reuellens
1395   Olli bis ternos discussit ab ore molares.
        Tali negotio dirimuntur prelia facto.
        Quemque suum uulnus atque aeger anhelitus arma
        Ponere persuasit. quisnam hinc inmunis abiret,
        Qua duo magnanimi heroes tam uiribus aequi
1400   Quam feruore animi steterant in fulmine belli?
        Postquam finis adest, insignia quemque notabant,
        Illic Guntharii regis pes palma iacebat
        Waltharii nec non tremulus Haganonis ocellus.
        Sic sic armillas partiti sunt auarenses.
1405   Consedere duo, nam tertius ille iacebat,
        Sanguinis undantem tergentis floribus amnem.
        Haec iter timidam reuocat clamore puellam
        Alpharides, ueniens quae saucia quaeque ligauit.
        His ita conpositis sponsus praecepit eidem:
1410   'Iam misceto merum Haganoni et porrige primum,
        Est athleta bonus fidei si iura reseruet:
        Tum praebeto mihi reliquis qui plus toleraui,
        Postremum uolo Guntharius bibat, utpote segnis
        Inter magnanimum qui paruit arma uirorum
1415   Et qui Martis opus tepide atque eneruiter egit.'
        Obsequitur cunctis Heririci filia uerbis.
        Francus at oblato licet arens pectore uino:
        'Defer' ait 'prius Alpharidi sponso ac seniori
        Uirgo tuo, quoniam fateor, me fortior ille est.
1420   Non solum mihi sed cunctis super eminet ille.
        Hic tandem Hagano spinosus et ipse Aquitanus
        Mentibus inuicti licet omni corpore lassi
        Post uarios pugnae strepitus ictusque tremendos
        Inter pocula scurrili certamine ludunt.
1425   Francus ait: 'iam dehinc ceruos agitabis amice,
        Quorum de corio wantis sine fine fruaris:
        At dextrum moneo tenera lanugine conple,
        Ut causae ignaros palmae sub imagine fallas.

Wah! sed quid dicis, quod ritum infringere gentis
1430 Ac dextro femori gladium agglomerare uideris
Uxorique tuae, si qua adeo cura subintrat,
Perverso amplexu circumdabis euge sinistram ?
Iam quid demoror ? en posthac tibi quicquid agendum est
Laeua manus faciet.' Cui Walthare talia reddit :
1435 ' Cur tam prosilias admiror lusce Sicamber :
Si uenor ceruos, carnem uitabis aprinam.
Ex hoc iam famulis tu suspectando uidebis
Heroum turbas transuersa tuendo salutans.
Sed fidei memor antiquae tibi consiliabor :
1440 Iam si quando domum uenias laribusque propinques,
Effice lardatam de multra farreque pultam :
Hoc pariter uictum tibi confert atque medelam.
His dictis pactum renouant iterato coactum
Atque simul regem tollentes ualde dolentem
1445 Inponunt equiti et sic disiecti redierunt :
Franci Wormatiam patriamque Aquitanus adiuit.
Illic gratifice magno susceptus honore
Publica Hiltgundi fecit sponsalia rite
Omnibus et carus post mortem obitumque parentis
1450 Ter denis populum rexit feliciter annis.
Qualia bella dehinc uel quantos saepe triumphos
Ceperit, ecce stilus renuit signare retusus.
Haec quicumque leges stridenti ignosce cicadae
Raucellam nec adhuc uocem perpende sed aeuum,
1455 Utpote quae nidis nondum petit alta relictis.
Haec est Waltharii poesis.   uos saluet Ihesus.

1431 amodo P.   1443 cruentum P.—1456 nos, I H̃ C P.

III.
CHRONICON NOVALICIENSE.*
(Lib. II., cap. vii–xiii.)

CAP. vii.

DICITUR autem in hoc monasterio prisco habuisse tempore monachum quendam olitorem, nomine Waltharium,[1] nobili ortum stigmate ac regali procreatum sanguine. Famosissimus enim valde ubique fuisse adletham,[2] ac fortis viribus refertur, sicut de eo quidam sapiens versicanorus scripsit:

> Waltarius fortis, quem nullus terruit hostis
> Colla superba domans, victor ad astra volans.
> Vicerat hic totum duplici certamine mundum,
> Insignis bellis, clarior ast meritis.
> Hunc Boreas rigidus[3] tremuit quoque torridus Indus,
> Ortus et occasus solis eum metuit.
> Cuius fama suis titulis redimita coruscis,
> Ultra caesareas scandit ab hinc aquilas.

Hic post multa prelia et bella, quae viriliter in seculo gesserat. cum iam prope corpus eius senio conficeretur, recordans[4] pondera suorum delictorum, qualiter ad rectam penitentiam[5] pervenire mereretur. Qui cum in monasterio, ubi districtior norma custodiretur monachorum, explere melius animo de liberasset, continuo baculum queritans perpulchrum, in cuius summitate plurimis configi precepit anulis, qui per singulis[6] ipsorum anorum[7] singulis[8] tintinnabulis appendi fecit; sumensque habitum peregrini, atque cum ipso pene totum peragrans mundum, ut exploraret cum ipso studia vite monachorum atque regulam ipsorum, ad quorumcumque[9] pervenisset monasteria. Tuncque illam, quam olim ferunt[10] peregrinationem habuisse, aggressus

---

* The text of the 'Chronicon Novaliciense' is here reprinted from that published by Pertz, 'Mon. Ger. Hist.' Vol. vii, cap. 7–13. The varsants in Muratori (M.) are given below the text; those found in Piper (P.), but not in Muratori, are designated by the abbreviation P. (v). Differences of orthography have been omitted in noting the variants.

1 Waltarius.—2 fuisse refertur athleta ac fortis viribus sicut.—3 Hunc Heroa (per) tremuit.—4 recardatus.—5 *not read by* M.—6 singulos.—7 anulorum.—8 singulos.—9 quodcumque.—10 fertur.

est. Qui cum in qualiqumque ingrederetur Monasterium tempore,[11] quo ipsi monachi ad laudes Deo reddendas intrabant. Hoc enim ipse valde observabat percuciebat siquidem bis vel ter cum ipso baculo pavimentum ecclesiae, ut ad sonitum ipsorum tintinnabulorum discerneret illorum disciplinam. Erat enim in eo maxima calliditas, et sollertis[12] exploratio, ut sic monachorum disciplinam agnosceret. Qui cum, ut supra retulimus, prope totum peragrasset cosmum, venit utique ad novaliciensem, tunc in studio sanctitatis famosissimum[13] monasterium. Ubi cum ingressus esset[14] ecclesiam, percussit more solito, ecclesiae solum. Ad quem sonitum quidam ex pueris retrorsum aspiciens, ut videret, quid hoc esset,[15] protinus magister schole in eum prosiliens, alapa percussit pueram alumpnum. Ubi ergo Waltarius talia vidit, ingemuit illico et ait : " En ergo hic, quod[16] multis diebus nonnulla terrarum spacia quaeritans repperire talia adhuc non valui." Exiens igitur statim ab ecclesia, mandavit siquidem abbati, ut secum colloquium habere dignaretur.[17] Cui cum suam insinuasset voluntatem, in proximo habitum sumens monachorum, efficitur protinus cultor orti, sponti et voluntarie, ipsius monasterii. Ipse vero accipiens duas longissimas funes, extenditque eas per ortum, unam scilicet per longum alteram namque per transversum, tempore[18] estatis omnes noxias in illas[19] suspendebat erbas, videlicet radicibus[20] ipsarum desuper expandebat contra solis fervorem, ut ultra non vivificarentur.

CAP. viii.

H IC ergo Waltarius quis vel unde nuperrime fuerit, vel a quo patre genitus sit, non est bonum silencio abscondere· Fuit enim quidam rex in Aquitanie regnum nomine Alferus.[21] Hic de coniuge propria habuit filium nomine Waltarium,[22] quem supra nominavimus. Huius temporibus in Burgundie regnum alius rex extiterat nomine Eriricus,[23] qui similiter habuit filiam valde decoram nomine Ildegundam.[24] Hii vere reges iuramentum inter se dederant, ut quando ipse pueri ad legitimam etatem primitus venissent, se invicem sociarent, scilicet cum tempus nubendi illis uenisset. Qui ergo pueri antequam se sociarent,

---

11 in tempore.—12 solers.—13 florentissimum.—14 foret.—15 erat.—16 qui.—17 dignetur.—18 ac tempore.—19 illis.—20 radices.—21 Alferius.—22 Waltarius.—23 Criricus Mur. and Bethm., Eriricus P.—24 Ildegunde.

subiecta sunt regna patrum suorum atque ipsi obsides dati sub
dicione regis Atile Flagellum Dei, qui eos secum duxerat cum
Aganone obside regis Francorum nomine Gibico.

CAP. ix.

H II namque pueri Attila causa obsidionis a propriis accipiens
patronibus [25] cum maxima pecunia, ad sua cum suis
repetit [26] arva.   Sic quidam [27] metricanorus de ipsis ait :

> Tunc Avares gazis onerati denique multis,   93
> Obsidibus sumptis Haganone, Hilgunde puella
> Necnon Walthario, redierunt pectore laeto.   95
> Attila Pannonias ingressus et urbe receptus,
> Exulibus pueris magnam exhibuit pietatem,
> Hac [28] veluti proprios nutrire iubebat alumpnos.
> Virginis [29] et curam reginam mandat habere.   99
> Ast adolescentes propriis conspectibus ambos   100
> Semper inesse iubet,[30] sed et artibus imbuit illos,
> Presertimque iocis belli sub tempore habentis.
> Qui simul ingenio crescentes [31] mentis et aevo,
> Robore vincebant fortes animoque sophistas,
> Donec iam cunctos superarent fortiter Hunos.   105
> Militiae primos tunc Attila fecerat illos ;
> Sed non inmerito ; quoniam si quando moverat

bella per insignes regionum illarum, isti ex pugna victoria mica-
bant, ideoque princeps ille quidni [32] dilexerat illos?   Virgo
etiam, quae cum ipsis ducta fuerat captiva, Deo sibi prestante   110
reginae placavit vultum, et ipsa auxit illi amorem.   Ex [33] nobilis
ergo moribus et operum [34] habundans sapientiae, ad ultimum
vero fit ipsa regis et reginae thesauris custoda [35] cunctis

> Et modicum deest [36] quin regnet et ipsa ;
> Nam quicquid voluit de rebus fecit et actis.   115

Gybichus [37] interea rex Francorum defungitur, et regno illo
Cundharius eius [38] successit filius, statimque foedera Pannonia-
rum dissolvit, atque censum illi deinceps negavit.   At vero
Haganus exul, agnita proprii domini morte, ilico fugam parat.
Ex cuius discessum [39] rex cum regina multum dolentes, Waltha-   120
rium retinere nitentes, ne forte simili exitu illum ammittentes,[40]

---

25 patronis.—26 redivit.—27 quidem.—28 Ac.—29 reginae P. (*variants*).—30 For the following verses cf.—Muratori, Antiq. Ital.' iii,
Diss. 44, pp. 965-972.—31 crescentis.—32 quidem.—33 Ea P. *wanting
in* M.—34 operibus.—35 custodia.—36 deese.—37 Gybicus.—38 ei.—
39 discessu.—40 amitterent.

rogare illum coeperunt, ut filiam alicuius regis satrapis Pannoni-
arum summeret sibi uxorem, et ipse ampliaret illi rure[41] do- 136
mosque. Quibus Waltharius talia respondit verba : 138
" Si nuptam," inquid, " accipiam secundum domini preceptum, 150
  In primis vinciar curis et amore puelle, 151
  Aedificare domos cultumque intendere ruris. 153

Nil ergo, mi senior, tam dulce mihi, quam semper tibi inesse 158
fidelis, teque optime deprecor pater per propriam vitam atque 165
per invictam gentem Pannoniarum,

  Ut non ulterius me cogas sumere taedas." 167
  Cumque [42] haec dixisset, sermones statim deserit omnes.

Sicque rex deceptus, sperans Waltharium recedere numquam.
Moxque satrapae illi certissima venerat fama de quandam gen- 170
tem quondam [43] ab Hunis devictam [44] super se iterum hostiliter
ruentem." [45]

  Tunc ad Waltharium convertitur actio rerum ;
  Qui [46] mox militiam percensuit ordine totam, 174
  Et bellatorum confortat corda suorum. 175
  Nec mora, consurgit, sequiturque exercitus omnis. 179
  Et ecce locum conspexerat pugnae, 180
  Et numeratam per latos aciem campos ;
  Iamque congressus uterque infra teli iactum
  Constiterat cuneus. Tunc utique clamor ad auras
  Tollitur ; horrenda confundit classica voce,
  Continuoque hastae volitant hinc indeque densae. 185
  Fraxinus et cornus [47] ludum miscebat in unum,
  Fulminis inque modum cuspis vibrata micabat. 187
  Fulmineos promunt [48] henses clipeosque revolvunt. 192
  Inde concurrit acies, et postmodum [49] pugnam restaurant,
  Ibique pectora equorum partim rumpuntur pectoribus,
  Sternuntur et quasdam partes virorum duro umbone.
  Waltharius tamen in medio furit agmine bello,
  Obvia [50] quaeque metens armis, hac limite pergens.
  Hunc ubi conspiciunt hostes tantas dare strages,
  Acsi presentem metuebant cernere mortem ;
  Et quemcumque locum seu dextram sive sinistram 200
  Waltharius peteret, cuncti mox terga dederunt. 201

Cumque ex victoria coronati lauro Waltharius cum Hunis 210-212
reverteretur, mox palatini ministri arcis 215

  Ipsius laeti occurrerunt, equitemque tenebant,

---

41 rura.—42 quum P. (v.).—43 quadam gente P. (v.).—44 devicta.—
45 ruente.—46 Quos.—47 cornua,—48 premunt.—49 per modum.—50
Nunc.—51 coronatus.

Donec vir inclitus ex alta descenderent [52] sella.
Quique [53] demum forte requirunt si bene rés vergant.
Qui modicum illis narrans intraverat aulam.
Erat enim oppido lassus,[54] regisque cubile petebat.   220
Illicque in ingressu Hilgundem solam offendit residentem ;
Cui post amabilem amplexionem atque dulcia oscula dixit :
" Ocius huc potum ferto, quia fessus anhelo."
Illa mero tallum complevit mox.pretiosum,
Atque [55] Walthario ad bibendum obtulit :   Qui signans   225
                              accepit,[56]
Virgineamque manum propria constrinxit ; at illa
Reticens vultum intendit in eum.
Cumque Waltharius bibisset vacuum vas reddidit illi—
Ambo enim noverant de se sponsalia facta—
Provocat et tali caram sermone puellam : [57]
" Exilium pariter partimur iam tempore tanto.
Non ignoramus enim, quod nostri quondam parentes
Inter se nostra de re fecere futura."   233

Quae cum diu talia et alia huiusmodi audisset virgo verba,
cogitabat hoc illi per hyroniam dicere, sed paululum cum con- 235
ticuisset, talia illi fatur :

" Quid lingua simulas quod [58] ab imo pectore dampnas?
Ore mihi fingis, toto quod corde refutas,
Tamquam si sit tibi magnus pudor ducere nuptam."
Vir sapiens contra respondit, et intulit ista :   240
"Absit, quod memoras. Dextrorsum porrige sensum.   241
Scis enim, nil umquam [59] me simulata mente locutum.   242

Adest itaque hic [60] nullus, exceptis nobis duobus. Amodo 244
namque esto mente sollicita, quae extrinsecus es regis reginaeque 261
thesauris custoda.

In primis galeam regis tunicamque trilicem   263
Assero [61] loricam fabrorum insigne ferentem.
Diripe bina, dehinc mediocria scrinia tolle.   265
His armillarum tantum da Pannonicarum,
Donec vix releves unum ad pectoris honum,[62]
Inde quater binum mihi fac de more coturnum.   268
Insuper a fabris hamos clam posce retortos.   271
Nostra viatica sint pisces simul atque volucres.
Ipse ego piscator sed auceps esse cohartor.[63]
Haec intra ebdomede[64] caute per singula comple.
Audisti quod habere vianti forte [65] necesse est.   275
Postquam septenos Phoebus remeaverit orbes   277
Convivia laeta parabo   279b
Regi ac reginae, satrapis, ducibus famulisque,   278
Atque omni ingenio potu sepelire studebo,[66]   280

---

52 descenderet.—53 Quemque.—54 lapsus.—55 Quem.—56 recepit.
—57 sermone . . . . velli.—58 quid.—59 enim numquam.—60 Adest
heic.—61 Affer.—62 onus.—63 cohortor.—64 hebdomadem.—65 forte
wanting.—66 potus saepius illinire studebo.

ita ut nullus supersit,[67] qui [68] sciat vel recognoscat, cur uel ob quam causam factum sit tale [69] convivium.   Te tamen premoneo mediocriter vinum [70] utere, ut vix sitim extinguas ad mensam.   Reliqui vero cum surrexerint, tu ilico ad nota recurre opuscula.   At ubi potus violentia superaverit cunctos,   285

> Tunc simul occiduas properemus querere partes."
> Virgo vero dicta viri valde memor praecepta complevit.
>   Et ecce
> Prefinita dies epularum venit, et ipse
> Waltharius qui [71] magnis instruxit sumptibus escas.

Luxuria denique in media residebat mensa.   Rex itaque ingred- 290 itur aulam, velis undique septam ; heros [72] itaque solito more [73] salutans quem magnanimus [74]

> Duxerat ad solium, quem bissus compsit [75] et ostrum.
> Consedit, laterique duces hinc indeque binos
> Assedere iubet ; reliquos locat ipse minister   295
> Centenos simul accubitus, et diversas dapes libans   297 a 297
>   convivia [76] redundat,
> His sublatis alie referuntur edende,   298
> Et pigmentatos [77] crateres Bachus adornat.   301
> Waltharius cunctos ad vinum ortatur et escam.
> Postquam depulsa fames fuerat [78] atque sublata mensa,
> Waltharius iamdictus dominum letanter adhorsus   305
> Dixit : " In hoc rogito gratia vestra [79] ut clarescat
> In primis, atque vos reliquos laetificetis."
> Qui simul in verbo nappam dedit arte peractam,[80]
> Gestam referentem priorum [81] ordinem sculture ipsius.
> Quam rex accipiens uno austu vacuaverat.   310
> Et confestim iubet reliquos omnes tali bibitione imitari.[82]
> Tunc citissime accurrunt pincerne atque recurrunt :
> Pocula plene dabant et inania suscipiebant.   313
> Ebrietas fervens tota dominatur aula.[83]   315
> Balbutit madido facundia fusa palato.
> Seniores fortes videres plantis titubare :
> Taliter in seram produxit [84] bacchica noctem.

Nam ire [85] volentes Waltharius munere retraxit, donec pressi [86] 320 somno potuque gravati per porticibus sternuntur humo tenus omnes passim.   Eciamsi tota civitas igne fuisse [87] succense, et

---

67 superius sit.—68 ut.—69 fit.—70 vino.—71 *wanting.*—72 Heroës. —73 more *wanting.*—74 magnanimitas.—75 composuit.—76 conviva.— 77 pigmentatas P. (v.)—78 fuerat *wanting.*—79 gratiam vestram.—80 paratam.—81 prior . . . . ordinem.—82 incitari.—83 in aula.—84 perduxit.—85 Nam in re.—86 perfessi.—87 fuisset.

ipse [88] flamivoma super ipsos crassari videretur, scilicet minitans
mortem,

> Nullus remansit,[89] qui scire potuisset causam.
> Tandem dilectam vocat ad semet [90] mulierem,
> Precipiens causas citius [91] deferre paratas.   325
> Et ipse de stabulis duxit victorem [92] aequorum,
> Quem ob virtutem leonem vocitaverat ipse.
> Stat sonipes, ac frena ferox spumatia mandit,
> Postquam enim hunc caballam ligamentis solito circum-
>   dederat, ecce
> Scrinia plena gazae, quibus utrique suspendit lateri,   330
> Atque itinere longo modicella ponit cibaria,
> Loraque virgineae mandat fluitantia dextrae.
> Ipseque vestit [93] lorica more gygantis,
> Atque capiti inposuit suo rubras cum casside cristas,
> Ingentesque complectitur aureis ocreis
> Et levum femur ancipiti precinxerat hense,
> Atque alio dextrum pro ritu Pannoniarum.
> His tamen ex una tantum dat vulnera parte.[94]
> Tunc hastam dextra rapiens clipeumque sinistra,
> Coeperat invisa terra trepidus decedere.   340
> Femina duxit *e*quum, nonnulla talenta gerentem.
> Ipsa vero in manibus virgam tenet simul colurnam,
> In qua piscator [95] hamum transponit in undam.   343
> Nam idem vir maximus [96] gravatus erat undique t*e*lis ;   345
> Ob hoc suspectam habuit cuncto sibi tempore pugnam.   346
> Sed cum prima lumina Phoebus rubens terris ostendit,   348
> In silvis latitare student, et opaca requirunt.   349
> Ergo [97] tantum timor pectora muliebria pulsabat,   351
> Ut cunctos susurros, auras vel ventos horrerat,[98]
> Formidans collisos racemos sive volucres.   353
> Vicis diffugiunt, speciosa [99] novalia linquunt,   355
> Montibus intonsis cursus ambage recurvos.   356
> Ast *u*rbis populus somno vinoque solutus.   358
> Sed postquam surgunt, ductorem quique [100] requirunt,   360
> Ut grates faciant hac [101] festa laude salutent.   361

Attila nempe utraque manu caput amplexatur,[102] *e*grediturque
thalamo ipse rex ; Waltharium dolendo advocat, ut proprium
quereret forte dolorem.   Cui respondent ipsi ministri, se non   365
potuisse invenire virum ; sed tamen princeps sperat, eundem
Waltharium in somno quietum recubare tentum hactenus, hac

---

88 ipsa.—89 remansisset.—90 ad se mox.—91 quantocius.—92 melio:
rem.—93 vestitus.—94 partem.—95 discator.—96 maxime.—97 erga ?—
98 Ut *a*d cunctos s. aurae v. venti haereret.—99 Spatiosa.—100 quoque.—101 ac.—102 amplexatus.

occultum locum sibi delegisse sopori. Ospirin vero regina, hoc illi
nomen erat, postquam cognovit Hildegunde abess*e* nec vestem   37?
deferre iuxta su*e*tum morem, tristior satrape inmensis strepens
clammoribus dixit :

    " O detestandas quas h*e*ri sumpsimus *e*scas !
    O vinum, quod Pannonias destruxerat omnes !
    Quod domino regi iam dudum prescia dixi,
    Approbat iste dies, quem nos superare nequimus.   375
    Hen ! [103] hodie imperii nostri c*e*cidisse columpna
    Noscitur ; hen ! [104] robur procul ivit [105] et inclita virtus,
    Waltharius lux Pannoniae discesserat inde ;
    Hildgundem quoque mi [106] karam deduxit alumpnam ! "
    Iam princeps efferus [107] nimia succenditur ira.   380
    Mutant priorem laetitiam merentia corda.   381
    Sic intestinis rex fluctuatur undique curis,   385
    Atque ipso quippe die fastidit omnino potus [108] et *e*scam,   389
    Nec placidam curam membris potuit dare quietem.   390
    At ubi nox supervenit atra,
    Decidit in lectum, ubi nec lumina clausit,
    Vertiturque frequenter de latus [109] in latere
    Tamquam si iacula [110] transfixus esset acuta.[111]   394
    Indeque surgens discurrit in urbem,   397
    Atque thorum veniens, simul attigit atque reliquid.
    Taliter insomnem consumpserat Attila noctem.
    At profugi comites per amica silentia euntes.   400

Tunc rex votum [112] fecerat, ut si quis Waltharium illi vinctum   403
afferret,   404

    Mox illum aurum [113] vestiret saepe recoctum [114]   405
    Sed nullus in tam magna regione   408

Fuit inventus tyrannus, dux sive comes s*e*u miles sive minister,
qui quamvis proprias ostendere cuperet vires, Waltharium   410
aliquando iratum presumpserit armis insequi. Nota siquidem   413
virtus eius fuerat facta [115] prope omnibus terrae [116] habitatoribus. 415
Qui Waltharius, ut dixi, fugiens noctibus ivit, atque die saltus 419
requirens et arbusta densa. Hic[117] vero arte accersita pariter volu- 420
cres arte capit, nunc fallens visca,[118] nunc fisso denique ligno.
Similiter in flumina inmittens hamum, rapiebat sub gurgitibus
predam.

    Sicque famis pestem pepulit tolerando laborem.   425
    Namque toto tempore fugae se virginis usu

---

103 Heu.—104 en.—105 procubuit et.—106 Hildegunde mihi.—107
effera.—108 potum.—109 latere.—110 iaculis.—111 acutis.—112 notum.
—113 auro.—114 recocto.—115 facta fuerat.—116 terrae *wanting*.—117
Heic.—118 visco.

Continuit vir Waltharius, laudabilis heros.

Et ecce quadraginta dies sol per mundum circumflexerat,

Ex quo Pannonia fuerat digressus ab urbe.

Ergo eo [119] die, quo numerum clauserat istum,   430
Venit ad fluvium iam vespere mediante,
Cui nomen est R<i>g</i>num,[120] qua cursus tendit ad urbem
Nomine Warmatiam, regali sede nitentem.
Illic pro naulo pisces dedit antea captos ;   435
Cumque esset transpositus, graditur properanter anh<i>e</i>lus.

Orta vero dies,
Portitor exsurgens [121] prefatam venit in urbem,
Ubi regali coquo, reliquornm certe magistro,
Detulerat pisces, quos vir ille viator dederat.   440
Hos vero dum pigmentis condisset et apposuisset
Regi Cundhario, miratus fatur ab alto :
" Ergo istiusmodi pisces mihi [122] Francia numquam ostendit.   444
Dic mihi quantotius, cuihas [123] homo detulit illos ? "
At [124] ipse respondens narrat, quod nauta dedisset.   445
Tunc princeps hominem iussit accersire eundem ;
Et cum venisset, de ré quesitus eadem
Talia dicta dedit et causam [125] ex ordine pandit :
" Uespere enim preterito [126] residebam ego litore Rh<i>e</i>ni.   450
Conspexi, et ecce viatorem vidi festinanter venire,
Tamquam pugne [127] per membra paratum.
Aere [128] etenim poenitus fuerat, rex inclite cinctus ;
Gerebat namque scutum gradiens,[129] et hastam choruscam,
Viro certe forti similis fuit, et quamvis ingens   455
Asportaret honus, gressum tamen extulerat acrem.
Hunc incredibili [130] forme puella decorata nitore   457a
Assequebatur, ipsaque caballum per lora rexit robustum,   458

bina quidem scrinia non parva ferentem dorso. Quae scrinia,[132]   460
dum cervicem sonipes ille [131] discutiebat ad altum, voluminaque
crurum superba glomerare cupiebat, dabant sonitum quasi quis
gemmis illiserit aurum. Hic miles mihi presentes pro munere
dederat pisces."

Cumque his [133] Hagano audisset verbis [134] — residebat quippe
ad mensam—

Laetus [135] in medium prompsit de pectore verbum :   465
" Congaudete mihi, queso, quia talia [136] novi.
Waltharius collega meus remeavit ab Hunis."   467
Cundharius vero princeps atque superbus ex hac ratione [137]   469
Vociferatur, et omnis ei mox [138] aula reclamat :   468

---

119 ea.—120 Rhenus.—121 pariter exsurgens.—122 mihi *wanting.*—
123 quinam.—124 Et.—125 causamque.—126 per terram.—127 pugnare.
128 qua re.—129 gratiens.—130 incredibilis.—131 scrupes—ille.—132
voluminaque *wanting.*—133 hoc.—134 verbum.—135 cuius.—136 utilia.
—137 oratione.—138 mox ei.

"Congaudete mihi, iubeo, quia gazam, quam Gybichus rex pater 470
meus transmisit Attile regi Hunorum, hanc mihi cunctipotens 139
huc in mea regna remisit."

Qui cum dixisset talia, mensam pede perculit,140 et exiliens
ducere 141 aequum iubet et sellam componere ilico sculptam;
atque de omni plebe elegit duodecim viros, viribus insignes et 475
plerumque animis probatos, inter quos simul ire Haganone iubebat. Qui 142 Hagano memor antiquae fidei et prioris sotii,143 nite-
batur transvertere rebus. Rex tamen *e* contra instat et clamat: 480
"Ne tardate, viri! 144 precingite corpora ferro!" 145   481

Instructi itaque milites t*e*lis nam iussio regis urgebat, exiebant 146 484
portis, ut Waltharium caperent, sed omnimodis Hagano prohi- 485–
                                                             487
bere studebat. At infelix rex coepto itinere resipiscere 147 non
vult. Interea vir inclitus atque magnanimus Waltharius de
flumine pergens venerat in silvam Vosagum 148 ab antiquis tem- 490
poribus vocitatam; nam nemus est ingens et spatiosum, atque
repleta ferarum plurima habens ibi suetum canibus resonare
tubisque. In ipsa itaque sunt bini 149 montes in secessu ipsius
atque propinqui, in quorum medium 150 quamvis angustum sit 494
spatium, tamen specus extat amoenum.

Mox iuvenis ut vidit, "Huc" inquit "eamus."   498
Nam postquam fugiens Avarorum arvis 151 discesserat, 500
Non aliter somni requiem gustaverat idem,
Quam super innixus clipeo vix clauserit 152 oculus.

Tum demum bellica deponens 153 arma, dixit virgini, in cuius
gremium fuerat fusus:

"Circumspice caute, Hildegund,154 et nebulam si tolli videris 505
atram, tactu blando me surgere commonitato.155 Etiamsi magnam conspexeris ire catervam, ne subito me excutias a somno, 508
mi kara, cav*e*to; sed instantem cunctam circa explora regionem."

Haec ait, statim oculos conclauserat ipse, desiderantes frui 510
iamdiu satis optata requie.

Ast ubi Cundharius vestigia pulvere vidit,
Cornipedem rapidum saevis calcaribus urguet, dicens: 156   514
"Accelerate uiri! iam nunc capietis eumdem.   516
Numquam hodie effugiet: furata talenta relinquet."

Illico inclitus Hagano contra mox reddidit ista:

"Unum tantum verbum dico tibi, regum fortissime:

---

139 cuncta potens.—140 percutit.—141 duodecim elegit viros vita insignes et animis.—142 quos.—143 sortis.—144 vestra.—145 ferris.—146
exibant.—147 respicere.—148 Vosagum *wanting*.—149 binae.—150
medio.—151 armis.—152 clauserat.—153 depones.—154 Hildegunda.
—155 commone.—156 dicens *wanting*.

Si toties tu Waltharium pugnasse videres,   520
Quotiens ego nova caede furentem,
Numquam tam facile spoliandum forte putares.
Vidi Pannonicas acies, cum bella agerent [157]
Contra aquilonares sive [158] australes regiones.
Illic Waltharius propria virtute choruscus,   525
Hostibus invisus, sociis mirandus obibat.
Quisquis ei congressus erat, mox Tartara vidit,
O rex et comites, experto credite, quantus [159]
In clipeum surgat, qua turbine [160] torqueat hastam."
Sed dum Cundharius malesana mente gravatus   530
Nequaquam flecti posset, castris propiabant.[161]
At Hiltgund de vertice montis procul aspiciens,
Pulvere sublato [162] venientes sensit ; ipsum
Waltharium placido tactu vigilare monebat.   534
Eminus illa refert quandam volitare phalangam.[163]   536
Ipse vero oculos tentos summi [164] glaucomate purgans,
Paulatim rigidos ferro vestiverat artus.   538

Cumque paululum properassent, mulier corusscantes ut vidit 542
hastas, stupefacta nimis " Hunos hic" [165] inquit " habemus."
Qui [166] ilico in terram cadens effatur talia tristis :

"Obsecro, mi senior, mea colla seccentur,   545
Utque non [167] merui thalamo sociari.
Nullius iam ulterius paciar consocia [168] carnis."   547

Cui Waltharius :

"Absit quod rogitas ; mentis depone pavorem, Ipse Domi- 551
nus, qui me de variis sepe eduxit [169] periculis, ille [170] valet hic
hostes, credo, confundere nostros."

Haec ait, oculosque adtollens effatur ad ipsam :

"Non assunt hic Avares, sed Franci nebulones, cultores 555
regionis."

Aspicit, et gnoscens iniunxit [171] talia ridens :

" En galeam Haganonis! meus collega veternus [172] atque
socius."

Hoc heros introitum [173] stationis hadibat,
Inferius stanti predicens sic mulieri :   560
" Coram hac porta verbum modo iacto [174] superbum " :

Hinc nullus rediens Francus, quis [175] suae valeat nunciar uxori,
qui tante [176] presumpserit tollere gazae."

---

157 egerent.—158 seu.—159 quantum.—160 quam bene.—161 properabant.—162 pulverem sublatum.—163 quasdam phalanges.—164 tonsos
somno.—165 hinc.—166 et.—167 utque tuo.—168 consortia.—169
eduxerat.—170 is.—171 adiunxit.—172 veteranus.—173 introitus.—174
iacta.—175 qui.—176 tantum.

Nec dum sermonem conpleverat, et ecce humo tenus corruit,
et veniam petiit, quod talia dixit. Postquam autem surrexit, 565
contemplans cautius dixit : [177]

"Omnes [178] horum quos video nullum timeo, Haganone remoto.
Nam ille meos per prelia scit mores, iamque [179] didicit, tenet et
hic etiam sat calidus artem. Quem si forte volente Deo intercepero [180] solum ; ex aliis namque formido nulla." 570

Ast ubi Waltharius [181] tali statione receptum 572
Conspexit Hagano, satrapae mox ista superbo
Suggerit verba : "O senior,[182] desiste lacessere bello
Hunc hominem! Pergant primum [183] qui cuncta requirant. 575
Et genus [184] et patriam nomenque et locum relictum,
Vel si forte petat pacem prebens [185] sine sanguine." 577

Qui licet invitus dicta [186] Haganoni acquievisset, misit ilico e
suis,[187] mandans Walthario, ut redderet [188] pecuniam quam
deferebat. Ad quos [189] Waltharius talia fertur dedisse verba :

"Ego patri suo eam non tuli neque sibi. Set si voluerit eam
capere, vi defendo eam fundens [190] alterius sanguinem."

Cumque hec denunciata essent Cundhario, protinus missit, qui
eum oppugnarent. Vir autem ille fortis ut erat, viriliter se ab
ipsis modicum defendens, ilico interfecit. Rex autem ut vidit,
et ipse protinus feroci animo cum reliquis [191] super eum venit.[192]
Waltharius vero nichil formidans, sed magis ut supra viriliter
instabat prelio. Cepit autem et ex illis Waltharius victoriam,
occisis cunctis preter regem et Haganonem. Qui cum eum
nullatenus superare possent, simulaverunt [193] fugam. Sperans
ergo Waltharius eos inde discedere, reversus in statione accep-
taque omni suppellectili sua, et ipse mox cum Ildegunda [194]
ascensis equis cepit iter agere. Cumque Waltharius egressus
esset ab antro quinque vel octo stadia, tunc leti posterga ipsius
recurrentes memorati viri, quasi victum eum iam extra rupe [195]
cogitabant. Contra quos ilico Waltharius quasi leo insurgens,
armis protectus [196] fortiter debellabat bellantibus sibi. Qui diu
multumque invicem pugnantes ac pre nimia lassitudine et siti
deficientes, iam non valebant virorum fortissimum superare.

177 dixerat.—178 Omnes *wanting*.—179 atque.—180 valentem dum
intercepero.—181 Waltharium.—182 O rex, mi senior.—183 primo.—
184 gentem.—185 prebens *wanting*.—186 dicto.—187 e suis *wanting*.
—188 Waltharium | reddere.—189 quod.—190 effundens.—191 cum re-
liquis *wanting*.—192 vertitur.—193 simulaverant.—194 Hildegunda.—
195 rupem.—196 pertectus.

Et ecce respicientes viderunt a sagma Waltharii vasculum vini dependere.

CAP. X.

INTEREA in eodem monestario consuetudine [197] eisdem temporibus dicitur habuisse plaustrum ligneum mire pulchritudinis operatum, in quo nichil aliquando fertur portasse aliquid, preter unam perticam, quae sepissime configebatur in eo, si necessitas cogeretur.[198] Sin autem tollebatur, et alio in loco recondebatur. In cuius summitate ferunt, qui videre [199] vel audire a videntibus potuerunt, habuisse tintinnabulum appensum valde resonantem. Cortes vero vel vicos ipsius monasterii, quae erant proximiores monasterio per Italiae tellus [200] in quibus ministri monachorum opportunis temporibus congregabant granum aut vinum. Cum autem necessitas vehendi exigeret ad monasterium, eundem sumptum [201] mittebatur plaustrum hoc cum predicta [202] pertica in eo conficta cum skilia ad predictos vicos, in quibus scilicet vicis inveniebantur nonnulla alia plaustra congregata, plerumque centena, aliquando etiam quinquagena, quae deferebant frumenta vel vinum ad antedictum coenobium. Hoc vero plaustrum dominicale nil ob aliud mittebatur, nisi ut agnoscerent universi magnates, quod ex illo inclito essent plaustra monasterio. In quibus erat nullus dux, marchio, comes, presul, vicecomes, aut villicus qui qualicumque violentia [203] auderet eisdem plaustris [204] inferre. Nam per foros Italiae annuales, ut tradunt, nullus audebat negotia exercere, donec eundem [205] plaustrum vidissent advenire mercatores cum skilla. Contigit autem quadam die, ut ministri ipsius Ecclesiae cum supradictis plaustribus [206] oneratis solito venirent more ad monasterium. Qui venientes in ipsa valle in quodam prato invenerunt familiam regis . . . pascentes equos regios. Qui statim ut viderunt tanta bona Servis Dei ministrare [207] fastu superbiae inflati insurgunt [208] illico [209] super eisdem hominibus, auferentes ab eis omnia, quae deferebant ; qui defendere volentes se et sua, incurrerunt in maiorem ignominiam, perdentes omnia. Qui statim mittunt legatum ad monasterium, qui ista nunciaret abbati et fratribus.

---

197 per consuitudinem.—198 cogeret.—199 viderunt.—200 tellures.— 201 idem supradictum.—202 plaustrum hoc cum supra dicta.—203 qualemcumque violentia.—204 plaustribus.—205 idem.—206 plaustris.— 207 munstrari.—208 insurgant.—209 illic.

CAP. xi.

A BBAS autem mox jussit congregari fratres, quibus insinuavit omnem rei eventum. Erat autem tunc pater congregationis eiusdem monasterii, nomine Asinarius, vir sanctitatis egregius Francicus genere, multis fulgens virtutibus. Cui cum unus nomine Waltarius, cui,[210] superius memoriam fecimus, respondisset, ut diligeretur illic [211] predictus pater sapientes fratres, ob quorum precacionem tanti sumtui [212] dimitterent iamdicti predones invationem. Respondit protinus eidem abbas, et ait:

" Quem prudentiorem et sapientiorem te mittere possimus, omnino ignoramus. Te autem, frater, moneo ac iubeo, utcelerius ad eos pergas, nobisque victum vi raptum quantocius reddere festinent moneto: alioquin citissime in gravi ira incurant Dei."

At Waltarius cum sciret conscientie sue illorum contumacia [213] ferre non posse, respondit: se denudandum ab ipsis tunicam, quam gestabat, Predictus vero pater, cum esset religiosus, ait:

" Si abstraxerint a te tunicam, da illis et cucullam : dicens, preceptum tibi [214] fuisse a fratribus."

Cui Waltarius:

"Ergo de pellicia, ac de interula quid facturus sum?"

Respondit venerandus pater et ait:

" Dicito, et ex illis tibi a fratribus aeque a fratribus fuisse imperatum."

Tunc Waltarius:

Obsecro, mi Domine, ne irascaris, si loqui addero. De femoralia [215] quid erit, si similiter voluerint facere, ut prius fecerunt?"

Et abbas:

" Iam tibi predicta suffitiat humilitas : nam de femoralibus tibi aliud non precipiam, cum magna nobis videatur fore humilitas priorum vestium exspoliatio."

Exiens vero Waltarius cum talia audisset a tanto patrono, coepit a familia queritare monasterii, an haberetur ibi caballum,[216] cui fiducia inesset bellandi, si necessitas cogeretur.[217] Cui cum famuli ipsius aecclesiae respondissent, bonos et fortes habere pœne se essedos, repente jussit eos sibi adsistere. Quibus

210 cujus.—211 dirigeret illuc.—212 sumtus.—213 contumaciam.—214 dicito tibi.—215 femoralibus.—216 caballus.—217 cogeret.

visis, ascendit mox cum calcaribus, causa probationis, supra sin-
gulorum dorsa ; cumque promovisset primos, et secundos, et
sibi displicuissent ; rennuit eos extemplo narrans illorum vitia.
Ille vero recordans secum nuper deduxisse in monasterio illo [218]
caballum valde bonum, ait illis :

" Illum ergo caballum, quem ego huc veniens adduxi, vivit,
an mortuus est ? "

Responderunt illi :

" Vivit, Domine," [219] inquiunt " iam vetulus est. Ceterum ad
usum pistorum deputatus est, firens quotidie annonam ad molen-
dinum, hac [220] referens."

Quibus Waltarius :

Adducatur nobis, et videamus, qualiter se habetur." [221]

Cui cum adductus *ess*et, et ascendisset super eum, ac promovisset ait :

" Iste,"[222] inquit, " adhuc bene de meo tenens [223] nutrimentum,
quod in annis iuvenilibus meis illum studui docere."

Accipiens ergo Waltarius ab abbate, et cunctis fratribus, bene-
dictionem, ac valedicens, sumens secum duos vel tres famulos,
propere venit ad iam dictos predatore ; quos cum humiliter salu-
tasset, coepit illos monere, ne iam servis Dei ulterius talem
inferrent injuriam, qualem tunc fecissent. Illi autem cum dura
Walthario coepissent respondere verba Waltharius *ę* contra [224]
sepissime illis duriora referebat. Hii vero indignati hac [225]
superbiae spiritu incitati, cogebant Waltharium exuere vesti-
menta, quibus indutus erat. At Waltharius humiliter ad omnia
illos obaudiebat iuxta preceptum abbatis sui, dicens a fratribus
hoc sibi fuisse imperatum. Cumque exspoliassent eum, coeperunt *ę*tiam calceamenta et caligas abstrahere. Cum autem
venissent ad femoralia, diutius institit Waltarius, dicens sibi a
fratribus minime fuisse imperatum, ut fœmoralia exueret. Illi
vero respondentes nulla sibi fore cura de precepta [226] Monachorum : Waltharius vero e contra semper asserebat nullo modo sibi
convenisse ea relinquere. Cumque coepissent illi vehementis-
sime vim facere. Waltharius clam abstrahens a sella retinacu-
lum, in quo pes eius antea herebat, percussit uni eorum in capite,

218 unum.—219 Domine sed.—220 ac.—221 habeat.—222 Ait "Iste."
223 tenet.—224 econtra.—225 ac.—226 nullam sibi fuisse curam de
praeceptis.

qui cadens in terram, velut mortuus factus est, arreptaque ipsius [227] arma, percutiebat ad dexteram, sive ad sinistram. Deinde aspiciens iuxta se vidit vitulum pascentem, quem arripiens, abstraxit ab eo humerum, de quo percutiebat hostes, persequens ac dibachans eos per campum. Volunt autem nonnulli, quod uni eorum, qui Waltario plus ceteris importunius insistebat, cum se inclinasset, ut calceamenta Waltharii a pedibus eius extraeret, hisdem [228] Waltharius illico ex pugno in collum eius percutiens, ita ut os ipsius fractum in gulam eius caderet. Ex illis namque plurimis occisis; reliqui vero in fugam versi, reliquerunt omnia. Waltarius autem adepta victoria, accipiens cuncta et sua, et aliena, repedavit continuo ad monasterium cum maxima preda oneratum.

Abbas autem talia, ut ante audierat, vidit, illico ingemuit ac se in lamentum et precibus cum reliquis pro eo dedit fratribus, increpans eum valde acrius. Waltarius vero exin poenitentiam accipiens a predicto patrono, ne de tanto scelere superbiretur [229] in corpore, unde iacturam pateretur in anima. Tradunt autem nonnulli, quod tribus vicibus cum paganis superirruentibus pugnaverit, atque victoriam ex illis capiens, ignominiose ab arva expulerit.

Nam ferunt aliquanti, quod alio tempore, cum de prato reverteretur ipsius monasterii, quod dicitur Mollis de quo eiecerat equos regis Desiderii, quos ibi invenerat pascentes, ac vastantes herbam, qui [230] cum multos ex illis debellans vicisset, ac reverteretur, invenit iusta [231] viam columnam marmoream, in qua percussit bis ex pugione, quasi laeto animo ex victoria, qui [232] maximam ex ea incidens parte [233] deiecit in terram. Unde usque in hodiernum ibi dicitur diem, Percussio vel ferita Waltari.

CAP. xii.

OBIIT interea vir magnanimus atque inclitus comes et aleta [234] Waltharius, senex et plenus dierum, quem asserunt nostri multos vixisse annos, quorum numerum collectum non repperi; sed in actibus vitae suae cognoscitur, quibus exstiterit temporibus. Hic sicut legitur in hoc fuisse aevo prudentiæ, corporis ac decore vulti [235] strenuissime adornatus, ita in predicto monasterio post militie conversionem, amoris, obedientiae et regu-

---

227 ejus.—228 idem.—229 superbiret.—230 quod.—231 juxta.—232 quam.—233 partem.—234 athleta.—235 vultus.

laris disciplinae oppido fervidissimus fuisse cognoscitur. Inter alia etiam, quae ipse in eodem gessit monasterio, fecit siquidem, dum vixit, summitate cuiusdam rupis sepulcrum in eadem petra laboriosissime excisum. Qui post suae carnis obitum in eodem cum quodam nepote suo, nomine Rataldo, cognoscitur fuisse sepultas. Hic filius fuit filii Waltharii, nomine Ratherii, quem peperit ei Hildegund premonita puella. Horum ergo virorum ossa post multos annos defunctionis suae sepissime visitans, pre manibus habui. Nam huius Rathaldi capitis [236] quedam nobilis matrona, cum illo causa orationis cum aliis convenisset ex Italiae tellus [237] occulte in braciale supposuit suo, atque ad quendam [238] castrum suum deportavit. Quod cum quadam die igne supposito concremaretur, post multa [239] adustionem, illum [240] recordans capite,[241] foras traxit, atque contra igne [242] tenuit, qui mox mirifice extintus est.

CAP. xiii.

POST itaque incursionem paganorum, quae ultima contigerat vice antequam hisdem locus reaedificaretur, ignorabatur omnino supradicta sepultura Waltharii ab incolis loci, sicut ceteras alias.[243] Eratque tunc vidua, nomine Petronilla, in civitate Segusina quae ob nimiam senectutem totam, ut ferunt,[244] incedebat curvam,[245] cuius quoque oculi iam pene caligaverant. Haec vero mulier habuit filium nomine Maurinum, quem pagani de predicta valle secum, vim facientes, deduxerunt cum ceteris concaptivis. Cum quibus, ut dicebat, amplius quam triginta in illorum manserat arva annorum.[246] Postmodum vero licentia a proprio accepta domino, ad domum remeavit propriam, in qua inveniens [247] matrem iam senio confectam, ut supra diximus, quae cotidie [248] ad solis residere erat solita temporem supra [249] quamdam amplissimam petram, quae proxima erat civitati. In huius ergo femine circuitu veniebant viri cum femine civitatis, scisitantes ab ea de antiquitate ipsius loci, quae referebat illis multa, maxime de Novalicio monasterio. Dicebat enim illis multa et inaudita, quae viderat, vel audierat a progenitoribus, et quantos abbates, quantasve destructiones ipsius loci facte a paganis fuerant. Haec igitur quadam die deduci illic [250] se fecerat a

---

236 caput.—237 tellure.—238 quoddam.—239 concremaret post multam.—240 illius.—241 capitis.—242 ignem.—243 ceterae aliae.—244 fertur.—245 curva.—246 annorum spatio.—247 invenit.—248 quae ut diximus quotidie.—249 super.—250 illuc.

quibusdam viris, quae ostendit illis sepulturam Waltharii, quae aute ignorabatur, sicut ab antenatis audierat; quamquam enim nulla foeminarum olim appropinquare illo in loco audebat. Referebat etiam, quantos puteos nuperrime in illo habebantur loco; nam vicini agebant praetaxatae mulieris, ducentos prope vixisse annos.

IV

WALTHER UND HILDEGUNDE.*

1   DIE mir in dem winter fröide hânt benomen,
      sie heizen wîp, si heizen man,
  Disiu sumerzît diu müez in baz bekomen.
  ouwê daz ich niht fluochen kan!
  Leider ich enkan niht mêre
  Wan daz übel wort 'unsælic.'   neinâ! daz wær alze sêre.

2   Zwêne herzelîche fleüche kan ich ouch:
  die fluochent nâch dem willen mîn.
  Hiure müezens beide ' esel' und ' der [1] gouch'
  gehœren ê si enbizzen sîn.
  Wê in denne, den vil armen!
  wess ich obe siz noch gerûwe, ich wolde mich dur got
      erbarmen.

3   Wan [2] sol sîn gedultic wider ungedult:
  daz ist den schamelôsen leit.
  Swen die bœsen hazzent âne sîne schult,
  daz kumt von sîner frümekeit.
  Trœstet [3] mich diu guote alleine,
  diu mich wol getrosten mac, sô gæbe ich umbe ir nîden
      kleine.

4   Ich wil al der werlte sweren ûf ir lîp:
  den eit den sol si wol vernemen:
  Sî mir ieman lieber, maget oder wîp,
  diu helle müeze mir gezemen.
  Hât si nû deheine triuwe,
  sô getrûwet si dem eide und senftet mînes herzen riuwe.

5   Hêrren unde friunt, nû helfent [4] an der zît:
  daz ist ein ende, ez ist alsô.
  Ich enbiute iu mînen [5] minneclîchen strît.

---

* The text is here reprinted from Wilmanns (Walther von der Vogelweide No, 53, 2. Ausgabe Halle 1883.) Essential variants of Pfeiffer's edition are to be found below the text.

1 den.—2 man.—3 troste.—4 helfet.—5 i'ne behalte mînen.

ja enwirde[6] ich niemer rehte frô :
Mînes herzen tiefiu wunde
diu muoz iemer offen stên, si enküsse mich mit friundes
munde.

mînes herzen tiefiu wunde
diu muoz iemer offen stên, si enheiles ûf und ûz von grunde.

mînes herzen tiefiu wunde
diu muoz iemer offen stên, sin werde heil von Hiltegunde.

---

6 so'n wirde.

V.

NIBELUNGENLIED.*

268.3 DÂ von ich wol erkenne   allez Hagenen sint.
     ez wurden mîne gîsel   zwei weltlîchiu [1] kint,
     er und von Spâne Walther :   die wuohsen hie zu man.
     Hagenen sande ich widere : Walther mit Hildegunde
     entran.

274.4 Er [Hagen] unt der von Spâne,   die traten manegen
     stîc,
     dô si hie bî Ezelen   vâhten manegen wîc
     zen êren dem Künege.   des ist von im vil geschehen : [2]
     dar umbe muoz man Hagene [3]   der êren wol von schul-
     den jehen.

358.2 Dô sprach meister Hildebrant [4]   'zwiu verwîzet ir mir
     daz ?
     nu wer was der ûfme schilde   vor dem Waschensteine saz,
     dô im von Spâne Walther sô   vil friunde [5] sluoc ?
     ouch habt ir noch ze zeigen   an in selben genuoc.'

---

* From the text of Zarncke's fifth edition (1875).

1 wætlîchiu L., B.—2 vil von im geschehen L ; des ist vil geschehen
B.—3 Hagenen L ; Hagenen der êren pillîche jehen B.—4 Des ant-
wurte Hildebrant B.—5 vil der friunde L., B.

VI.

GRAZ FRAGMENT.*

. . . . michel vn.[1]

First page, first column.

1 . . . . ie[2] getan.

Do sprach[3] (der starche Hagene : ze w)ev[4] sold din din
lip?

. . . . inne, wem liezst (du daz wîp,
diu) din mit solhen e(ren[5] unz her gebiten) hat?
si wær[6] wol (mit krône ein k)eyserinne,[7] die sold(u min-
nen :

dêst) min rat

2 Do . . . mte[8] Walther n[8] . . .

First page, second column.

1 . . . . (be) stætet[9] vnd ir vater[10] lant
ich stunt[11] da man ivch mæhlt beide, iz ist mir
allez wol erkant.

2 O we mich miner leide, sprach Walther[12] sa ze stunt,
daz miner gvten dienste min vrou[13] Hiltegvnt.
ist also verteilt[14] her vil manigen[15] tac.

---

*The text is here reprinted from Haupt [*Zeitschrift*, xii 280 f) with Heinzel's additions
enclosed in parenthesis, and the variant readings (including those of Schoenbach, *Zeitschrift*, xxv, 181) given below the text. The earlier order of Weinhold and Müllenhoff has
been retained. The arrangement of the fragments is discussed in another place.

1 *These two words close a page and verse that are otherwise lost ;
they, together with three letters* ret *read by* Schönbach (*Zeitshrift*,
xii, 182) *yield no sense.*—2 Weinhold *read the remains of a letter
before* ie.—3 *spch*, Weinhold ; *sprach*, Heinzel.—4 *v*, Weinhold ; *ev*,
Schöbach.—5 *ren* Müllenhoff, Heinzel.—6 *ir er*,Weinhold.—7 *k*, Müllenhoff, Heinzel.—

Dô sprach [diu kuneginne : 'zw]u solde dir din lîp?
[war taete du die s]inne? wem liezest [du din wip,
diu] dîn mit solhen ê[ren hie gebiten] hat.
si wære wol [ein rîchiu k]eyserinne ; die sold
[. . . . deist mîn] rât.' —Bartsch.

8 *read by* Schönbach. Dô [sprach der herre] Walther. Bartsch.—
9 Müllenhoff, Heinzel.—10 Heinzel ; *vat*[1] MS.—11 Heinzel *.stüt* MS.—
12 Heinzel ; *Walth*[1] MS.—13 Heinzel ; vrŏ MS.—14 *verteilet*, Heinzel.—15 Heinzel ; *manegē* MS.

swen ich (iemer) mit minne ir [16] wolde [17] (swîchen),   daz
        wær den êren mîn ein slac).

Second page, first column.

1   .   .   .   .   (den kunec und sîn) wip.
    dar nach neig er in vil flizichliche   vnd hiez
            vil sælich sin er lip.

2   Die do die næhsten waren [18]   bi im von Hivnen lant
    den gab der snelle Hagene   div ross vnd [19] daz gewant
    daz silber zv dem golde   swaz mans im fvrgetruch [20]
    er sprach niemen [21] sold icht mit mir (vliesen: daz
            wær ein michel ungevûch).

Second page, second column.

1   .   .   .   .   .   han ich
    not v(nde kumber   het ich) ie dvrch dich
    w(em wilt du mich lazen,   troutgeselle (mîn?)
    (woltstu) daz ich von hinn(en [22] mit dir scheıde)
            umb dich diende (ich jâmers pîn)

2   (Dô het) der starche Hage(ne [23]   daz mære) wol vernomen
    di   .   .   .   chet   nummer vor [24]   .   .   .

---

16 Heinzel.—17 Schönbach, Heinzel; *lde* Weinhold.—18 Heinzel;
warē MS.—19 *d* Heinzel *vn̄* MS.—20 *für getruch*, Heinzel.—21 Heinzel; *nemen*, Schönbach.—22 *hinnen*, Müllenhoff, Heinzel.

lazen, troutgeselle [min
und ist] daz ich von hinn[en müese scheiden, daz wil
ich] umb dich diende [sin.'
Dô spr_ch] der starche Hage[ne : ' ich hân daz] wol
        vernomen.   —Bartsch.

23 *Hagene*, Müllenhoff, Heinzel.—24 *all of the verse except* d *deci-
phered by* Schönbach.

VII.

VIENNA FRAGMENT.*

I.—WALTHERS UND HILDEGUNDEN HEIMKEHR.

a

1 . . . . . ín.)
  wol gehelfen. si rv̇hten mînen wín.
  von míner hende nemen an. (ic)h gan iv deste baz.
  daz ir vns leitet nah den iwern siten. daz svle wir dvlden
    ane haz.
2 Si enphiengen Volkere. vnd ovch die sine man,
  sehzec siner degene. die waren mit im dan.
  gevolget von dem Rine. dvrch den wasechen walt.
  er laítte so den gast vnd ovch die sine. daz ers vil wenich
    enkalt.
3 Do sprach der ellende. nv helffet mir bewarn.
  daz wir die twerhen strazen iht ī den landen varn.
  wir svln gen leng^{r}s. da ist d^r vater min.
  des antwrt Volk^r der vil kv̊ne. des sol ich hvt^r sin.
4 Swie wir anders ríten. so ist daz div lere min.
  daz wir da ze Metzen geste niht ensin.
  Ortwin hete drinne / wol tovsent kv̊ner man.
  swaz der kvnic hernach darvmbe geredete. mit strite wrdē
    wir hestan.
5 Er hete wol geraten. si líezens ane strit.
  so er aller beste chvnde, so leít er siv sit.
  di . . . . di ez sahen daz er da míte reit.
  die mohtē do dem helde noch d^r vrȯwen vor ī geratē dehei-
    niv leít.
6 Wa si die nahtselde. næmen dvrch div lant.
  mit volk^{r}e dem heldē. daz enwart mir bechant.

---

*The text is that of Massmann (*Zeitschrift für deutsches Alterthum*, ii, 216 ff.). The orthography has been retained as found in Massmann's reprint. Variants include the additions of Bartsch (*Germania*, xii,88–89), and of O. Jänicke (Haupt, *Zeitschrift*, xiv,448).

1, 3. nâch den iwern êren, Bartsch.—6, 3. sînem gvote, Haupt and Karajan.

dᵣ kvnic mit sinʳ gvte ím schone dînen hiez
Volkʳ dʳ was in also werden mv̊te.   daz er sin wenic vʳliez.
7 Ovz Ortwines lande dvrch Bvrgonde dan.
braht si do volkʳ dʳ vil kv̊ne man.
ob ma daz sin geleite.   so starch niht het geschen.
so mv̊s in ouf der selben straze dikche sín michel arbeit
geschehen.
8 Nv hôrt ovch wîe der reke frᷓt í(n sime) lant.
die boten die er hete dem kuníge gesant.
die rîten rôss div gvten.   vn̄ fv̊rten spæhiv kleit
die sagten indem lande.   daz er kôme vn̄ ŏch vrŏ Hildegʳt
div meit.
9 Do der khvnic alker.   gehorte diese sage.
do entweich im vngemv̊te.   vnd ovch sin langiv klage.
die boten er vlízichliche enphie. vnd ovch. sîn wîp.
si wrden harte grozer vrevden riche.   dvrch den waltheres
lip.
10 Do sprach dʳ vogt von Spanyge so wol mich iwer sage.
ich hete sorge manige. lang mine tage.
daz sin s(in in der) fremde. was mir wol tᵒvsent iar /
ich sih ín gern. sweᴘ ī got sendʳ div red ist entlichen war /

b

11 DO ez div kvniginne. het mit im vernomen.
ir was von lîeben mæren. vil de træhʳen komen.
von herzen indiv ovgen. weinde si do saz.
si riet wie man si bede wolde solde enphahen. vnde tet vil
willechlichen daz.
12 Do sprach aber der rekche ír svlt mich hôren lan.
wie Etzele vnd frŏ Helche zv zin haben getan.
do sprach der boten eîner daz wil ich iu sagē
walthʳ ist vo dem kvnige so gescheiden. daz ez die Hivnen
ímmer mvzen klagen.
13 Ir ettelichʳ drvnder. daz si ī wæren holt.
er hat an svmelichen. vil wol daz versolt.
daz si ím ímmer flvchen. wand er hat ín erslagen.
an siner verte vil ir lieben mage. ich kan ív andʳs niht ge-
saǵ.

8, 1. in siniu lant, Haupt; ûz síme lant, Bartsch; fröute . . lant
Wackernagel.—10, 3. daz sîn s]tân in der] fremde, Bartsch.

14 Do sprach der kvnic edele. ich sol mich vrewen sin.
er mvz wesen herre. inden landen min.
er wirt der Hvne purgetôr.
swes Ezele vnd sine rechen ie begvnden. da was er ze
    allen zîten vor.
15 Den chvnic sprach zv den reken. wol òf alle mine man.
vnd rîtet ím begegene. er hat mir liep getan.
swer ī nv gerne díenet. des vrívt (wi)l ich wesen.
div lant svlt ir mit vns beiden bowen. ir mvgt bi walth^r
    wol genesē.
16 Man sagt im daz in leite. d^rch Gvnth^rs lant.
Volk^r der vil kvne. d^r was im wol erkāt.
vnd ovch des kvniges reken. driv hvndert od^r baz.
do bat er sîn gesinde zv im gahen. di tatē willechlichen daz.
17 Do hiez ovch sich bereîten des edeln kvniges wîp.
ia wolde si beleiten. d^r Hild^rgde lîp.
so si aller beste kvnde. ze Leng^res índie stat.
ir vrowen si do wol kleiden begvnde. des si der kunich
    selbe bat.
18 Sin warten sine lîvte. mit g°zer vngebite.
dar nach ín chvrzen stvnden. man sagt im daz da ríte.
daz Gvnth^rs gesinde. mit ín indaz lant.
do kom d^r wirt mit stolz^r massenye. da er vròn Hild^r. vant.
19 Div kvniginne fvrte. wol sehzec megedin.
die aller schônisten. die d^r mohten sín.
vñ ovch d^r hohsten mage. di mā do bi ín vant.
do fvrten och des alten kvniges helde. Vil harte herlich
    gewant.
20 E si vol drîe mîle komen waren dan.
von der stat ze Leng^res. ín volgen tvsent man.
od^r dannoch mere. die zv den gesten riten.
wand si d^r kvnigínne here. heten.

2.—HILDEGVNDE BRVTE.

1 NV was ze hove níemen. wan di da solden sín.
    het gesehen íemen. ein schôner magedin.
denne wær Hildegvt do si da heîme saz.

20, 4. Wande si der künigiune hère heten vil müelîche erbiten,
Jänicke.

da ír des ivngen kvniges reken dīeten.   ich gelovb mv̌lich
    daz.
2   Swaz man wesse vnpilde.   di îemen het getan.
    er wære denne wilde zereht mvse^r stan.
    da walther d^r vil kvene sines vater lant besaz.
    er phlach des landes nach der krone rehte.   wande ím riet
        div ivnchfröwe daz.
3   Die Walthers mv̊ter.   zaſte wol die meît.
    daz sach der degn gvter.   iz was im niht leît.
    si schvf ir hovegesinde.   vil schŏniv magedîn.
    die bî Hildegvnde.   ze allen ziten mit grozē zvhtē mvsē sin.
4   Do div magt edele in ir heinliche saz.
    so getet ir chvrzwîle/nie dekeine baz.
    wa so si des gedahte waz ir d^r chv̊ne degen.
    ê daz er si vo den Hívnen bræhte.   het gedíenet ovf den
        wegen.
5   Dar zv sach er si diche.   vrŏ was in d^r m°v̊t.
    ir trivtlich^r bliche siv beide dovhte gv̊t
    er liebte swie er kvnde.   daz min*nechliche kint.*
    *daz man lobes mv*se iehen . . . . *Hilde*gvnde.   *der*
        *ivnc*vrowen sint.
6   Swa îe des fvrsten b*otê ri*ten.   dvrch daz lant
    ez wart den livten allen.   mit *sime* tv̊n bechant
    er wolde *hoh*zite.   mit Hildegvnd*e han.*
    der riche kvnich mi*lte mit* sînen vrevnden, dar *zv̊* bereiten
        sich began.
7   Gestvle hiez do wrchen *der her*re alpker.
    ahzec hêr g*esellen.*   vnt wæn dannoch í*nder mer.*
    . . . . der ies*l*ichen wol zwe*i hvn*dert man.
    die mit de . . . . sche chomen solden.   *des wer*ches gahen
        man be*gan.*
8   Er schvf ovch allentha*lben.* iâget inden walt.
    v*f ma*nic tŷer wilde. der he . . . . enkalt.
    ouch mv̊sen *vischæ*re. ovf wage vnmv*zic we*sen.

6,2. er hiez den liuten allen mit vîlze tuon bekant, Haupt.—6, 4. mit
den sînen vriunden, Haupt.—7, 2. ahzec hêrgesidele (*oder* hergesi-
dele) unt wæn donnoch mêr Jänicke ; inder *omitted by* Haupt.—7, 3,
4. [und mit] der ieslîchen (= ieslîchen) wol tzwei hundert man, die
mit de[n ze ti]sche chomen solden. Bartsch.—8, 2. vil manic tier
wilde der hêrschaft enkalt, Haupt. v[il ma]nic tyer wilde der he[lde
dô] enkalt, Bartsch.

si fvnden ir vil . . . . . . in den vnden. die von in enkvnden
    genesen.

9 Die sinen valchnære. der fvrste peizen hîez.
  wie vil man der nezze. mv̆zichlichen lîez.
  . . . hiez(e)n a . . . . . . snelle . . . . a . . . . .
  . . . . în s . . . .

10 E . . . .
  wîe . . . . . . icher de . . . . eʳ daz.
  . . . . gesniten.
  di(e) da lieber rôss gewnnē der kom vil manigʳ dar geritē.

11 Die hohzite walther dʳge . . . . do der walt gelovbet was
  . . . . . . vnd daz die blv̆mē vnd daz gras
  stvnden allenthalben ŏf den wisen breit.
  daz im dʳ sîne geste kŏmen. so was allez da bere(it.)

12 . . . . . vnmv̆zic waren híe. ze Spaníe lant.
  da h . . . nv . . . Hildegvnt. kom heím . . . gesant.
  ze Arrogŏn dem lant div mære hîez si sagen.
  daz si in chvrzen ziten wolde krone. bi dem kvninge walthere tragen.

13 Wol was iz in allen. (de)n si / den grv̆z enbôt.
  ovch mv̆s in wol gevallen. daz si von mangʳ nôt.
  zen Hîvnen was gesceiden. vnd daz si brahte dan.
  der hʳ walthere so rehte lobliche. da vō er erē vil gewan.

14 Des kuniges íngesinde. be(rei)te sich zer vart.
  wol . . . sa(z)te er di reken. wol geziret ŏf rôssen vn(ge-
  sp)art.
  . . . . vrowen vo . . . . ᴧher.
  . . . .

8, 4. die vor in, Haupt.—9, 2. wie wênic oder wie lützel, Haupt.—9,
4. [si] hiezen a[lle deste] snelle[r gâhen], Bartsch.—10, 1. 4. Ê daz
der fürste rîche mit in ze tische saz die da [guot]er rosse gewunnen,
Bartsch.—11, 4. sô waere, Haupt. 11, 1-4.

> [Sine hôc]hzite Walther dô geb[ot,
> Sô]der walt geloubet [wære] und daz die bluomen [rot
> st]üenden allenthalben [ûf de]n wisen breit,
> daz im [danne] sîne geste kœmen : sô[wære]allez dâ bereit.
>   —Bartsch.

12, 1. dô h[et ouch] nu [vrou] Hildegunt boten heim [gesant],
Bartsch.—12, 2. ze Arr. dem lande mære (oder diu mære), Haupt.—
13, 1. Liep was, Haupt.—14, 2 wol [ge]sach [man] recken ziere [ûf
r]ossen un[gesp]art, Bartsch.—14, 4. her W., Haupt.—15, 1. ze En-
gellande rîten man ouch die boten hiez, Jänicke.

15 Ze Engellant. man riten och die boten híez.
die wege *man vil witen. gar vn*mv̊zic (lie)z.
zNauarren vn Chǣrlíngen. da wart ez ovch bechant.
do rihten si sich gen der hohzite. ī daz waltheres lant.
16 Walthere gie zerate. ob si daz devhte gv̄t.
sine man vn sine mage. ob niht vbele gemv̊t.
Ezel da vo w°rde. ob er die boten sin.
im vnd der kvniginne Helch'n sande. vn ouch daz schon
magdin.
17 Daz wider riet im niemen, da von wart ez sit getan.
sine brieve schriben. man dar zv̊ began.
die er da wolde senden in Ezelen lant.
den selben boten lîe man niht gebresten. man gab in rosse
vnd ŏch gewant.
18 Mit den hiez man do ritē. di da solten an den Rin.
Gvnthʳ wol gedahte. vnd ovch die vrevnde sìn.
wie er sinív mǣre. hete dar gesant.
bi volkere dem stolzen videlære. in der Bvrgŏnde lant.
19 Do sprach der vogt von Rine. vnd wǣr iz niht schande *min.*
*het i*ch *nv* tovsent miner helden. so wold ich gerne sin.
ze siner hohzitē. wær ez dʳ Hagne rat.
so wold ich dar

15, 2. allenthalben, Jänicke,—19, 2. mit tûsent miner helde, Jänicke.
—19, 4. sô wold ich dar [mit mînen recken rîten, als ez mir lobelîche
stât,] Bartsch.

VIII.

BITEROLF UND DIETLEIB.*

Walthêr sô was er genant:
er was der künec von
Spanjelant.
der was von Hiunen her bekomen,
als ir wol habt ê vernomen.

581-798

Dem jungen helde was geseit
daz hie mit zwelf gesellen reit
in rehter mâze ein alter man.
im wart ouch kunt daz getân
daz si âne helme niht enriten.
586 einen garzûn hiez er si des
biten,
daz si ım enbuten mære
war ir geverte wære.
dô sprach Biterolf der degen
'der mich frâget, wie ich ûf
den wegen
591 rîte und die gesellen mîn.
dem saget daz wir geste sîn
und wellen rîten durch diu
lant,
ich tuon im anders niht bekant.'
Der garzûn sagte dem künege
daz
596 'herre, ich weiz niht umbe waz
er iu anders niht enbôt :
âne ertwungenlîche nôt
rîte er swar in dunket guot.
er hât sô hêrlîchen muot
601 unde ouch die gebære,
sam ez im zorn wære,
daz ich in gefrâget hân.'

dô sprach der künic 'daz lât
stân.
ich wil in gerne selbe sehen,
606 in swelher fuoge ez mac geschehen,
sît im mîn name ist unbekant.
und füere er alsô durch diu
lant,
des müese ich immer laster
hân.
nu wil ich in daz sehen lân :
611 wirt noch nâch mæren zim
gesant,
er enbiut mirs heim in mîniu
lant.'
Sîne man er dâ belîben hiez.
der fürste dô daz niht enliez,
er hielt gên im ûf den wegen.
616 dô sach ouch Biterolf de degen
an dem schilde guot genuoc
bî dem ¹ wâpen daz er truoc,
daz er was von Spanjelant.
dô gedâhte er sâ zehant
621 daz wider komen wære
Walthêr der degen mære
ûz hiunischen rîchen,
im selben angestlîchen
und den sînen niht ze guote.
626 in bêden in ir muote.
herter wille was gestalt :
des wurden ûf daz gras gevalt
sît ir mœre beider.
den gesten wart nie leider
631 und ouch denWalthêres man.
der alte sît dâ von gewan

---

* The text is from ' Deutches Heldenbuch ' (i. Theil, S. Jänicke, Berlin, 1866.) Only the important variants are given.

1 waffen.

einen grimmigen muot:
dô spranc er an den helt guot,
an Walthêrn den jungen.
636 dô sluoc er Welsungen,[2]
durch einen helmen rîchen
harte krefticlîchen
unz ûf ein hîubel guldîn.
daz im genas der lîp sîn,
641 daz hât man noch für wunder.
dô truoc ouch dâ besunder
Walthêr ein wâfen an derhant,
daz vil wîten was erkant
646 zeinem dem aller besten
daz si dô inder westen.
ze strîte kunde er als ein
degen:
er hete senfte sich bewegen.
den künec von Bergen[3] er dô
sluoc
651 daz ûz der sarwæte truoc
diu ecke heiz fiuwer rôt.
dem fürsten witze daz gebôt
unde ouch sîn bescheidenheit:
dô er sô hêrlîchen streit,
656 dô bat den zorn lân
der alte disen jungen man:
'Waz hulfe,ob ich slüege dich
·ode ob du houbetlôsen mich
tætest mit der dînen kraft?
661 unser bêder meisterschaft
wære ringe hie gelegen.
bist duz Walthêr der degen,
sô hou ûf mich niht mêre.
ez ist ein kleiniu êre,
666 der den andern sô bestât,
daz der schulde niht enhât.'
er sprach 'ir habt mich rehte
erkant:
ich bin Walthêr genant.'
dô sprach Biterolf der degen
671 'sô sol man senfte mir gewegen:
mîn swester was diu muoter
dîn,
und ob du vor den handen mîn
alsô ze tôde wærst erslagen,

sô möhte ich nimmer dich
verklagen.'
676 Dô sprach der kindische man
'sô ist mir liep daz niht gewan
iuwer lîp dervon diu meil,
und ist ouch unser beider heil:
wan habt ir Welsungen hie,
681 so genas als zeichenlîchen nie
in der werlt nehein man,
dann ich vor iuwer hân getân.
œheim, sît mir willekomen.
mir ist liep daz ich hân vernomen
686 daz ir noch sît sô wol gesunt.'
ir liuten winkten si zestunt,
den vil liebe dâ geschach,
dô man die stæten suone sach.
dô si heten daz vernomen
691 wie diu suone was bekomen,
dem fürsten nigen al zehant
die guoten helde ûz Spanjelant.
Walthêr dô Biterolfen bat
daz er ze Pârîs in die stat
696 wider rite hinder sich;
dô sprach der degen 'nein ich.
ze Pârîs ich nu niht enwil:
ich hân ze reden mit iu vil,
des sult ir mich niht verdagen
701 er sprach 'ich wil iu gesagen
swes ir mich hie gefrâget,
wan mich des niht betrâget.'
Si sâen nider ûf den plân.
den recken frâgen er began
706 von hiunischen rîchen.
vil bescheidenlîchen
sagt er im daz im was erkant,
der heiden site und wie daz
lant
berihtet mit ir herren was,
711 und daz vil lützel der genas
die er in sîne æhte nam,
und wie der küniginœe zam
ir leben in hiunischen rîchen,
und wie rehte wünniclîchen
716 die recken lebten dar enlant,

---

2 Welfungen, H.—3 von den Pergen.

und wie sich des heldes hant
hete ervohten an dem Rîn.
des smielte sâ der neve sîn.
Walthêr dô herbergen hiez,
721 die geste er von im niht enliez,
man enschüefe in ruowe unde
gemach.
der junge helt zem alten
sprach
' friunt und lieber œheim mîn,
ir sult durch kurzwîle sîn
726 bî uns hie doch drîzic tage,
unz ich iu allez daz gesage
daz ich mit iu ze reden hân ;
daz kan sô gâhes niht ergân,
alsô ir des habt gedâht.
731 mich hât mîn ellende brâht
ûf sô grôzen ungewin
daz ich im immer vîent bin.'
Die hütten hiez er ûf daz velt
spannen unde diu gezelt
736 dâ si under solden ligen.
diu sunne diu was nu gesigen
den bergen alsô nâhen,
dô si gerihtet sâhen
gesidele ûf einem anger wît.
741 der mit liebem gaste sît
ze tische wirdiclîchen saz,
die koste gap er âne haz :
vor dem er kûme ernerte den
lîp,
der bevalch im lant und ouch
sîn wîp.
746 die helde sliefen deste min,
diu naht gienc in alsô hin :
ê daz si sâhen aber den tac,
der helt mit frâge bî im lac
wie stüende Rüedegêres leben
751 ode waz im hete der künec
gegeben
Wider Arâbî daz lant,
er sprach 'dâ stêt in sîner hant
allez daz der künic hât.
er hât urliuges rât
756 nâch sînem erbe an sînen tôt

daz Etzelen golt rôt
mac er geben swem er wil.
er hæt mir ouch wol alsô vil
gegeben unde mêre ;
761 Helche diu hêre,
diu bôt mir tugentlîche
krône und lant rîche.
sô bedâhte ich mich baz :
ich wiste âne zwîvel daz,
766 daz ich selbe hete lant.
Etzelen unde Helchen hant
heten mir und Hildegunde
verlihen in der stunde
swes wir heten dâ gegert
771 von Etzelen wir nâmen swert,
bêde ich unde Hagene.
umb uns ellende degene
liez sichz der künic hêre
kosten michels mêre,
776 ze tûsent marken 4 oder baz,
und tete vil williclîchen daz.'
Dô sprach Bitrolf der wî-
gant
' ich wil ouch hiunischiu lant
und die recken schouwen
781 und Helchen die frouwen
von der ich wunder hœre sagen,
wie si in ir hôhen tagen
lebe und in ir zîten,
daz si âne widerstrîten
786 sî daz miltiste küneges wîp,
diu noch ie gewan den lîp.
nu solt du, Walthêr, neve mîn,
fride meister mînes landes sîn.
lâ dir bevolhen sîn mîn guot,
791 sô friunt dem andern dicke
tuot.
ich wil bevelhen dir mîn wîp
und lâz ouch mîner recken lîp,
vil lieber friunt der guote,
sîn in dîner huote.'
796 er sprach ' got müeze iuch
dort bewarn,
ir sult hie heime wol gevarn :
an aller hande dingen

_____
4 ze dreissig tausend march.

sô sol iu wol gelingen.'

799-808

Urloup nam er von im dan.
dô sâhen wol des fürsten man
daz vil friuntlich scheiden
geschach dô von in beiden.
Biterolf der kêrte dan,
804 Walthêr und die sîne man
ze Pârîs kêrten in die stat.
wol leiste er des er in gebat :
ez hete der degen guote
sîn lant in friundes huote.

2104-8

der frumen lützel wære ge-
nesen,
wær der von Kärlingen niht :
swaz ie den liuten dîn geschiht,
Walthêr ez heizet widertuon.
der ist dîner basen 5 suon.

3038-42

her künec, daz irs gewarnet
sît :
sol Bitrolf inder erben hân,
sô sippet der vil junge man
an Walthêr den wîgant,
den recken ûzer Spanjelant.'

5082-98

sô kumet iu ouch mit sîner
kraft
der fürste dâ von Spanjelant,
Walthêr der wîgant ;
der lobte, ob daz geschæhe
swenn man in gerne sæhe
5087 ze Wormez bî dem Rîne,
daz er und al die sîne
iu ze dienste wolden komen :
daz habet ir selbe wol vernomen.
wer mac iuch danne twingen?
5092 her bringet 6 von Kärlingen
der künec alle 7 sîne man,
di sint im dienstes undertân :
Arragûn und Nâvarren lant,
daz stêt gar in sîner hant ;
5097 dâ von er bringet helde

her in iuwer selde.

6219-24

dar nâch hiez er springen
und Walthêren bringen,
den helt ûzer Spanjelant.
mit dem kômen al zehant
sîner undertânen drî
künege die im stuonden bî.

6273-6306

her Walthêr lachende gie
dâ er den marcman enphie :
er gedâhte an diu mære
wie er gescheiden wære
von hiunischem rîche :
6278 si redeten schimphlîche.
er frâgte an der stunde
nâch der schœnen Hilde-
gunde.
dô sprach Walthêr der degen
' diu ist hie in Gunthêres phlegen.
6283 welt ir, daz mac vil wol geschehen,
daz ich iuch lâze die gesehen.'
Den boten wunderte sêre
wie Hildegunt diu hêre
zuo dem Rîne was bekomen :
6288 der helt hete noch niht vernomen
der unglouplîchen mære
daz ir dâ mêre wære.
im sagte der helt von Spanjelant
'Gunthêr hât nâch uns gesant:
6293 die dâ heizent küneges kint,
daz unser vierzehen sint,
der habent siben hie ir wîp :
des ist der Hildegunde 8 lîp
bî den andern hie gesehen.
6298 wir hôrten sîne boten jehen,
wir solden zeîner hôchzît.
nu riuwet mich daz immer sît
daz ich sô smâhe her gereit,
und ist mir doch ze mâzen leit.
6303 sul wir wern im sîn lant,

---

5 deines vaters.—6 der Öringen.—7 den kunig und.—8 Hildepurgen
H.

sô sol dienen hie mîn hant
sô wol sîn brôt und ouch den
    wîn
daz si mir holt müezen sîn.'

6423-34

dô sprach ûzer Spanjelant
Walthêr der wîgant
'her künec, hæt ir mich wiz-
    zen lân,
dô ich mit juncfrouwen dan
von Spanje her zem Rîne reit,
6428 wie sêre iu sî hie widerseit,
sîn möhte dannoch werden
    rât.
ob man iuch mit strîte bestât,
ich bræhte niun tûsent man :
die wîle und ich der einen hân
6433 und ouch ich selbe lebendic
    bin,
ûf iuwer helfe stêt mîn sin.'

6774-77

Walthêr sprach 'sô ist niht rât
ern küsse ouch Hildegunde
diu in in vil langer stunde
mit mir zen Hiunen hât er-
    kant.'

7644-50

sô sol daz Etzeln golt rôt
dienen der helt Rüedegêr :
von Spanjelant den künec hêr
sol er mit sîner hant bestân.
daz er froun Hildegunden dan
enphuorteHelchen der richen
er richet ez ouch billîchen.'

7655-59

'waz wîzet ir mir, Hildebrant?
wær iu Walthêr alsô wol be-
    kant
als mir ist der küene degen,
ir hæt mich nimmer im gewe-
    gen
ze einem widerstrîten.

7660-63

Jâ lieze ich in noch rîten,
und næme er mir tohter mîn,
sô solde er ungevangen sîn
immer von der mînen hant.

7664-68

er rûmte mînes herren lant

gar âne alle schande
daz ich sô rehte erkande
sîne site, des jungen man :
des muoste ich in dô rîten lân.'

8436-41

'sô wil ich lâzen schînen,'
sprach Walthêr von Spanje-
    lant,
'daz uns turnieren ist bekant:
ich wil ouch lâzen hundert
    dar.
si werdent schiere wol gewar
wie wir turnierens kunnen
    phlegen.'

8770-79

gên den sach man dô wenden
hundert Walthêres man.
dô begunde enstete stân
dâ daz ritterlîche spil
für diu hâmît 9 an ir zil.
8775 Vil schiere komen wâren
die von Bechelâren
gegen den von Spanjelant,
den ze helfe man dô vant
die von Arragûne lande.

8958-60

Walthêres 10 wîgande,
sibene fuorten sie sît
der Rüedgêres durch diu hâ-
    mît.11

9075-82

Sîfriden frâgen man began
und ouch den Hildegunde 12
    man,
Walthêren von Spanjelant.
dô sprach der recke sâ zehant
'wes frâget ir mich eine'?
9080 dô sprâchens al gemeine
'wir lâzenz alsô hine gân.
nu si niht frides wellen hân.'

9576-96

Walthêr der wîgant
sprach 'lat iur sorge under
    wegen.
hie sol ein ieslîcher degen
wane mir volgen mite.
ich wil daz man si lîhte erbite
9581 daz si den vinden sîn ze wer.

---

9 hannt.—10 Walther H.—11 handt.—12 Hildegunden.

und gesiget hie der Hiunen
  her,
ich weiz die helde alsôgemuot,
wir hætenz alle gelîche guot.
dâ von sol ein ieslîch man
9586 hie strîten als er beste kan.'
Walthêr redete mêre sider
'ê si mich zen Hiunen wider
fuorten âne mînen danc,
ich lieze se zehen lande lanc
9591 noch herverten fürbaz ;
wan Etzel wolde sînen haz
allen rechen ane mir.
edel künec, ich râte dir
daz wir mit gelîchen scharn
9596 âne sorgen zuo in varn.'
9904-92
'hie kumet daz Alpkêres kint.'
sprach der marcgrâve rîche,
'mit spangen snêgelîche,
im volget her von Spanjelant.
die êrsten tjost sol mîn hant
9909 tuon vor der Hiunen her :
dar nâch rihten sich ze wer
die Hiunen, swie man hie getuo,
sô muoz ich Walthêre zuo,
sît mich des wolde niht erlân
9914 des fürsten Dietrîches man.'
Dô sprach der recke Diet-
  leip 13
'mir ist doch lange her geseit,
und hôrte in selbe des verje-
  hen,
dô ich in næhste hân gesehen
9919 dô ich reit zuo der Hiunen
  lant,
daz Walthêr der wigant
wære mîner basen kint.'
der mære verjach im sint
Biterolf der vater sîn
9924 'sîn muoter was diu swester
  mîn.
wie sich daz verkêret hât
daz er nu Gunthêre gestât !
er füert ein kreftige schar.

wir solden einen boten dar
9929 senden der im kunde gesagen
daz wir im holden willen tragen,
swie halt uns der helt getuo.
Rüedegêr der gap duo
eines lôrboumes zwî
9934 einem garzûn der stuont dâ bî
und hôrte gar diu mære
waz hin enboten wære :
der lief dô balde vor in dar.
Walthêr hielt vor sîne schar
9939 sam er nu strîtes wolde phlegen
der Hiunen, unde sach der
  degen
den boten tragen an der hant.
daz er im wære dar gesant,
des verdâhte er sich duo :
9944 er sprach dem boten balde zuo
'saget an, waz mære bringet
  ir '?
er sprach 'herre, zeiget mir
hie den künec von Spanje-
  lant.
dem habent die zwêne mich
  gesant,
9949 Bitrolf und Dietleip der degen,
durch wen er welle sich bewegen
sô guoter friunde sô si sint.'
dô sprach daz Alpkêres kint
'ich bin Walthêr genant.'
9954 'sô sî iu daz bekant
daz si bêde klagent daz,
daz ir in alsô sît gehaz
daz ir durch ieman si bestât
und die verchsippe lât
9959 zwischen iu und sînem kinde.
die helde und ir gesinde,
die wæren iu vil gerne bî :
daz ir si liezet schaden frî,
daz wolden si ze liebe hân.'
9964 dô sprach der tugenthafte man
'so bræche ich mîn sicherheit.

---

13 vil gemait.—14 im.

wurde ez nimmer in¹⁴ geseit,
mînem œheim und dem sune
sîn,
sô leiste ich in die triuwe mîn
9969 die wîle ichz leben mac ge-
hân.
wie wolde er sînen wirt verlân
der im schankte sînen wîn?.
ich hete die nahtselde sîn
vil undegenlîche genomen,
9974 wold ich im niht ze helfe komen.'
Zuo dem boten er dô sprach
'ich leiste des ich im verjach,
dô ich nu jungest von im reit.
im sol daz niht wesen leit
9979 swa er hœre von iemannes
sage
daz ich lop unde krône trage.
geselle, got gesegene dich,
und bite daz niht zürnen mich
mîn neve und ouch der vater
sîn.
9984 dar under si suln hüeten mîn
swâ wir uns samenen in den
scharn:
sô sol ouch ich daz wol bewarn
daz in mîn kraft iht widerste;
ja bestüende ich einen Krie-
chen ê,'
9989 der bote brâht diu mære dan,
als er im hete kunt getân.
dô dûhte dise helde guot
Walthêres sin und ouch sîn
muot.
10112-32
dô sach daz Alpkêres kint
der marcgrâve Rüedegêr:
die Etzeln helde liez er
unde reit Walthêren an.
dô hete ouch sîn der junge
man
10117 vor den Hiunen war genomen,
si mousten zuo einander komen
als ez den helden wol gezam.

daz dâ den tôt niht ennam
der marcgrâve hêre,
10122 des wundert mich vil sêre.
ouch kom im ze heile daz,
daz ûf dem rosse gesaz
der marcgrâve rîche.
ze helfe im snelliclîche
10127 kômen dô die sîne man:
hæt er den niderwanc getân,
sô kunde er nimmer sîn gene-
sen.
wie mohte ez grimmer gewe-
sen,
dô ez diu Rüedegêres hant
versuochte an den von Spanjelant.
10396-494
dô heten die von Spanje-
lant,
als wir diu mære hœren sagen,
baz danne tûsent erslagen
der hiunischen schützen.
swie wol si kunden nützen
10401 ir hornbogen bî der schar,
ir kocher wâren lære gar:
der was geschozzen von ir
hant
sô vil daz der von Spanjelant
vil maneger tôt was beliben.
10406 des heten si sô vil getriben
daz von den wunden rossen
sider
muose vil manic helt nider
ûf die füeze in die schar.
des hete wol genomen war
10411 der marcgrâve Rüedegêr,
daz Walthêr der degen hêr
mit den sînen ûfez gras
von den rossen kumen was.
Swaz dô der edel wîgant
10416 der küenen Hiunen bî im vant͵
die mante er wol ze strîte.
siben schar vil wîte,
die volgeten Rüedegêre.
Blœdelin der hêre,
10421 der erbeizte nider neben sîn.
dô truobte der sunnen schîn

der nebel von der helde hant.
dô kam der helt von Hiunen
      lant
dâ er Walthêren sach.
10426 der guote marcgrâve sprach
'nâher alle die ich hân.
kumet der Hildegunde man
ûz der Gunthêres schar,
sô müezens die andern gar
10431 bieten hiute ir sicherheit.'
dô Rüedegêr der helt ges-
      treit
daz er wart Walthêre bekant,
dô sprach der herre ûz Span-
      jelant
'hie kumet der Gotelinde
      man:
10436 möhte ich mich¹⁵ mit êren dan
von dem helde gescheiden,
man gesæhe von uns beiden
tâlanc deheinen¹⁶ swertes
      swanc.
Hildebrant der habe undanc
10441 der mîch zuo im gemezzen
      hât:
wir¹⁷ hetens bêde gerne rât.
ich schiet alsô von Hiunen
      lant
daz mir der mære wîgant
nie beswêrte mînen muot:
10446 nu muoz ich den helt guot
under mînen danc bestân.
swaz er mir liebes hât getan,
des wolde ich im nu lônen,
und kunde er mîn geschonen,
10451 sô wurde schaden deste min.
er lât mich nu niht komen hin,
sît mich der küene hât gese_
      hen,
sô muoz under uns geschehen
des ich vil gerne enbære
10456 ob ez mir êre wære.'
Nu was ouch komen Rüede-
      ger.
dô sprach der marcgrâve hêr

'got weiz, her künec von
      Spanjelant,
hie muoz unser eines hant
10461 bejagen schaden oder fru-
      men.'
vil manic swert sach man dru-
      men
und bî in beiden bresten,
dô man die nôtvesten
sach zuo einander springen.
10466 dô hôrt man lûte erklingen
ir beider wâfen an der hant.
dô wurden die von Spanjelant
umbe gekêret mit ir schar.
ez was vil degenlîche dar
10471 komen der guote Rüedegêr.
do versûmte sich der künic hêr
daz diu Rüedegêres hant
den helt erreichte über rant.
er sluoc in durch den helm
      guot
10476 daz im gezwîvelt der muot,
und sich wunden dâ versan
von dem Etzelen man.
Walthêr der küene wîgant
huop dô hôher an der hant
10481 ein schœnez swert daz er
      truoc:
dem marcgrâven er daz sluoc
durch schilt und durch sar-
      wât,
do er des niht mohte haben
      rât,
daz sêre sweizen began
10486 des künic Etzelen man.
ouch was Walthêr worden
      wunt.
dô kam in vil gâher stunt
der herzoge Râmunc
und ander manic helt junc,
10491 die drungen Rüedegêre
von dem künege hêre:
dô weich der Hildegunde man
von Etzelen schar dan.

---

15 euch.—16 einem.—17 weit, H.

10780-83
ouch kam von Francrîche sît
vil manic tiurlîcher degen :
dâ was in Waltheres phlegen
von Arragûn manec helt guot.

11001-42
Gunthêr nam es vil wol war,
Witege wîste sie dar.
dô wânde des der wîgant,
wand er den helt von Spanjelant
hie vor Dietrîche sach,
11006 daz durch sînen ungemach
alle wolden komen dar.
er hiez der Burgonde schar
alle kêren zuo in hin :
' nu helft Walthêren von in,
11011 sô rehte liep ich iu sî :
wan 18 gestüende wir im niht
bî,
sô slüegen in die geste.
seht wie der sturmveste
vor den andern allen stât,
11016 daz er des lützel sin hât
daz er wîche von in dan.'
alle Gunthêres man
huoben schilde in henden.
wer möhte daz verenden ?
11021 si kômen in den herten strît :
zesamene brâhten sie sît
vierzehener künege hervanen.
dô mohte man si lîhte erman⁻
en
daz grimmer strît von in geschach,
11026 dâ iegelîch den sînen sach
zuo deme er was gezalt.
si wæren junc oder alt,
si kâmen zuo einander gar :
sô dôz 19 ez über al die schar,
11031 sam ez nâch doners blicke
tuot.
wie dicke sich die recken
guot
mit slegen underliefen !
genuoge ' wê, wê ' riefen :

die andern sprâchen ' nâher
dar ' !
11036 sich heten alle die schar
gesamenet dâ daz swert lac :
vil maneges jungester tac
was im unz dar gespart.
daz velt über al dô wart
11041 geverwet mit dem bluote :
dâ sturben helde guote.

11686-707
Gunthêr der sprach sint
'der wæn wir inder drizic hân.'
dô sprach der Hildegunde
man,
Walthêr von Spanjelant
' nu bin ich eine doch genant
11691 über zehen künege rîche :
ich wil iu sicherlîche
bî mir zeigen zweinzic man
die lant und fürsten namen
hân.'
Dô sprach der herre Sîfrit
11696 in einem hôchvertigen sit
' ich boute ê eine grâfschaft,
ê wir des wurden lügehaft,
wirn 20 gewunnen sam manegen man.
driu künicrîche diu ich hân
11701 müezen 21 werden zwelf her-
zentuom,
ê daz si hæten den ruom
daz wir gestrîten möhten 22
niht.
swaz halt anders hie geschiht,
man sol uns bî einander sehen.
11706 hœrt wes 23 iu die andern jehen,
die ouch fürsten sint genant.'

11922-38
Walthêr der wîgant,
der sach Rüedegêren an :
dô sprach der Hildegunde
man
' des weiz got wol die wârheit,

18 und.—19 daz.—20 wir.—21 ez müezen.—22 mohten gestaten.—23
waz.

mir ist inniclîchen leit
11927 daz ich dem helde gewegen
bin.
füert er nu den prîs hin,
des hân ich lützel êre :
slah aber ich Rüedegêre,
sô hât der alte friunt mîn
11932 übel bestatet den sînen wîn
den ich ze Bechelaren tranc :
sô habe diu wîle undanc
daz des spils ie wart gedâht.
sîn tugent hât mich dar zuo
brâht
11937 daz ich ofte den lîp mîn
wâgte durch den willen sîn.'
12200-6
Walthêr von Spanjelant
unde ouch Herbort der degen,
mit den aller meisten slegen
der ie gephlâgen küneges
kint,
dâ mit si von der porten sint
12205 drungen Dietrichen
daz er in muoste entwîchen.
12285-7
Walthêr von Spanjelant
der truocWasgen an der hant,
der kam dar gesprungen.
12647-58
Dô sprach der guote Rüedegêr
'ob ir, küniginne hêr,
mich überhüebet der scham,
mich hât gemachet im 24 sô
zam

der degen ûz Spanjelant :
12652 hæt ir hie twalm an der hant,
den trunke ich, unde gebüte
er daz.
ez was nôt daz âne haz
uns der wirt sô hât gelabet.
mich hât alsô ze hûse gehabet
12657 der schœnen Hildegunde man
daz ichs vergezzen niene kan.'
12801-17
Dô sprachdiu schœneHilde-
gunt
'wiste wir nu hie zestunt
waz wir Rüedegêre
möhten bieten êre
nâch friuntlîcher minne,
12806 er und diu marcgrâvinne
hânt uns sô dicke liep getân,
wir kunden night sô guotes
hân
wir enteilten ez im gerne
mite.'
dô sprach er ' frouwe, des ich
bite,
12811 des gewært mich,vil edel wîp.
swie mir verhouwen sî der lîp
von des küenen recken hant,
sô wil ich von iu beiden sant
in friuntschefte urloup hân.'
12816 dô sprach Hildegunde man
'got phlege iuwer,Rüedegêr.'
12998-13000
dô kam für den künec gegân
Walthêr und frou Hildegunt :
urloup si nâmen an der stunt.

_____

24 in.

IX.

ALPHARTS TOD.*

77. 1-3   DÂ saz Amelolt und Nêre,   die zwêne küene man,
                Walthêr von Kerlingen,   Helmnôt von Tuscân,
        als der vogt von Amelungen,   si hete ûz erkorn.

307   Walthêr von Kerlingen   in engegene gie,
        dâ man die recken   harte wol enphie,
        und Hûc von Tenemarke,   ein ûz erwelter degen.
        vünfhundert burcmanne   enphie[1] die recken ûz
        erwegen.

317. 1-2 Dô sprach von Kerlingen   Walthêr der degen
        'hilfe ich im, des[2] keisers hulde   hân ich mich
        erwegen.'

334. 1-2 Dô sprach von Kerlingen   Walthêr der degen,
        'ich und der münich Ilsam   weln schiltwahte phlegen.'

356. 3-4 Walthêr von Kerlingen   und der müenech Ilsam
        die kômen mit gewalte   anderhalben hîn dan.

372-373 Dô streit vermezzentlîchen   Walthêr der degen.
        sîn swert hôrt man erclingen.   dô vaht er sô eben
        und streit ouch gar sêre   âne allen wanc.
        mit lîbe und mit guote   seite mans im sider danc.
        Daz tete der vogt von Berne,   der küene wîgant.

        Walthêr von Kerlingen   vuorte an sîner hant
        ein swert daz in dem sturme   als ein glocke erdôz,
        Walthêres ellen[3] was ûzermâzen grôz.
380. 4   dô tete wol daz beste Walthêr und Hûc von Tenemarc.

400   'Wis got wilkomen, Hildebrant,   lieber meister mîn,
        und der herzoge Nîtgêr,   der sol mîn ôheim sîn :

---

* From the text of ' Deutsches Heldenbuch ' (ii Theil, E. Martin, Berlin, 1866).

1 entphingen.—2 dün ich jm no holffe des.—3 elende.

Walthêr von Kerlingen   und Hûc der küene man,
dar nâch die recken alle,   die ich niht genennen kan.

426   Dô sprach von Kerlingen   Walthêr der degen
‘ich wil des vorstrîtes   noch hiute hie phlegen
durch hêrn Dietrîches willen,   des vürsten, sâ ze hant.
ich tuon ez wol mit êren :   ich bin geborn ûz Diutsch-
       lant.’

434   Walthêr von Kerlingen   und Hûc von Tenemarc,
die zwêne ritter junge,   ez wâren helde starc :
si hiewen durch die ringe   daz vliezende bluot,
ez lac von ir handen   manic ritter guot.

448   Walthêr von Kerlingen   und Hûc von Tenemarc,
die zwêne ritter junge (ez wâren helde starc),
Hildebrant der alde und der münic Ilsam,
die kêrten alle viere gein den zwein küenen man.

X.

DER GRÔZE RÔSENGARTE.*

32–33 DER zehende heizet Walther von dem Wasgenstein,
er ist an dem Rîne der küensten fürsten ein.

235–36 der zehende daz ist Walther von dem Wasgenstein,
er ist an dam Rîne der küensten recken ein.

407–14 'Noch weiz ich einen vor dem ich¹ sorge hân,
wer sol uns in den rôsen den zwelften helt bestân?
der ist geheizen Walther von dem Wasgenstein,
und ist an dem Rîne der küensten recken ein.'
'Dem ich sînen kempen, weizgot, niht finden kan,
412 ez sî dan Dietleip von Stîre, der ist ein starker man.
hulf uns der junge herzoge, vil lieber herre mîn,
sô möhten wir mit freuden wol rîten an den Rîn.'

1402–57 Dô sprach der küneg Gibech 'waz sal nû mîn leben,
daz ich unser keime den prîs al hie mag geben!
wan ich weiz einen recken, der ist ein starker man,
der mag uns wol gerechen, als ich gesagen kan.'
Dô sprach der küneg Gibeche 'nu rich mich, edeler
Walther,
1407 ein herre von Wasgensteine, setze dich ze wer.'
'vil gerne', sprach dô Walther, einen buckelære nam
er in die hant
mit vil zornegem muote, sîn güete im gar verswant.
Hiltebrant hielt bî dem ringe, dô rief er al zehant
'wâ bistu nû, Dietleip, ein herre von Stîrer lant'?
1412 er hielt bî küneg Etzel under einer banier rôt:
daz fuorte der von Stîre als im diu schult gebôt.

* The passages from 'Der Grôze Rôsengarte' are reprinted from W. Grimm's edition
(1836). The variant passages from the "Rosengarten Fragments" are taken from the texts
published by Bartsch in *Germania* (No. 1, from 'Der Rosengarte,' *Germania* iv, 1-33; No.
2, from "Bruchstücke aus dem Rosengarten," *Germania* viii, 196-208).
1 sich C.

'Ich wil mit ime strîten,' sprach der junge man,
'swie er bî sînen zîten sô vil grozer dinge habe getân.'
Des danket ime der von Berne und er Hiltebrant.

1417 den schilt begund er fazzen, den helm er ûf gebant:
er sprang in den garten, als wir ez hân vernomen:
wol gar schierere Walther was gegen ime komen.
Dô sprach der von Wasgenstein, 'bistu Bitterolfes
barn?
wer hât dich ze strîte her gein mir erkorn?
1422 du bist niht gewahsen noch zuo einem man:
wie wiltu eime recken mit strîte vor gestân'?
'Des breng ich iuch wol innen,' sprach der junge man,
'nu schônet mînes lîbes niht, sô tuon ich iu daz sam.'
Er sprach 'guotiu triuwe an tôren lützel helfen kan.'
1427 dô sprungen si ze samen die mortgrimmegen man,
sie striten mit ein ander, als ich iu sagen wil:
manheit unde sterke sie beide hâten vil.
Ir helm und ire brünne dô liezen iren schîn,
dar durch ran ir beider bluot, des lachte diu künegîn.
1432 ir goltvaren schilden schrieten sie von der hant,
daz sie mit kleinen stücken von in stuben ûf daz lant.
sie liezen von irme schirmen die zwêne küenen man:
helm und ouch ir schilde zerhiuwen sie ûf den plân.
Dô sprach meister Hiltebrant 'sehent ir, frou künegîn,
1437 wie dise recken strîten? ez muoz ir ende sîn.
ir einer mag dem andern niht gesigen an:
sie slahent tiefe wunden: von schirmen hânt sie gelân.'
Dô sprach diu küneginne 'nu sage mir, du wîser man,
wie sal ich sie nu scheiden die recken lobesan?
1442 'jehent in siges beiden, wol edele künegîn,
unt gebent ir ieglîchem ein rôsen krenzelîn.'
Krîmhilt diu küneginne langer dô niht beitete,
mit zwein krenzelînen sie sich dô bereitete.
sie sprach 'ir beide habent dane, ir sît zwên biderman,
1447 ir hânt in den rôsen daz beste beide wol getân.
nu lânt von iuwerme strîte, ir sulnt gesellen sîn,
sô geben ich iuwer ieglîchem ein rôsen krenzelîn.'
Sie bunden abe die helme, unt nigen der künegîn,
ûf saste sie ir ieglîchem ein rôsen krenzelîn:
1452 ein helsen und ein küssen gab sie dô ie dem man.

dô wurden eitgesellen die stolzen recken wol getân.
Dô sprach der von Berne, 'ir hânt beide wol gestriten
in deme rôsengarten nâch ritterlîchen siten.
der anger ist bekleidet mit iuwer beider bluot :
1457 Krîmhilt diu küneginne ist vil diu baz gemuot.'

ROSENGATEN FRAGMENTS.

1.

65 D AZ vîrde daz ist Hagene,   Alriânis kint,
daz vunfte daz ist Walthêr,   geborn von Kerlinc.

290 Orlob nam dô Hildebrant   umm einen mitten tac,
her gâcht zum rôsingarten   dâ manic recke lac.
do enphingen in Walthêr   [und] Sîfrit von Niderlant,
do enphingens in gemeine,   den alden Hiltebrant.

' 25 Dô sprach der konic Gibeche   'dir sî gecleit, Walthêr,
und beite hî niht lenger   und richte dich zu wer.'
Walthêr drabt in den garten . . . .
'wâ ist nû von Berne   der alde Hildebrant?
Wer sal mit mir vechten ?   der ist mir unbekant.'
630 [mit] 'Hertinc von Rûzen,   den ich ûch habe genant.'
Hertinc der kûne   drabete vast dort her,
her fûrte an sîner hende   ein armdickez sper.
Her dâcht 'nû sal ich vechtens   hûte werden sat,'
her fûrte ûf sîme helme   von golde ein michel rat.
635 ir strîten wart michel   und starc . . . .
daz ir iclîcher   mit den rossen belac.
Do di forsten ûf sprungen   zusamen in daz gras,
mich wundert daz ir keiner   vorm andern ie genas.
si striten mit heldes handen,   di swert si hôch zogen,
640 daz des fûres flammen   kein den luften flogen.
Si slûgen durch di schilde,   daz iz lûte irclanc
und daz si beide striten   mit ellenthafter hant.
si vâchten mit ein ander   ein vil lange stunt,
daz si zu beiden sîten   worden sêre wunt.
645 Ir kein konde dem andern   mît strîte ane gesegen,

si hatten sich mit strîte   alsô sêre irwegen:
ûf stûnt di schône Krîmhilt   und schît di zwêne man.
dô mûste ir iclîcher   von der heide zu sîm frûnde dan.

2.

(1ᵃ)   D ER eine schilt vil rîcher   den der ander was.
            von edelme gesteine   swas man dar ane vant,
        di wêrn al um und umme   geleit ûf des schildes rant.

        Walter sprach zu Witgen   'nu nim du einen schilt
5   under disen beidin   swelhin sô du wilt.'
        'vorslûg ich daz' sprach Witige, 'des mohtich mich
            schemen.
        nemt ir den armen,   ich wil den rîchen nemen.'

        Sich hûb ein nûwez vechtin,   di schilde gar zuclobin
        die steine gein dem vrouwen   hôch in di venster stobin.
10   Walter der stunt ebene   Witige wart gewunt:
        ir hende slûc zusamene   di schône Hiltegunt.

        'Waz sal des . . . . . .   dâ ni . . . . . .
        Wal(ter) . . . .
        . . . .
15   . . . .   (1ᵇ) und habt ûch deste baz.'

        'Wî lobis . . . .'   sprach her Dîterîch.
        Witige sprach 'mîn vechtin   ist gein im ungelîch.
        ichn rîte nimmer mêre   nâch rôsin in diz lant.'

94-101 'waz ist ûch, hêre mûter   sprach ver Crêmilt.
        dar umme hîz ich her kumen   vil mangen nûwen schilt.

        Daz ich wolde schouwen   wer vrowen dînen kan.
        dar um hân ich gesamnet   vil mangen werden man.'
        'diz mûz sîn,' sprach Walter,   'man râte vorbaz.
99   si mûzenz baz vorsûchin,   vor wâr sô wizzet daz.

        'Wer sal mit Ectwart vechtin?   der schaffe sînen rât.
        er wil zum êrstin vechtin,   her mir enboten hât.'

ADDITION TO PAGE 88.*

3.

I^b

Hie klagt Gi Kunig Gibich gegen
Graf Walhther von Waxenstein

17-114 Ach gott was soll Ich heben an,
      Meiner fursten mag kayner bestan,
      Ich ways noch ein rysen,
20   Der wierdt den streydt nit verliesen,
      Er liess sy (*l.* sich) nie erschreckchen,
      Waltherr ein gefurster graff ob allen rekgen,
      Vnd ein lanndtherr zw waxenstain,
      Eer fürcht weder gros noch klain,
25   Wallherr Richstw mier mein hertznlaydt,
      Ich gib dier ein kunigin hochgemaydt,
      Zw ainem weyb mach ich dierr vnntertan,
      Die allerpest als Ich sy Inn meynem Reich han,
    Kunig gibich   Graff Wallther von Waxenstain
(*mit dem scepter in der linken hand*) (*trägt als riese eine stange in der rechten*)

II

Anntwort Wallherr von Waxenstain
Kunig Gibich Hinnwider

Genedigster kunig, Ich habs Ewern khunigklichen
      genaden vor gesagt,
30   Da maynt ewr gnad Ich wär vertzagt,
      Ich habs nit darumben than,
      Gern will ich den meyn bestan,
      Hiett man geuolgt dem Ratt meyn,
      Vnd hiett nit der khunigein,
35   Yern muetwillen gelan,
      Das wär weyslicher getan

*Reprinted from *Zeitschrift* ii, 243-7 ; 552.

Annder leytt haben auch khraft,
Vnnser grosse hochfardt macht vns vnsighaft,
Vnnd die verachtung die wier treyben,
40   Ladt gott vngerochen nit beleyben,
Nw̄ habt yer offt gehordt,
Wie Troya wardt Erstordt,
Von wegen hochfardt vnd des vbermuett,
Der thuet hewt noch nymermer guet,
45   Doch Es ist geschehen,
Mann soll daz best dartzw yehen,
Herrn yer sollt vnnerschrökhen sein,
Ich thue ewch die hilffe mein,

Hie manndt Hillibrant der maister
Hertzog Dietlieb von Stey[r]

Hertzog Dietlieb von Steyr nw wolher,
50   Vernembt mich lieber herr,
Ich bitt ewch yer welt bestan
Graff Wallther den grossen man,
Gar hart thuet er warten,
Hie zu disem Rosenn Garten,
55   Sein hertz Ist zornes vol,
Herr Diettlieb Nw thuet allso,
Wie Ich ewch gelernnt hann,
So mag ewch nyemandt widerstan,

Anntwurt Herrtzog dietliep von Steyr
dem Berrner vnnd Hilliprant wider

Herr jer dorfft mich nit bitten,
60   Ich bin doch darumb her gerytten,
Das Ich manndlich wel streytten,
Wie wol walltherr bey seynen zeytten,
Gross sachen hatt getan,
Darumb will Ich Inn gern bestan,
65   Daran wag Ich meinen leyb,
Von wegen aller schöner weyb,
Ach zw geuallen dem allerliebsten půelen mein,
Mues es manndlichen gefochten sein,
Wol herr gesell, vnd wer dich mein,
70   Alls lieb dier dein leben mag sein,

Dann dw muest mich gewern,
Gar pald will dier scheern,

II^b

Hertzog Dietlieb　　　　　Graff Wallther
　von Steyr
　　　　Krimhilt
　　(*gibt jedem einen rosenkranz*)
Hie Schaidt Kunigin Krimhillt die
zwen fursten. vnd gibt yedem ein cranntz

Hört Auff yer zwen fursten guet,
Es bryngt mier grossen vnnmwt,
75　Es gylt auch Ewr payder leben,
Ich bitt ewch yer wellt frydt geben,
Ich gib ewch bayden gewunnen,
Kainer Ist dem anndern enntrunnen,
Yer seydt bayd zwen Redlich Man,
80　Inn dem garten habt yer das pest getan,
Mein Cränntzelein tayl Ich ewch mit
Durch gott nw habt frydt.

III

Graff Wallther　　　Kunig Gibich　　　Graff Völkhher
(*auf den schild mit der*　(*mit dem reichsapfel und*　von Altzen
rechten gestützt)　*scepter in den händen*)　(*mit der stange in der rechten*)
Hie dannkht Kunnig Gibich dem
Fursten von Waxestain

Hab ymmer dannkht dw Edler furst von Waxenstain.
Mit ganntzen trewen Ich dich mayn,
85　Das best lanndt das ich han,
Will Ich dier mächen vnntertan,
Wann dw hast manndlich gestrytten
Vnd wass dw mich thuest bitten,
Das solldtw gewert seyn,
90　Von mier vnnd der khunigeyn,

III^b

Hie dannkht der von Waxenstain
　dem kunig Seinner gab
Gott dannkh ewrn khunigklichen Mayestat.

4

Das mier ewr gnad geben hat,
Ich hab mein bestzs hie getan,
Vnnd wills ewr khunigklich gnad han,
95   So will Ich noch mit ainem schlahen,
Gar klain acht Ich den schaden,
Der mir von yen möcht geschen,
Dann gern wolt Ich Rechen,
Die fursten die hie erschlagen sein,
100   Sy rewen mich In dem herrtzen mein,

Anntwort Kunnig Gibich dem
Fursten vonn Waxenstain

Nayn dw furst lobysan,
Dw hast deinen Ern genueg tan,
Dw soldt deiner Rue phlegen,
Ich ways ainen Risen verwegen,
105   Das jst ain starker furste herr,
Mit namen graff Völkherr,
Layd mag er vnns wol Ergetzen,
Denn wil ich ann sy hetzen,
Er hat erschlagen manichen man,
110   Wolherr Graff lobysan,
Nw gedennkh an den buelen dein,
Vnnd thue mier hilffee scheyn,
Gar furstlich wille ich dich begaben,
Des solldtw kainen zweyffel haben.

4.

617-18   Wer bestat mir Walth' ein helt vo Kerling genant
Den bestat Hartnit ein kug vfser rüfsen lant.

XI.

DIETRICHS FLUCHT.*

5902-3   I U kumet von Lengers Walther
           und Hagen der vil starke,

7359-64   her Gotel und her Helphrîch,
           Walther der ellens rîch,
           si sint reht alle wol gesunt.'
           'sælic müeze sîn dîn munt'!
           sprach vrou Helch diu guote
           mit tugentlîchem muote.

8589-8602   Hie bî im beleip her Paltram,
           Nuodunc unde Sintram,
           Îrinc unde Blœdelîn,
           Helphrîch unde Erewîn,
           und Hornboge von Pôlân,
8594   her Îsolt und her Îmîân,
           Hûnolt unde Sigebant,
           Walther der wîgant,
           Gotel der marcman,
           von Ôstervranken Herman,
8599   Dancwart unde Hagene,
           von den[1] wol zimt ze sagene,
           si wâren zwêne degene
           in strîte vil bewegene.

8629-64   daz was der starke Liudegast,
           dem an sterke niht gebrast,
           und Liudegêr der unverzagt,
           von dem man grôze manheit sagt.
           dâ was Rûmolt der starke
8634   und Diezolt von Tenemarke,

---

* From the text of ' Deutsches Heldenbuch ' (ii Theil, E. Martin, Berlin, 1866).
1 dem, A.

von Norwæge Hiuzolt,
von Gruonlande Diepolt,
Fridunc von Zæringen,
Walther von Kerlingen,[2]
8639   Sturmgêr von Engellant,
Sigemâr von Brâbant,
Tûsunc von Normandîe
und sîner bruoder drîe,
Marchunc von Hessen,
8644   die ouch ze strîte wol wessen,
und von den Bergen Ladiner,[3]
der hete dâ ein starkez her,
Râmunc von Îslande,[4]
des ellen man wol bekande,
8649   Môrolt von Arle[5]
und sîn bruoder Karle[6]
(den guoten Karle mein ich niht,
von dem man saget manec geschiht)
Gunthêre von Rîne,
8654   Gernôt der bruoder sîne,
Tîwalt von Westevâle,
Marholt von Gurnewâle,
von Dietmarse Môrunc,[7]
der manheit ein ursprunc:
8659   Heime und Witegouwe,
als ich der mære getrouwe,
Witege und Witegîsen.
noch wil ich iuch bewîsen,
Madelolt unde Madelgêr
8664   daz wâren zwêne recken hêr.

9244-7   von Lengers[8] Walther
der bestuont den starken Hiuzolt.
si arnten[9] alsô daz golt,
daz ez si sûre muoste an komen.

9870   Walthêr unde Erewîn.

---

2 Baltheir von Chedingen, A.—3 Ladimer, W.—4 unnd Yslande, A.
—5 Albarle, W.—6 Barle, A.—7 Maysunck, A.—8 Lennges, A.—9
ordneten, A.

XII.

RABENSCHLACHT.*

47–48 WALTHER der Lengesære[1]
         sprach dô al zehant
'dêswâr,[2] her Bernære,
und wæren nâher mîniu lant,
ich bræhte iu helde guote.
die hulfen iu mit unverzagtem muote.

48 Doch wil ich daz niht lâzen,
ich welle mit iu dar.
ob ez iu kumt ze mâzen,
so geleiste ich noch wol, daz ist wâr,
aht hundert werder recken.
jâ helfent iu vil gerne die kecken.'

551–574 Hinevür trat mit gewalde
her Walther zehant.
der küene und der balde
sprach wider den künec von Rœmisch lant
'vil edeler Bernære,
dû solt ouch hœren mîniu mære.

552 Vrou Helche diu milde
hât dir gesendet her
vümfzec tûsent schilde,
(ich wæn aber wol, ir sî mêr)
und als manic ors verdecket.
Ermrîch wirt mit riuwen erwecket.

553 Der houbetman sol ich sîn,
si wartent mîner hant.
Etzel der herre mîn
hât den vanen her gesant,
der ze Hiunisch lant gehœret.
die vînde werdent noch hiute gestœret

---

* From the text of 'Deutsches Heldenbuch' (ii Theil, E. Martin, Berlin, 1866).
1 Lennges here, A.—2 dêswas, A.

554   Mit jâmer und mit leide,
dazz muoter kint beweinen muoz.
noch hiute ûf dirre heide
mache wir lebens mit tôde buoz
und manegen satel lære.'
'daz vüege got!' sprach der Bernære.

712   Nû hœret starkiu mære,
die ich iu tuon bekant.
Walther der Lengesære
der bestuont mit ellens hant
Heimen [3] den vil starken.
si sâzen bêde ûf zwein guoten marken.

---

3 Hevnen, R.

XIII.

THIDHREKSAGA OR WILKINASAGA.*

P. Ch. 84. U. Ch. 241.

ATTILA konungr af Susa var bæði rikr [oc feolmennr.¹ oc
vann morg riki. Hann leggr vingan við Erminrik konung. er þa² reð Puli. þessir .ii. konungar leggia vingan sin a
mæðal. sua at Attila konungr sendir Erminrik konung(i) sinn
frænda Osið með .xii. riddara. Erminrik(r) konungr sendir i
gegn³ Valltara af Uaskasteini sinn systurson með .xii. riddorum.
þa var Valltari .xii.⁴ uetra.⁵ þar dual diz hann .vii. uetr. Tveim
uetrum siðarr kom þar. [en Valtari com til Susa.⁶ Hilldigundr⁷
dottir Jlias iarls af Greca. oc var send at gisling Attila
konungi. þa var hon .vii.⁸ vetra gomul. [þessir enir ungu
menn⁹ unnuz mikit. oc veit þat þo æigi Attila konungr.

P. 85. U. 242

þat er .i. dag at veizla rik er i grasgarði¹⁰ Attila konungs oc
[danz rikr.¹¹ oc þa hellt Valltari i hond Hilldigundi. þau talaz
við marga luti. oc þat grunar ængi maðr. Nu mællti Valltari.
Hve lengi skalltu vera ambatt [Erca drottningar.¹² oc væri bætr
fallit. attu fœrir heim með oss til minna¹³ frænda. Hon mællti
Herra æigi skalltu spotta mic. þo at ec se æigi hia¹⁴ minum
frændum. Nu suarar Valltari. Fru. þu ertt dottir Jlias iarls [af
Greca. oc þinn er fauðurbroðir Osangtrix konungrVillcinamanna
oc annar i mikcla Ruzi.¹⁵ en ec em systurson Ærminrix konungs
af Romaborg. oc annar er minn frændi þiðrecr konungr af Bern.
oc hvi skal ec þiona Attila konungi. Ger sua uel. far heim með

---

*In this reprint from Unger's text of the Thidreksaga (Saga Didrik Konungs af Bern
1853) variants are given below the text. The abbreviations MSS. and the [have been
retained as employed by Unger. In the numbering of chapters P. refers to Peringskiold
(whose designation is followed by v. d. Hagens translation) and U. to Unger.

1 [af fiolmenni, A.—2 i þann tima, A, B.—3 Attila konungi add. A,
B.—4 cf. A, B; .iiii., Mmb.—5 gamall add. A, B.—6 [want. A, B,—7
Hilldigunn, A.—8 .xii., A.—9 þauValltari, A.—10 garði, A.—11 [danz-
hringr, A, B.—12 [Attila konungs, B.—13 varra, A, B.—14 með, A,
B.—15 [want. A, B.

mer. oc [16] sem ec em þer hollr. sua se guð mer hollr. þa suarar
hon. þægar ec ueit þinn vilia at sœnnu. þa skalltu oc vita [mic
oc [17] minn uilia. [þa var ec .iiii. uetra gomul. er ec sa þic et
fyrsta sinni. oc unna ec þer þægar sua mikit at œngum lut i ver-
olldu [18] meira [19] oc fara vil ec með þer þangat er þu villt. þa
suarar Valltari. Ef sua er sem þu sægir. þa kom þu a morgin er
sol rennr vpp til ens yzta borgarliðs. oc haf sua mikit gull með
þer. sem þu mat mest bera a [20] annarri henndi þinni. firir þui at
þu ueiz allar fehirzlur Erka drottningar frænkonu þinnar. Oc hon
sægir sua vera skulu. Oc nu verðr Attila konungr æcki varr við
þetta ra ɔ. fyrr en Valltari hæuir ut riðit af Susam. oc með honum
Hilldigundr. oc hofʒu nu mikit fe i gulli.[21]   Oc .ii. riðu [22] ut af
borginni oc [ængi var þeirra sua goðr vinr. at þau tryði til
þessa at vita sina færð.[23]

P. 86.   U. 243.

Oc nu verðr við varr [24] Attilla konungr. at Valltari er brot
riðinn oc Hilldigundr. oc nu biðr hann sina menn .xii. riða æptir
þeim [Hilldigundi oc Valltara oc skulut [25] aptr haua fe þat allt er
brot er tecit. oc sua hofuð [26] Valltara.   Oc af þessum [27] var .i.
maðr Haugni. son Alldrian konungs.   Oc nu riða þessir .xii. rid-
darar æptir þeim skyndilega.[28] oc sea nu huarir annarra reið. Nu
lœypr Valltari af sinum hæsti með mikilli [kurteisi oc rœysti. oc
tekr ofan sina fru Hilldigundi oc þeirra gersimar.   Nu lœypr
hann a sinn hest [oc setr sinn hialm a hœfuð ser. oc snyr fram
sinum gladil.[29]   Nu mællti Hilldigundr [við sinn sœta [30] lafarð.[31]
Herra harmr er þat. er þv. skallt .i. beriaz við .xii. riddara.   Rið
hælldr aptr [32] oc forða [33] þinu liui.   Fru sægir hann. grat æigi. set
hævi ec fyrr hialma klofna. skiolldu skipta.[34] bryniur sundraðar.[35]
oc menn stœypaz af sinum hæstum haufuðlausa. [oc allt þetta
hæui ec gort minni hendi.[36] oc æcki er mer þetta ofrefli.[37]   Oc
nv riðr hann i moti þeim.   Verðr nv mikill [38] bardagi. oc fyrr er
myrct af nott en lokit se viginu.

---

16 sua add. A, B.—17 [want. A. B.—18 ann ek add. B.—19 [at þegar
fyrsta tima er ek sa þik .iiii. vetra gomul. unna ek þer, A.—20 i, B;
want. A.—21 ok oðru add. B.—22 þau add. A, B.—23 [engum truðu
þau her til, A.—24 cf. A, B; varar, Mmb.—25 skulu þeir, A, B.—26
cf. A, B; hafit, Mmb.—27 .xii. add. A, B.—28 sem hvatligast, B.—29
sinu gladieli, B; [vel herklæddr, A.—30 liufa, B.—31 [want. A.—32
undan, A, B.—33 hialp, A; hallt, B.—34 skyfða, A; styfða, B.—35
sundrrifnar, A; rifnar, B.—36 [want. A. B.—37 at heriaz við bessa .xii.
riddara add. A, B.—38 hinn harðasti, A, B.

P. 87. U. 244.

En Valltari er nu sarr mioc. oc drepit hævir hann nu .xi. riddara. en Hœgni komz undan [oc komz i skog. En [Valltari
hittir nu sina fru. oc buaz þar³⁹ um við skoginn.⁴⁰ Valltari slær
þa ælld við tinnu oc gerir þar [mikinn ælld.⁴¹ oc þar við steikir
hann .i. bœysti villigalltar. Oc nu mataz þau siðan. oc [luka
æigi fyrr en allt er⁴² af beinunum. Nu snyr Hœgni or skoginum
oc [til ællzens.⁴³ er Valltari sat hia. oc hyggr at hann skal drepa
hann. oc bregðr nu suerði. Hilldigunnr mællti til Valltara.
Vara þic. her ferr nu .i. af [þinum ovinum. er þu barðiz við i
dag.⁴⁴ Oc nu tecr hann vpp bœystið uilligalltarens. er af uar
etit. oc kastar at Hœgna. oc lystr sua mikit hogg. at þægar fellr
hann til iarðar. oc kom a hans kinn. sua at þægar rifnaði holl-
dit⁴⁵ oc ut sprac augat. Oc nu stendr⁴⁶ hann upp [skiott a fœtr
oc lœypr a sinn hæst. oc riðr við þetta heim til Susam [oc sægir
Attila konungi vm sina ferð. Valltari stigr nu a bac. oc riða þau
suðr um feall a fund Ærminrix konungs [oc sægir honum nu allt
af sinum ferðum. Oc þo fa þeir [Attila konungr⁴⁷ halldit sinu
vinfengi með⁴⁸ fegiofum. er Ærminrikr konungr gaf Attila
konungi.

P. 104. U. 128.

[Nv. mælti einn riddari. sa het Valtari af Vaskasteini. hann er
systorsvnr Erminrics konungs oc þetmars oc allra kappa mestr i
konungs hirð at afli oc atgorvi.⁴⁹ Hvat kann þessi maðr fleira at
gera [segir Valtari. en eyða fe eða eta oc drecca. kanntv noccot
skapti⁵⁰ skiota eða steini varpa. þetleifr svarar. þat vænti ec.
at ec gera hvartveggia við hvern yðarn er vill. þa sagði Valtari
af miklu cappi. þa scaltv þessa leika við mic fremia. En ef þv
leikr betr.⁵¹ þa scaltv firir raða mino hofði. en ef þv kant eigi⁵²
sem þv lætr. þa scaltv⁵³ [at visv her⁵⁴ lata lif þitt með osœmð.
oc aldrigi siðan scaltv [eyða iammiclv fe sem nv logaðir (þv). oc
engvm hofðingia siðan gera þvilica neisv. sem nv hevir þv
konongenom gort. er þat segir maðr manni. at þin veizla var

---

39 þau, A.—40 [want.B.—41 [mikit bal, A,—42 [aðr letti var allt
holld, A, B.—43 [at elldinum, A.—44 [af þeim er þu laust til iarðar,
A.—45 want. A, B.—46 spratt, A.—47 [cf. B; konungar, A; þiðr.
konungr, Mmb.—48 storum add. A, B.—49 [cf. B; þa tok V. af. V.
sva til orðz, A.—50 spiotskapti, B.—51 en ec ad. B.—52 þessa leika
add. B.—53 cf. Mmb.—54 [ekki i (við B) dyliaz at þu skalt, A, B.

halv(u) rikvlegar veitt at allvm lvtvm en konongsens sialfs. oc er
slict diorfvng mikil at gera manni eigi meira firir ser en mer
syniz þv vera. þetleifr⁵⁵ svaraði. Miskvnnar mvn hverr a sinv
mali þvrva. En albvinn em ec at fremia þessa leika oc freista
hversv at ferr. hvat man þa meirr ef ec kann ecki. at þa lata ec
lif mitt. enda er œren soc til at sv se. mvn oc frændom minvm
þyckia litill sacnaðr eptir mic vera. ef ec em ecki at manna. ef
noccorir ero þeir er dvgandi menn se. en ec ætla at vist engi se.⁵⁹

P. 105.   N. 129.

Ganga ⁵⁷ þeir nv vt a [voll noccorn ⁵⁸ oc taca stein einn. er eigi
stoð minna en .ii. scippvnd.   þann stein toc Valtari oc kastaði fra
ser .ix. fet. en þetleifr kastar .x. fet.   Nv kastar Valtari .xiii. fet.
þa kastar þetleifr .xviii. fet.   Nv vill Valtari eigi optarr til ganga.
oc hevir þetleifr nv vnnit þenna leic. oc finnz allvm mannvm
mikit vm.   Nv taca þeir [eina merkistong. en þa atti Atila
konongr. er Ærminrikr konongr hafði þingat boðit til sinnar
veizlv. firir þvi at þar var goð vinatta milli þeirra.   En sv merkistong var allra þeirra skapta þvngast ⁵⁹ er þar varo þa komin.
Nv skytr Valtari þesso scapti ivir konongsholl sva at annarr
endir kœmr niðr a hallarveginvm.⁶⁰   Nv mæltv allir þeir menn
er þetta sa. at fvrðv sterklega er scotið. þetleifr tecr nv scaptit
oc skytr aftr ivir hollena. oc er hann hevir scotit. þa rennr hann
i gegnvm hollina [er tvidyr var.⁶¹ oc toc a lopti spiotscaptit. oc
gengr nv i brot við sva bvit.   Nv mælto þat allir er sa. at þetleifr hevir vnnit þessa tva leica. oc at hann hevir oðrlaz havuð
Valtara.   Konongrenn ⁶² Erminrikr mælti. þv goðr drengr. ec
vil leysa havuð frænda mins með gvlli oc silfri oc goðom gripvm.
[sva dyrt sem þv villt ⁶³ þa mælti þetleifr. Hvat scal mer
havuð frænda þins. hann er goðr drengr. oc vill ec geva þer
hera havuð hans. en lavna þv sem sialfr villtv. en æ verðr þv at
leysa vapn herra mins oc hans lagsmanna. en ecki scaltv her
meira firir gialda en [sialfr villtv.⁶⁴ þa mælti konongrenn. þenna

55 þetleifr vill fremia þessa leika. Sups. Mmb.—56 [glutra sua
miklu fe sem nu fortu (með add. B). Nu lezt hann (þetleifr B) albuinn
at reyna þessa leika, A. B.—57 Nv reyna þeir afl sitt Valtari oc
þetleifr. Sups. Mmb.—58 [viðan voll, A, B.—59 [merkistong (Er-
menriks add. B) konungs, firir þvi at þat var þyngst skapt þeira, A,
B.—60 hallarvegginn, A, B.—61 [want. A, B.—62 Ærminrikr konongr
leysir havuð Valtara. Sups. Mmb.—63 [ef þu villt þat þeckiaz, B ;
want. A.—64 [sialfum þer þikir vel, B.

kost vil ec giarna þeckiaz. oc haf firir micla gvꝍs þocc oc mina.
þetta scal ec þer vel lavna. Nv lætr konongr taka sva mikit fe
sem mest hafꝍi [hann neytt⁶⁵ oc leysir vt vapn oc hesta⁶⁶ þeirra
felaga. er at veꝍi lagv. oc þar a ovan gefr hann hanom hinn gafv-
glegsta bvnaꝍ. oc [sva mikit fe gefr hann hanom siꝍan sem hann
kostaꝍi af sialfs sins.⁶⁷ oc eptir þat dvbbar konongrinn hann til
riddara. Nv segir þetleifr nafn sitt oc alla ætt sina. oc verꝍr
hann [viꝍfrægr vm oll⁶⁸ lond af reysti sinni. Ov tecr þiꝍricr
hann ser til felaga [oc kallar hann sinn iafningia. Oc skiliaz
þeir nv at veizlvnni. oc heitr þar hverr aꝍrom sinni vinattv.⁶⁹
Riꝍr nv þiꝍicr konongs svn heim til Bernar oc meꝍ hanom þet-
leifer oc allir hans menn er þangat fylgꝍv hanom [oc Jsvngr
havuꝍloddari meꝍ þeim.

P. 130. U. 151.

Oc nv er morna tecr. þa lætr þiꝍricr konongr segia frænda
sinvm Erminric kononge fall iarlsens. Oc þegar er hann verꝍr
sannfroꝍr at þvi. þa lætr hann blasa allvm lvꝍrvm sinvm oc vapna
alla riddara sina. oc siꝍan [veita þeir atgangv at borginni⁷⁰ meꝍ
valslœngom oc meꝍ lasbogom oc skoteldi⁷¹ oc allzconar velvm.
Nv sia borgarmenn engan sinn cost vænna. en a hond at ganga
oc leggia sitt mal a konongs vald oc geva vp borgena. En
konongrenn [gefr þeim lifsgriꝍ oc fear sins.⁷² en hann eignaz
sialfr staꝍinn oc setr þar ivir hofꝍingia Valtara af Vascannsteini⁷³
frænda sinn. Nv riꝍa þeir heim konongarnir [oc gætir nv hvarr
sins rikis. Ærminricr konongr i Romaborg en þiꝍricr konongr
i Bærn meꝍ sina kappa. Oc liꝍr nv sva vm riþ noccora. at
þiꝍricr konongr er heima oc sitr vm kyrt. en þvi a hann
sialdan at rosa a sinvm aldri. þotti hanom oc þa at eins vel eꝍa
hvgr sinn ror. er hann skyldi i storræ ꝍvm lvt eiga. i orrastvm
eꝍa i einvigom þeim sem allan aldr mætti vppi vera.⁷⁴

P. 307. U. 330.

Ok⁷⁵ nu er mornar oc alliost er orꝍit. stendr þiꝍrekr konungr
upp oc lætr blasa [sin bosun.⁷⁶ oc þægar i staꝍ lætr viꝍ kvæꝍa

65 [þetleifr eytt (neytt B) þessa stund, A, B.—66 ross, A, B.—67 [aptr
lætr hann gíallda .xxx. marka (er þettleifr atti *want.* B) A, B.—68
[frægr viꝍa um, A, B.—69 [*want.* A, B.—70 [gera þeir mikla atgongu til
borgarinnar, A, B.—71 elldi, A. B.—72 [lætr þa halda lifi sinu ok fe,
A, B.—73 Vaskasteini, A, B.—74 [Erminrekr ok þiꝍrekr, A, B.—75
fra þiꝍreci konungi oc Erminriki konungi. *Sups.* Mmb.—76 [ollum
sinum luꝍrum, A, B.

iunkherra þether sina luꝺra. oc slict sama margræifi Roðingæirr.
oc standa nu upp allir oc vapna sik. Oc er þæir koma a sina
hæsta. þa riꝺr firir mæistari Hilldibrandr ok bærr i sinni hændi
merkistong þiꝺreks konungs. oc þægar eptir honom riꝺr þiꝺrekr
konungr. oc hverr eptir aꝺrom allir hans menn. oc riꝺa til þessa
vaꝺs. er aꝺr um nottina hafði yfir riðit Hilldibrandr. Oc er þat
sia Aumlungar, letr Sifka blasa [basun Erminriks konungs.⁷⁷
Oc er þetta hæyrir Viðga oc Ræinalld. þa lata þæir blasa ollom
sinom mannom ⁷⁸ til at vapnaz oc bua sik til orrosto. Oc nu
læypr Viðga a sinn hest Skemming meꝺ allum sinum vopnom oc
er albuinn at bæriaz. slict sama Reinalld meꝺ sinn hær. Valltari
af Vaskastæini er nu kominn a sinn hæst oc bærr i hendi ser
mærkistong Erminriks konungs. þat mærki er a þa lund gert.
at hinn [ytri lutr ⁷⁹ mærkisins er [suart silki ⁸⁰ sem ramn. en
annarr lutr er silki litt sem gull. en hinn þriði lutr mærkissins er
grænn sem gras. oc utan viꝺ þat mærki er saumat [siautigir dynbiollor af gulli.⁸¹ sua ringir þetta merki oc glymr. at hæyrir um
allan hærinn. þegar [er riðit er merkit ⁸² eꝺa vindr bærr þat. Oc
her eptir riꝺr Sifka meꝺ alla sina fylking .vi.⁸³ þusundrat riddara
oc mikinn fiolꝺa sargenta.⁸⁴ Oc er þiꝺrekr konungr ser merki
Erminriks konungs oc hann væit at þar fylkir ⁸⁵ Sifka. þa kallar
hann at ⁸⁶ mæistari Hilldibradr skylldi bera þar i mot hans merki.
þat er gort af huito silki. þar stendr i leo af gulli meꝺ korono. oc
þar fylgia dynbiollor [af gulli ⁸⁷ æigi færi en [.vii. tigir.⁸⁸ þetta
merki hæfir Erka drotning latiꝺ gera oc gaf þiꝺreki konungi.
Nu riða saman þessar tvær fylkingar. Ræinalld riꝺr [með
sinom ⁸⁹ flokk. hans mærki er a þessa lund buit. þat er raut silki
sem bloꝺ. oc firir ofan [a millom oc ⁹⁰ spiotzins ero þrir knappar
af gulli. oc hann stæfnir sinom hær i gegn margræifa Roðingæir.
Oc þa riꝺr Viðga meꝺ sinn hær. hans mærki bar hinn sterki
Runga. er engi risi fekz [sa er honom væri iamsterkr.⁹¹ þetta
mærki er suart oc af [hvitom stæini ⁹² hamar ok tong ok stæði.
Her i gegn riꝺr hærtogi Nauꝺung oc bærr i sinni hændi mærki
huit oc a [markat leo ⁹³ af gulli. ok þat merki gaf Erka drotning
þether. Oc þar eptir riꝺr iunkhærra þether oc tvæir synir Attila

77 *want.* A.—78 [luðrum, A, B.—79 [yzti litr, A.—80 [suart, A:
svartr, B.—81 [dynbiollur, A ; .lxx. dynbiollur, B.—82 [at er riðit með
merkit, A ; riðit er, B.—83 .vii., B.—84 skardiant, A ; annars liðs, B.
—85 fylgir, A, B.—86 *add.* A, B.—87 [*want.* A, B.—88 [.lx., A ; lxxx.,
B.—89 [við sinn, A, B.—90 [milli ok, A ; milli, B.—91 [honum sterkari,
A.—92 [hvitu silki, A.—93 [markaðr leo, A, B.

konungs Erpr oc Ortvin. ok hinn go꞉i riddare Hialprik er allra
riddara er kurtæisaztr oc vaskastr.[94] þæirra [skor er buin allt[95]
meꝩ rauꝥo gulli sua[96] at liominn stendr af sem a loga sei.

P. 308. U. 331.

Nv[97] riða þessar .vi.[98] fylkingar saman. þiðrekr konungr af
Bern ri꞉r nu fram [meꝩ sinn hæst Falka oc sitt goꝥa sverð
Ækkisax.[99] oc hoggr a tvær hli꞉ar ser menn oc hæsta. oc fællir
hvern yfir annan. allt þar sem hann færr. Ok fyr honom riðr
mæistari Hilldibrandr meꝩ hans merki ok drepr margan mann
annarri sinni hændi. ok þæirra goꝥi felagi Vildifer fylgir þæim
alldrengiliga. ok er þesssi orrosta en harꝥasta. oc falla nu miok
Aumlungar af lidi Sifka. Ok nu kallar þiðrekr konungr hatt
ok eggiar sina menn ok mællti. Fram hart varir menn ok bæriz
nu af kappi miklu ok drengskap. þer hafit optlega bariz við
Ruzimenn eꝥa Vilcinamenn oc fengum ver þa optaz[100] sigr. en
nu i þessi orrosto sœkium ver vart land oc riki. ok her af me-
gom ver hæita miklir[101] menn. ef ver fam vart æiginland. Oc
heꝥan af verðr þessi [væizla miklu[102] akavare. Oc nu riðr þiꝥ-
rekr konungr i miꝥia fylking Sifka oc drepr menn ok hæsta ok
alt þat sem firir honom verðr. oc sua fram i gegnom þæirra fylking oc aptr aðra læið. Hann hræðaz nu allir ok engi þorir firir
honom at standa huar sem hann riꝥr. ok þa hæfir hann drepit utal
manna. A annan veg i miðri fylking Aumlunga riðr Villdifer oc
firir honom falla Aumlungar. oc hvar sem hann kom i hærinn.
þa hælldr ængi maꝥr sinom hesti ok sinom vopnom firir honom,
ok nu hæfir hann drepit marga rika hofðingia. ok er hann enn
æigi [sárr drava.[103] þætta ser hærtogi Valltari af Vaskastæini.
hverso mikinn skaða Villdifer gerir a Aumlungum. oc firir
honom flyia Aumlungar hvar sem hann kemr fram. ok riðr i gegn
honom allkapsamlega[104] ok leggr merkispiotino firir hans briost.
ok spiotið gengr i gegnom hann oc út um hærðarnar. Ok nu
hoggr Villdifer af ser spiotskaptið oc riðr at Valtara oc hoggr a
hans lær við sauðlinom. ok sundr tækr bryniuna sua at i sauꝥli-
nom nam staðar. ok sinn væg fell huarr af sinom hæsti dauðr a
iorð. Oc nu er Sifka ser at hans merki er fallit oc drepinn er

---

94 traustastr, A; hraustastr, B.—95 [skari er buinn allr, A.—96 *add.*
A, B.—97 Er þiðrecr konungr bersk við Sifka. *Sups.* Mmb.—98 .iii.,
A.—99 [a sinum hesti Falka, A.—100 iafnan, A, B.—101 mestir, A;
meistara, B.—102 [orrosta halfu, A. B.—103 [saardrafa, A; sar, B.—
104 allakaflega, A, B.

hinn matki¹⁰⁵ kappi Valtari. snyr hann sinom hæsti undan ok
flyr. oc þar eptir allt hans liþ. En þiðrekr konungr oc allir hans
menn ræka flottann oc drepa þa¹⁰⁶ oc fylgia þæim allan þann
dag langa læið.¹⁰⁷ ok skiliaz æigi við fyrr en dræpinn er mæstr
luti þæssa hærs. oc er þat [langa rið at¹⁰⁸ þiðrekr konungr
riðr¹⁰⁹ aðr hann skiliz við oc hann snyr aptr.¹¹⁰

1.

OLD SWEDISH VERSION.*

KAP. 222.

Om konung Aktilius' vänskap med konung Ermentrik.

Koning Atilia war en riker konung . han haffde mýkin winskap mz
ermentrik . koning / han satte sin frende till ermentrik konung . som
osid het . mz xij riddara . konung Ermentrik fik hanum sin frende
igen som walter het aff waldsken han war tha ekke mesta gamall . En
5 iomfrw war mz Attilia konung . hon het hildegulla . jarlens dotter aff
greken . hon war tit sat till gisl¹ . walter haffde henna ganszke ka'r.

KAP. 223.

Walter af Wasekensten rider bort med Hildegunna, jarlens dotter
af Grekland.

Et sinne haffde Aktilia konung manga ga'ster . oc mýkin gla'di mz
dans oc alskýns² lek . walter hiolt i jomfruna hand . hildegunna . oc
sagde till henne . hwat heller wiltw fýlgia mik . eller wara konung
attilia frilla . Hon swarade/ ware thz ether alffwara tha will iak engen
5 heller haffua a'n ider/ han swarade/ gud warde mik sa hwll som iak
skall wara ider hull . Jomfrwn sagdis wilia gerna góre hans wilia/ han
sagde . kom i morgon som [thz] ³dagas vtan for löna porten/ oc haff
mz tik gull oc silff oc tina cla'der . hon sagdis thz göra wilia . Eý
10 wiste konungen för a'n the bada borte wore . Tha kom portaneren oc
sagde hanum thz.

KAP. 224.

Huru Walter drap konung Aktilius' riddare.

hagen war tha mz attilia konung . oc war tha ganske vnger
konungen sagde till hanum . rid effter iomfrvna' . oc walter . han fik

---

* The text is reprinted from the edition of Hyltén-Cavallius ('Sagan om Didrik af Bern.'
Stockholm 1850–1854), chapters 222-225, 128-129, 147, 280-281. Substitutions for Hyltén-Ca-
vallius signs, are : ö for o with inclined stroke, z for ʒ (=Old Swedish composite sign).
The variants are those of B.

105 mesti, A; mikli, B.—106 margan mann, A.—107 hrið, A, B.—
108 [long leið (er *add.* B), A, B.—109 rekr, B.—110 fra hernum *add.* A.
1 gelss.—2 helskóns.—3 Bl. 101.

hanum xj riddara mz sik . the rido skẏndeliga' effter wolter/ tha
wolter fik them atsee . tha steg han aff sin ha'st . oc tog nid iomfrwna .
5 Sidan sprang han a sin ha'st igen/ oc bant fast hielmen a sit huffuod .
Jomfrwn sagde/ thzte a'r stor harm . at tw skallt allene slass mot
xij . / flẏ hellre vndan oc redde tit liiff/ walter swarade gra't ekke
jomfrw . iak hauer för seet hielma . brẏnior oc skiolde kloffne . oc
mongen en huffuodlöss aff hesten störte offta haffuer iak warit ther
10 mz . tẏ grwffuar mik encte for thesse xij . sidan red han hardeliga mot
them . oc slogos gansze lenge . walter slog the xj i ha'll . oc hagen
rẏmde vndan i en skog . ther na'r lag.

KAP. 225.

*Huru Walter af Wasekensten slog ut ögat på Hagen, och red till
konung Ermentrik.*

walter kom i sama skog . oc iomfrwn mz hanum/ han giorde eld oc
redde matt . som walter sat oc att . aff et willegals böste . tha kom
hagen mz et dragit swerd oc liop at walter . jomfrwn ropade ware tik
herre . her . komber en aff tina owener walter sprang op oc tog böstet
5 oc slog hagen wid hans öga . sa at wtgik annat ögat/ oc han fioll om
kull . hagen sprang snart op oc steg vppa sin ha'st oc red hem till
attilia konung oc sagde hanum tidende/ oc haffde tha mist sit ena
öga . walter red till Ermentrik konung . oc war hanum welkomen oc
dwaldis ther om langa stund.

KAP. 128.

*Detzleffs måltid. Walter af Wasekensten manar Detzleff till
kamp i att skjuta stång och kasta sten.*

Detzleff swarade hwar iak haffuer warit i androm landom . for stora
herra/ tha wiste the alla stadz then hedher . at biwda fra'mede man
till bords oc giffua hanum matt om han wara' fastande/ för a'n the
sporde hanum tidende . konungen lot giffua hanum matt/ tha aat han
5 mer a'n iij the starkaste men/ sidan bar skenken fram ena gwll skaall
som han störst orkade ba'ra fulla mz starkasta wiin / then drak han
wt at enom drẏk/ konungen oc alla höffdingia talade oc vndrade ther
vpa . thz skötte detzleff encte . Sidan sagde walter aff wasekensten 4 .
konung ermentrikx oc konung thitmars systerson . han war starkiste
10 ka'mpe i konungens gard . kan thenne man enchte annat . vtan mẏkit
a'ta oc dricka oc forta'ra gots 5 . oc kantw skiwta stoug . eller kasta
sten . Detzleff swarade jak tror jak kan bada' a' mz hwilkom idrom
som torss mz mik prÖffwa . walter swarade Jak will thz mz tik öffwa' .
om thens wor huffuod . som tapar/ oc 6 winner iak tha skaltw aldre
15 forta'ra sa mẏkit mer . eller 7 göra nokrom första' tẏlke nesa som tw

---

4 volter aff vode vasekensten.—5 inte anath gôre vtan a'ta och
môkedh fforta're.—6 om ba'ggas vaare huffuodh.—7 Bl. 72.

hau*er* nw giort mi*n* h*er*re/ [8] tẏ folkit siger tit ga'stabud hau*er* wa*r*it
kosteligare a'n hans . Detleff swarade lekar iak a'ẏ som mik bör/ haut
skadar thz tha mer . a'n iak mist*er* mit liiff . litit mo*n*na' mẏ*n*a fra'nd*er*
mik sakna . a'n alt skall iak röna' om tw tor m*z* mik leka.

KAP. 129.

Detzleff segrar i leken. Konung Ermentrik löser Walters lif.
Detzleff säger sitt rätta namn, och blir upptagan till
Didriks jämning.

The gingo wt vppa wallen tha tog walt*er* en sten som wog ij
skipp*un*d oc kastade ix föter . Sidan kastade detzleff x föter Sa kastade walt*er* xiij föt*er* . Detzleff kastade xviij föter/ [9] tha wilde walt*er*
a'ẏ mer th*en* Iek . / Tha gingo the till k*onung* attilius bannera stang .
5 hon war störst oc tyngst aff all the spiwt som th*er* wore . tha sköt
walter stangena twert wtoffu*er* k*onungens* sall . thz sagde alla
konu*n*gxme*n* at thz war wa'll skut*i*t [10] . Tha tog detzleff stongena oc
sköt langx at salen i gömo*n* two dörr*er* oc löp sa snart efft*er* antha*n*
tog stongena för a'n hon nokorstadz mötte . ell*er* rörde/ oc gik sa jn
10 i salen . tha sagde alla' at detzleff haffde wu*n*net . the two leka . oc
walters huffuod . tha sagde k*onung* er*en*trik . tw goder dreng*er* vn
mik lösa huffuod fra'nda my*n*s iak will giffua tik th*er* for*e* gwll oc
klenodie sa mẏkit som tw bed*i*s . Detzleff swa*r*ade mik a'r encte om
thin fra'nda huffuod . tẏ ha*n* a'r en god*er* dreng*er* . iak will giffua thik
15 hans huffuod . oc lön mik [11] haut tik ta'kk*i*s . tog ward*er* tw lösa my*n*
h*er*ris wapn oc ha'sta' oc hans tia'nare [12] . thu skalt mik ekke a*n*nat
atbetale a'n som tw sialffu*er* wilt . k*onungen* agde haff th*er* thak for*e*
thz skall jak tik wa'll löna' . k*onungen* tog gwll oc silff oc löste ther*i*s
ha'sta oc harnisk ig*en* oc betalede alt thz detzleff fortarit haffde aff sit
20 egit . Sid*an* gaff ha*n* detzleff kosteliga cla'd*er* . oc slog hanu*m* till
riddar*e* . oc fik hanu*m* xxx mark guls so*m* [13] han forta'rit haffde aff sit
egit/ her didrik tok h*anu*m till sin iampnu*n*ger [14] . detzleff war tha be-
kender hwat hans naffn war / oc atha*n* war bit*er*wlff jarls son aff
twmmathorp . sida*n* wart ha*n* prjsat offu*er* alla land.

KAP. 147.

Widikes och Heyms träta och förlikning. Konung Ermentrik
vinner slottet Gerimshem.

Tha wredd*i*s wideke ok spra*n*g at heẏm oc grep mi*m*mi*n*gx
handfang . oc rẏkte swerd*i*t fra heẏm / Nagelri*n*g kastade han for
ha*n*s föter . oc böd hanu*m* strax till kamp . heim tog nagellri*n*g op .

---

8 gòr*e* naagen ffòrste tolken neese och skam ssaa ssom tu haffuer
giorth.—9 Sa ... xviii föter *omitted in* B.—10 alla men vell var*e* kastadh
och man*n*eliga skuthz.—11 och giff meg.—12 min herres vapn och hans
tia'nares vapn och ha'sta.—13 Bl. 72, Verso.—14 her didrek tog ha*nu*m
till stalbrod*er* och kallade honum sin iempnunge.

oc sagde/ iak a'r rede at kampa mz tik . konung tidrik sprang i
5 mellom . oc flere gode men . oc wilde thz a'ÿ till sta'dia . wideke
sagde Aldrey skall mimming komma i sina skida . för a'n han haffuer
skilt ¹⁵ hans huffuod . fra hans bwk/¹⁶ tÿ athan hauer mik offta hwgmod
giort/ som han oc giorde tha iak lag om kull slagen i wilcina land .
tha matte han mik wa'll hulpit haffua . sa/ at iak ekke haffde grepin
10 wordin/ han lot som han¹⁷ mÿn fiende¹⁸ war/ oc röffuade mik mit swerd
wtaff/ tÿ wet iak athan skall sin lön haffua . ther fore sa got a'r nw som
annat sin ¹⁹ . her tidrik talade till heim/ oc straffade hanum ther fore
. oc bad hanum forbidia wideke/ sidan swor heim en ed . at thz war
hans snak . oc gaman som han till widike talade . oc encte spot eller
15 hat ²⁰ . oc ther mz bliffuo the forlikte/ konung tidrik sporde widike/
wolte tw jarlans död . ja sagde wideke . han kom mot mik ²¹ sielff vjᵗᵉ
oc sidan han war slagin tha rÿmde the . v./ konung tidrik sagde . tw
skalt haffua ther god lön fore . oc myn kerleek . tw a'ft en rask man .
oc fultage ka'mpe / konung tidrik sende et bud till Ermentrik
20 konung . oc lot hanum sigia ²² at iarlen war död . tha han thz sporde /
tha lot han bla'sa i alla sina ludra . oc wapna alt sit folk . oc stormade
strax till slottit . sa lenge at jarlans men gaffuo slottit . sa at the aff
gingo mz harnisk oc haffuor./ konung Ermentrik annamede slottit oc
satte ther till höffuisman . wolter aff waskensten ²³ . sin sÿsterson./
25 Sidan redo konungana bade hem i thera egit land igen.

KAP. 280.

Konung Didrik och Seveke föro sina baner emot hvarandra.

Om morgonen arla stodh ha'r didrik op ok vapnadhe sik ok loth
bla'sa j piper ok basunar . tetmar hans brodher giordhe ok samaledis
ok tesslighchis margreffuen rödgher ok stigha pa sina ha'stha /
mesther hyllebrandh redh fram mz her didriks baner All ha'ren
5 fjldhe a'ffther . han ridh öffuer thz sama vadh som han hadhe om
nattena Ridhith/ tha seueke var thess var/ ok vidheke velanson/ tha
bla'sthe the j alla thera ludha/ ok badh thera folk/ vapna sik .
vidhekhe stegh pa sin hesth skimplingh teslikis giorde renaldh ok
valther aff vaskensten han förde konung Ermentriks baner thz var
10 badhe storth ok lancth ok manga gulklocchor/ oppa . thz baner
rykker [? rynger] saa fasth ath thz höra magh offuer all hera'n/ ther
vndher redh seueke mz viᴹ ²⁴ riddare . tha didrik saa konung
Ermentriks baner/ ok viste ath seueke var ther vndher / ta badh han
hyllebrandh föra sith baner ther j moth thz var giörth aff slwth
15 [? hwith] silke och lxx gul klokkor oppa / thz hafdhe a'rcha .
drotningh giorth ther stod eth förgylth leon oppo/ tho kom renaldh
mz eth röth baner som blodh / moth honum ridher margreffue

---

15 slitidh.—16 bak.—17 Bl. 77.—18 ffende.—19 paa en annan tidh.
—20 och icke hans alffuare som han till videke talade.—21 han mötte
meg.—22 fförstaa.—23 vollter van vaskinsten.—24 Bl.121, Verso.

rôdgher . tha redh videke fram ha*n*s baner war swarth / ok stodh
ha*m*ber ok tongh vti / thz fôrdhe en ka'*m*pe som rwnghe heth han
20 var stor ok stark som en rese/ moth ho*n*um ridh*er* h*er*togh nordu*n*gh
mz ma'rkar thetmarss*on*s baner th*er* stodh paa eth leon aff gul thz
gaff ho*n*um Ercha d*rotning* . th*er* a'pth*er* foldhe tetmar/ ok hin*a* vnge
h*er*rer ok godhe riddare hia'lprik / han var alla riddar*e* raskasth .
the*ra* vap*en* glimadhe so*m* solen.

KAP. 281.

Slaget vid Grans-port.   Wildefers och Walters af Wasekensten död.
Sevekes flykt.

The drogo til sama*n* mz tesse vi baner . h*er* d*idrik* sath pa syn
hesth falke ok hugh*er* mz sith godha swa'rdh ekke sax/ fôr ho*n*um
stôrthe ma*n*gen ma*n* . fôr ho*n*um ridh*er* hyllebrandh ha*n* drap ok
ma*n*ga*n* ma*n* ok godhe ridde*re* vildefa'r/ tho fiôl mykit aff seuekis
5 folk . h*er* d*idrik* ropadhe hôcth ok badh sina men goo hardeliga fram/
ok sagde vi haffua optha slagis mz rysserna/ ok vy*n*nit th*er* myk*i*t
sigh*er*/ nw vilia vi ok vi*n*na vort eghit landh j gen/ ok h*er* aff hetho
vi mycla me*n* . k*onung* d*idrik* ridh mith j seuekis h*er* / ha*n* dra'par
badhe ma'n ok ha'stha ok alth thz fôr ho*n*um var/ han for badhe
10 twa'rth ok a'ndelancth gyno*m* the*ra* h*er* ok alla ra'dd*is* fôr ho*n*um/ ok
haffu*er*²⁵ dra'pit otalighit folk/ ok anna*n* vegh ridh*er* vildhefer/ ok
hugg*her* ma*n*neligha hwaske vap*en* ell*er* ha's tha ha'ctha fôr honu*m*/
han drap mo*n*gha rika hôfdingha/ thz saa valth*er* aff vaskensten/ hwru
mykin skadha vildhefer giordhe/ ok ath alle flyddhe fôr ho*n*um .
15 valth*er* slogh sin ha'sth mz sporona/ ok satte sith spywth fôr vildhefers
brÿsth saa ath wth gik gyno*m* ha'rdener/ vildefer hugh spwth skapth*i*t
sy*n*dh*er*/ ok sydha*n* hugh han oppa valthers lar ok brynia*n* sy*n*dh*er*
ok larith aff saa ath swa'rdit stod j sadele*n*/ sydhe*n* storthe the bodhe
dôde ok th*er* fiôl k*onung* Erme*n*tr*iks* baner nidh*er* som valth*er*
20 fôrdhe/ tha seueke thz sagh ath valth*er* var slaghe*n*/ ok baneret lagh
nidhre a jorde*n*a tha flydde ha*n* alth thz ha*n* ku*n*dhe/ ok alla ha*n*s
ma'n sa mo*n*ge so*m* vndh*er* thz banere*t* var/ h*er* didrik ja'gadhe
a'pth*er* them ok slogh mesta delin j ha'l aff the*m*/ Sydh*an* va'ndhe
h*er* d*idrik* om.

2.

HLOD AND ANGANTHEOW'S LAY.*

Ár Kvóðo Humla Húnom ráða,
Gitzor Grÿtingom, Gotom Angantÿ,
Valdar Daõnom,¹ enn Vaõlom Kiár,
Alrekr inn frœkni Enskri þióðo.

---

* The text is that of Vigfusson-Powell ('Corp. Poet. Boreale' i, 349), verses 1-4.
25 Bl. 122.
1 Vigfusson amends the line thus:
Valdarr Vöskom enn Vǫlom Kiarr.

XIV

BOGUPHALI CHRONICON.*

ERAT enim temporibus illis urbs famosissima in regno Lechitarum, murorum altitudine circumsepta, nomine Wyslicia,
cujus olim princeps, tempore paganismi, fuerat Wyslaus decorus,
qui et ipse de stirpe regis Pompilii¹ duxerat originem. Hunc
quidam comes, etiam stirpis ejusdem, ut fertur, fortis viribus
nomine Walterus² robustus, qui in polonico vocabatur wdały
Walter,³ habens castrum Tynecz prope Cracoviam, ubi nunc
abbatia Sancti Benedicti per Casimirum Monachum regem
Polonorum seu Lechitarum fundata consistit, in quodam seditioso
conflictu captivaverat, captumque in vincula conjecit ac in
profundo turris Tynecensis mirae custodiae deputaverat tenendum. Hic Walterus quandam nobilem, nomine Helgundam,
sponsam cujusdam regis (Almanorum filii, et regis) Francorum
filiam, habuit in uxorem, quam, ut ajunt, clam versus Poloniam
non sine magnis corporis sui periculis abduxit. (Quum enim)
cujusdam Almaniae regis filius in curia regis Francorum, patris
Helgundae praedictae foveretur, gratia morum capessendorum,
Walterus prout erat animo perspicax ac industriosus, considerans
filiam regis Helgundam⁴ in regis Almaniae filium amoris affectum
avertisse, quadam nocte, moenia castri ascendens, vigilem castri
pretio convenit, ne ipsum quovis modo detegere praesumat, et
sic dulci melodia perstrepuit, quod ad hujus dulcem vocis
sonitum regis filia e somnio excitata, de lecto saliens, cum
caeteris puellabus, somni quietis oblita, cantui dulcissimo intenta,
manebat, donec cantor vocibus sonorose operam dabat. Mane
autem facto, Helgunda jubet vigilem accersire, perquirens dili-
genter, quisnam fuisset ille? Qui se omnimodo ignorare asserens,

---

* The text is from Bielowski's 'Monumenta Poloniae Historica' ii. 510-514, which has the
correct forms *Walczerz* and *Tynecz* instead of the incorrect forms *Walgerzs* and *Tyneg* of
Sommersberg's edition ('Rerum Silesiacarum Scriptores,' 1730: ii, 37-39) and of San Marte's
reprint ('Walther von Aquitanien,' s. 213 ff.). Bielowski's additions to the text are enclosed
in parenthesis. Important variants are given below the text.

1 Popeli in other MSS.—2 Valters iv, Walcerus v.—3 vdaly Walterz
ii, wdalj Walczerzs v, udali Valt, viii.—4 Algundam, ii.

Walterum prodere non praesumsit. Sed cum duabus noctibus sequentibus Walterus adolescens similia caute peregisset, Helgunda dissimulare amplius non valens, vigilem, ut cantorem prodat, minis et terroribus compellit. Qui cum prodere nollet, ipsum capitali sententia plecti jubet. Vigil itaque cum Walterum cantasse meminisset, ipsa in ejus amorem fervide exardescens, ad ejus vota se totaliter acclinavit, filium Almaniae regis omnimodo respuendo. Cernens itaque Almaniae regis filius se pudorose ab Helgunda abjectum, et Walterum in amoris alveolum esse subrogatum, nimio zelo contra Walterum accensus, ad patrem rediens omnia navigia Reni fluminis occupat, ac ne aliquis cum virgine nisi marcam aure pro navigio exsolvat, custodiri sollicite committit. Tracto igitur temporis spatio, Walterus cum Helgunda oportunitatem fugiendi captant, captamque inveniunt, et adveniente die optato aufugiunt. Sed postquam ripam Reni flumenis optate perveniunt, nautae marcam auri pro navigio exposcunt, receptamque, quousque filius regis Almaniae adveniat, transmeare contradicunt. Ille autem, sentiens ex mora periculum, mox bucephalum conscendit, et Helgundam retro se conscendere jubet, fluvium insiliens, sagitta velocius pertransit. Et cum aliquantisper a fluvio Reno viam peregisset, audis clamorem post terga Almani, ipsum insequentis et voce praecognita dicentis: 'O perfide! tam cum filia regis clam aufugisti, et, pedagio non soluto, Renum transmeasti? siste gradum, siste ut ineam singulare certamen, et qui victor exstiterit, victor existens, equum et arma ac Helgundam retinebit.' Cujus clamoribus Walterus intrepide respondens, ait: falsum est quod loqueris nam marcam auri nautis tribueram, et filiam regis non vi raptam sed ultronee me sequi volentem mihi sociavi. Et his dictis alter alterum lanceis animose impellit. Quibus confractis, ensium ictibus pugnant, et viriliter vires exaptant. Et quia Almano Helgundam ex opposito positam repraesentabat aspectus, idcirco ejus aspectibus hilariter confortatus Walterum retrorne coëgit, quousque retroiens Helgundam conspexit. Quam conspiciens, tam pudore incredibili persistit quam ejus amore nimio succensus, viribus resumptis, Almanum fortiter impetit, et ipsum protinus occidit. Cujus equo et armis receptis, itinere capto ad propria remeat, laeti honoris triumpho duplicitur trabeatus. Qui ad castrum Tinecense veniens prosperis itineris successibus feliciter peractis, aliquanto tempore medicandi gratia quieti indulsit, ubi ex querelis suorum intellexit Wyslaum decorum, principem Wysliciensem, in sui absentia suis quasdam injurias irrogasse. Quas grave ad animum revocans, causa ulciscendi contra Wyslaum insurgit, et tandam cum eo confligit, vincit, victumque, ut praemissum est, in profundo turris castri Tinecensis custodiae carcerali deputat mancupatum.

Post aliquam [5] vero temporis revolutionem ad exercendus actus bellicos, more militantium peragendos, remotas peragrat regiones. Et cum duorum annorum ejus absentiae circulus jam revolvisset, Helgunda de mariti absentia nimium auxiata, cuidam puellae, sibi secret iriae, vultu submisso referre fit compulsa, asserens, nec viduas nec maritatas esse, reputans illas, quae viris strenuis et bellorum certamina indagantibus matrimonialiter commiscentur. Secretaria vero, dominae suae luctuosam inopiam, pro qualitate temporis perpessam, pudore proditionali protinus abjecto, cupiens revelare, Wyslaum principem Wysliciae, formae elegantissimae et corpore venustum, in aspectu decorum, in turri nunciat mancipatum ; suadetque misera, ut ipsum de turri, noctis sub silencio, extrahi jubeat, et votivis amplexibus debriata, ad imma turris iterum caute remittat. Favet illa suasionibus secretariae, et periculosis eventibus angustiata, vitam et famam honoris exponere non metuens, Wyslaum de immo carceris extrahi praecipit. Ejus viso decoris aspectu nimium admirans, laetabunda efficitur, nec ipsum amodo ad imma turris mittere, sed cum ipso potius, cui jam sodalitio foedere sociata et indissolubili amoris vinculo compaginata est, ad urbem Wysliciensem fugam inire elegit, proprii viri thoro prorsus derelicto. Sic Wyslaus ad propria remeat, duplicem se sperans habere triumphum : qui tamen in eventu dubio utrique necis apportabat interitum. Nam post revolutionem brevis temporis, Walterus ad propria rediens, a castrensibus sciscitatur, cur Helgunda saltem ad valvas castri sibi non occurrit in suo jucundo adventu ? A quibus cum didicisset, qualiter Wyslaus de immo turris, custodum fretus auxilio, exsiliens, Helgundam secum asportasset, ipse nimio zelo furoris repletus, versus Wysliciam festine properat, casibus fortuitis se et sua exponere non pavescens, urbemque Wysliciensem insperate ingreditur, Wyslao protunc extra urbem venationi insistente.

Quem [6] Helgunda in urbem conspiciens, ei festine occurrit et

---

5 ii has the heading—Quomodo Helgunda—respuit Valterum.—6 ii has the heading—Quomodo Helgunda decepit Valterum.

prona cadens in terram de Wyslao, quod ipsam violenter
rapuerat, lamentabiliter querulatur; suadens Waltero ut ad
secretiora habitaculi ejus ascendat, spondens Wyslaum ejusdem
nutui subito tenendum praesentare.   Credit ille deceptrici, et
deceptivis suasionibus circumseptus, habitaculum firmum ingreditur, in quo Wyslao per deceptricem captus praesentatur.
Gaudet itaque Wyslaus et Helgunda, jocosis plausibus operam
dantes de successu prospero feliciter triplicato; gaudii extrema
minime perpendentes, quos frequenter luctus mortis occupari
consuevit.   Hunc ergo non carcerali custodia teneri voluit, sed
plus quam carceris squaloris coangustari decrevit.   Fecit namque
illum ad parietem coenaculi vinctum bogis ferreis, extensis manibus, collo et pedibus fortiter erectum, alligari.   In quo coenaculo
stratum sibi parari jussit, ubi aestivo tempore cum Helgunda
infra meridiem delectationes venereas exercentes quiescebant.

Habebat[7] autem Wyslaus quandam sororem germanam, quam
ob despicabilitatem ipsius nemo cupiebat in uxorem.   Cujus
custodiae Wyslaus prae caeteris custodibus Walteri plus con-
fidebat.   Haec Walteri afflictionibus nimium compatiens ipsum,
pudore puellari prorsus semoto, a Waltero percontatur, si ipsam
habere vellet in uxorem, si suae calamitati subveniret, a vinculis
liberando? Spondet ille et juramento confirmat, quod eam
maritali affectione, quoad vixerit, pertractet et contra Wyslaum
fratrem ejusdem gladio suo, ut eadem optaverat, numquam
dimicabit.   Hortaturque eam, ut ensem suum a fratris cubiculo
subtrahat, et ipsum apportet, ut cum ipso vincula dirumpat.
Quae mox, ense apportato, clavem cujuslibet bogae seu ferreae
ligaturae in parte extrema, ut Walterus jusserat, de ense praecidit,
ensemque inter dorsum Walteri et parietem reposuit, ut temporis
opportunitate captata securius possit abscedere.   Qui usque in
crastinum hora meridiei exspectatur, et Wyslaus cum Helgunda
jocosis amplexibus in lecto coenaculi dum uterentur, Walterus
contra morem eos alloquitur, dicens:

‘ Qualiterne[8] vobis videretur esse, si ego solutus a vinculis ensem meum stridentem in manibus gestans, ante lectulum vestrum
conspicerer vindictam de commissis inferre minando.’ Ad cujus
dictum Helgundae cor contabuit, et tremebunda Wyslao dixit:

---

7 ii has the heading—Quomodo Valterus a captivitate sive viculis
liberatur.—8 ii heading—Quomodo Valterus Helgundam cum suo
amaio cecidit.

'vae domine! ensem suum in cubiculo nostro non reperi, et tuis affectibus intenta oblita sum revelare.' Ad quod Wyslaus: 'etiamsi decem ensibus fulciretur, bogas ferreas rumpere, absque fabrorum industria, non valeret.' Ipsis sic inter se confabulantibus, Walterus, liber a vinculis, saliens, ense vibrato, ante lectulum stare conspicitur, et mox, datis improperiis, manum cum ense in altum erigens, ipsius ensem in ambos cadere permittit ; ˙qui cadens utrosque per medium scidit. Sic uterque eorum detestabilem vitam miserabiliori fine conclusit. Hujus itaque Helgundae sepulcrum in castro Wyslicensi omnibus cernere cupientibus in petra excisum, usque ad praesens demonstratur.

Huic 9 ergo urbi munitissimae Boleslaus rex illum Pannonium, putativum exulem, quem non ut profugam sed ut patriae alumnum benigne susceperat et caritativo modo pertractans, praefectivo officio gratiosissime insignivit.

9 ii hic redit ad propositum.

XV.

B. PAPROKCI.*

WALCERA hrabie z Tyńca wspominają historye: jako Andreas de Zarnow, wszakoż dowodniej Anonimos, to jest historyk, który kroniké polská, łacińskim jézykiem pisana, krom podpisu imienia swego zostawił, etc.,—dla tego, że był uniósł królewné francuzká imieniem Heligundé, tym sposobem : Służąc albo sié bawiác w postronnych krainach, dla przejrzenia spraw rycerskich, bédác méżem urodziwym i roztropnym, przypatrował sié na dworze króla francuzkiego porzádkowi. Tam bédác, okazował sié znacznym i w każdej potrzebie nad inne rycerstwo fortunniejseym, tak, że go onos zczeście wielkiej sławy człowiekiem rozniosło. Na tegoż króla dworze, było ksiáżé które on królewicem niemieckim mianuje, imieniem Arinaldus, który sié starał o oné królewné, ale go sama panna wzgardzała. Walcerus przed nim miał u niej wielká łaské, co baczác, zabawił sié służbá króla ojea jej, który mu zaraz dać kazał urzád u stołu, jeśliż podezastwo, albo misé stawiać, tego nie miarmje. Tam mn sié ona panna pilnie przypatrując, wielká chéć i uprzejmosć serdeczná k' niemu przyłożyła. Co on jawnie znajác, chcác já jeszeze wiécej do miłości przeciwko sobie prsyciágnáć, szedł w nocy pod pokoje jej, śpiewał i grał na lut nijako mógł napiékniej. Co usłyszawszy Heligunda, z łóżka wstawszy, szła do okna, słuchała tak długo. póki Walcerus nie odszedł, wszakoż ktoby to był taki, nie wiedziała. A Walcerus z razu niechciał sié jej w tem objawiać, owszejki jeszcze stróże przenajáł, aby tego nikomu nie objawiali. A gdy to drugiej i trzeciej nocy uczynił, panné oné do tego zniewolił, że go bezmiernie miłowała, posłała sobie po straż, a ktoby to u niej pod pokojem grał, pytała. Powiedzieli : Nie wiemy, ani znamy, bo tak nieznacznie twarz nakrywszy chodził. Ale panna chciała koniecznie wiedzieć od nich, ktoby to był taki. Wczém gdy stróże byli uporni, ona ich do więzienia wsadzic

---

* " Herby rycerstwa polskiego." Krakow, 1858. 4to. pp. 59-61.

In order to facilitate printing, á, é, ł=Polish ą, ę, ł respectively.

kazala i na gardle karać chciala. Potem z bojażni wyznali a wydali Walcera, który sié o to na nic nie frasowal. Heligunda już z myślá rozdwojona byla, nie wiedząc kogo miala wiécej milować, jeśli Walcera, którego osobé znala, jeśliż onego, którego glos tylko slyszala, a coby zacz byl, nie wiedząc. A dowiedziawszy sié, iż to już on byl, którego w myśli serdecznej miala, poczéla go dopiero zapaczliwiej (sic) milować, a potem do siebie na pokój wzywać. A gdy onych rozmów przez kilka czasów z sobá używali, umyślila z nim potajemnie zjechać. Czego Nicmice postrzegl, jednak milując oné panné bezmiernie, nie wydal jej i Walcera w tych sprawach, a to wiedząc, że przez jego państwo jechać mieli, byl tego pewien, że Heligundy mógl latwie dostać, a ucieszywszy sié w milości, oné niechéć jej przeciwko sobie oddać. A tak naprzód jachal do domu, zakazal na przewozie, aby mu przewoznicy znać dawali, kiedyby kto z panná od Francyi jechal, k'temu aby go dluźej zabawili, rozkazal, aby od takiego nie brali mniej za przewóz, jedno grzywné zlota, rozumieją c to o Walcerze, żeby sié z nimi mial o tak nieprzystojny przewóz targować. Walcerus upatrzywszy czas, zjechal z panná do Polski. A gdy na rzece Renie przewozić sié mial w państwie królewica onego, z fukiem przewoźnikom rozkazal, aby go co prédzej wozili. Którzy z preléknienia zapomnieli rozkazania pana swojego, wszakoz tego nie zapomnieli, co za przewóz wziáć mieli.

Walcerus dawszy im to co mu zacewili, precoz jechal. Oni dopiero wspomniawszy, znać dali o nim panu swemu. Krolewic bédąc zalosny dla despektu i dla milości na sercu niespokojoncj, puscilsié po nim prédko sam, ufają c szcséściu, że go mial przewódz. A gdy go z dalska rajżrzal, wolal nań : Stój zdrajco, przewozuś nie zaplacil i królewskás córké ukradl ! Na co mu Walcerus obcóciwszy sié odpowiedzial: Źle mówisz, przewózem zaplacil, a królewska córka sama ze mná dobrowolnie jedzie. Potem sié zjechawszy, rzekli sobie o panné z sobá czynić, a któryby którego zabil, mial wszystkie rzezy przespiecznie pobrać i dobrowolnie przec jachać. Wtem acz królewicowi zbytnia milość serca dodawala, wszakoż go Walcerus zabil. Przyjechal potem na zamek swój Tynice. Tam pomieszkawszy, o wielkie kszywdy skarżyli mu sié poddani na Wiślimiera opiekuna majétności jego. A tego Wiślimiera opowiada ksiáżéciem wiślickim, z narodu jeszcze Popielowego ; ten byl w niebytności

Walcerowćj wielkim zdziercá poddanych jego. O co z nim
naprzód Walcerus łaskawie mówił, a potem gdy sié im i jemu
z wszy usprawiedliwić niechciał, on go pojma pszywiózł na Tynic
i do wieże wsadził. Sam potem kwoli królowi albo monarsze na
służbé żołnierská jachał, zostawiwszy Heligundé na Tyńcu,
która była bardzo żałosna z odjechania jego. Wszakoż gdy w
wielkim dostatku chwilé była bez Walcera, poczéła sié przed
panná swojá uskarżać mówiác : Żem ja ani dziewka, ani wdowa,
etc. Panna ona żałujac pani, powiedziała jej : żc tu jest wiézień urodziwy, będziemyć go na noc wypuszczać do protochwile,
a na dzień go będziem do więzienia sadzać, tak że tego żaden
nie postrzeże. Owa namówiwszy sié to wczyniły, stróże co go
strzegli przenajáwszy. Heligunda obaczywszy Wiślimiera méża urodziwego, nie chciała go więcej dać do więzienia, owszejki
dowiedziawszy sié co zacz był zjechała z nim na Wiślicé. Wtem
przyjechał Walcerus, pytał, czemu Heligunda przeciw jemu nie
wyszła, jako to zwykła czynić. Powiedzieli słudry, że jej nie
masz. Dowiedziawszy sié wszystkiej sprawy, jachał do Wislice,
zastał tylko samé Heligunde, a Wiślimier w łowy był zajachał.
Upadła mu u nóg, proszác łaski i miłosierdzia, a proszác
aby sié schzonił do ko komozy jego, i sługom sié takze
schronić kazał, a ona mu go wydać obiecała, aby sié nad nim
pomścił krzywdy swojej. A gdy on tak uczynił, Wiślimier przyjechał, ona wybieżawszy powiedziała mu o Walcerze,
kédy go skryła. On go zatem z sługami nabieżawszy, pojmał i
wsadził do więzienia, potem nań włożył okowy jakie rozumiał
najtéższe, k'temu jeszcze do muru przykować dał, a nie rozumie-
ják sobie wierniejszego stróża i przyjaciela do tego, siostrze
swojej rodzonej oddał klucze od niego, coby z wiadomościá jej
tylko w onej komorze tak go w pécie na potrzebé wypuszczano.
W czem ona panna przez kilka czasów wiaré bratu swojemu
strzymała statecznie. Potem ulitowawszy sié Walcera, z mowé z
nim tajemnie uczyniła, jeśliby já chciał sobie wziáć za żoné,
rzekła go z więzienia wypuścić; a była ta panna Rynga tak
żadna (brzydka), że jej żaden człowiek równy jej w zacnosci nie
chciał do stanú małżeńskiego. Co Walcerus uczynił, chcác być
wolen z wiecznego a okrutnego więzienia, bo siedział na
żelezie nakształt woła uczynionem, a jeszcze do tego w oko-
wach. A gdy już té zmowe z sobá mieli, panna Rynga
wolnym go uczyniła i miecza dodała; wszakoż on siedział

na onem żelezie, jakoby niewolny. A gdy Wiślimier z
Heligundá według zwyczaju szli sié przelegać, rzekł do nich
Walcerus: " Kiedybym ja też teraz nad wami pomścił sié
krzywdy swojej"?—Poczéła sobá Heligunda trwożyć ala Wiślimier já upominał, a rzekł do Walcera: " Już ci odpuszczé, chocia
mié i zabijesz"—a to dla tego mówił, że ufał wierności siostry
swojej.

Dla wiétszego żalu Walcerowego, nczynił mu był z onego
sklepu jego okno do pokoju swego, że na czas każdy na nie
patrzał, kiedy z sobá żartowali. A gdy po onych rozmowach
Wiślimier z Heligundá tak sié zabawili przespiecznie, że Walcerus czas miał do pomszczenia krzywdy, skoczył prédko z
onego wołu, przypadłszy oboje mieczem ku ziemi na łożu przebił,
potem sam wolno z Ryngá na Tyniec wjachał, wszystkie skarby
pobrawszy co ona panna tak sprawowała, że słudzy Wiślimierowi
tego nie postrzegli iże pan ich zabił, aż na Tyniec odwieźli one
wszystkie rzeczy, a Walcera chodzác wolnego ogládali.

Tej Heligundy ciało tam w Wiślicy schowano i twarz na
kamieniu wyciosano, która była w roku 1242 na zamku, czego
potwierdza Andreas de Zarnow. Ale ten pomieniony historyk,
Walcera, dowodnie opowiada z domu Toporów, jakoż tego
potwierdzają pewne zaki, że Tyniec ze wszystká włościá był tej
familii Topoiow. Bo tam gdy na gwałt wołają we wsiach
starodawnych Tyńcowi należácych, tedy krzyczá: Starza! starza!
albo: Stary koń! stary koń! a te familie obie z wieka dawnego
jednej sá dzielnice, o czem niżej czytać bédziesz.

XVI.

M. BIELSKI.*

O tej Wiślicy piszá, że kiedyś to miasto było barzo budowne i obronne (jakoż ma miejsce po temu), ale natenczas było przez Ruś z gruntu zburzone. Piszá i to o niem zwłaszcza Anonimos jeden, że tam było niejakie ksiáżé, Wisław, a tego grabia niejaki z Tyńca, który był z domu Toporów, poimał i u siebie wiéził, którego użaliwszy sié jednego czasu żona jego w niebytności méża swego z wieży wyciągnéła. A ta była Francuska, jednego francuskiego króla córka, imie jej było Heligunda, do któréj grabia z Tyńca Walcer tym sposobem przyszedł: Bédác na dworze króla francuskiego upodobała go była sobie ta panna, a gdy jej ojciec zań dać nie chciał, że to był cudzoziemiec, nabrawszy z niá klejnotów i skarbów zjechali potajemnie w nocy. Czego mu zajrzał Niemiec jeden, co tej pannie też rad służył, gonił go i czynił z nim o panné, jednak zabit Niemiec a Walcer i z krolewná do Polski przyjechał. Ta tedy, jako sié raz dała wziáć jednemu, dała sié wziáć potem i drugiemu, zjechała także z tym Wisławem wiślickim ksiázéciem, gdy méża jej doma nie było dwie lecie, bo jako sié był zwykł przedtem służbami bawić, tak i ożeniwszy sié siedzieć go było doma teszno. Potem gdy przyjechał do domu, dziwował sié temu barzo, że żona przeciwko jemu nie wyszła, która była zawżdy zwykła to uczynić; spyta o niá, powiedzá mu, że z ksiéżéciem wiślickim precz zjechała; z wielkiego gniewu zaraz do Wiślice bieżał, chcác jako prédko i niespodziewanie zbiéżéć Wisława i zemścić sié tego nad nim, by mu też tam i gardło dać. Wisława natenczas doma nie było, w łowiech był, ale żona wyźrzawszy oknem użrzy go z strafunku i zbiéży prédko do niego, i obimała jako méża swego, skarżác sié z płaczem przed nim, iże já gwałtem wział; i aby sié tego nad nim zemścił, radzi mu aby sié do komory na chwilé skrył, a gdy bédzie czas po temu, da mu znać, aby go mogł tém łatwiej zdrajce swego pożyć i z niá bezpieczniej uść. Uwierzył nieborak.

---

*"Kronika," tom ɪ, p. 175-177. wyd. Turowskiego. Sanok 1856. 8vo.

A gdy Wisław przyjechał, ukazała mu Walcera méża swego, którego on poima wszy, kazał tak dobrze żelazem opatrzyć, że niepodobna rzecz, aby miał kiedy wyniść. Ktemu na żałość większá kazał go w kuné sadzać tam, kédy z Heligundá legał. A straż nad min siestrze zlecił, która jeszcże była panná, bo że na dziwy była szpetná, nikt jej pojáć nie chciał. Jál já tedy sobie namawiać po cichu on grabia, obiecując já pojáć i z niá mieszkać dobrze do śmierci, by tylko z wiézienia wyszedł, co gdy jej poprzysiágł, odemknéła go i miecz z głowy wyjáwszy bratu, gdy spał, onemu go dała. Także gdy sié ocuci Wisław i z swojá Heligundá, rzecze do nich Walcer grabia: Cobyście wy też rzekli, kiedybym ja te péta i kuné złamawszy was pozabijał? Zléknie sié zaraz Heligunda i do ksiáżecia Wisława poszeptem rzecze: Miły! wieréć broni twej w głowach niemasz. Odpowie jej Wisław: Nie boj sié miła! trudnoćby mu te kłódki otworzyć i té kuné złamać. On tego domawia, a Walcer grabia z mieczem gołym do nich prosto skoczy tak, że ich obu wespól przebił a żalu i despektu swego znacznie sié zemscił. Pisze historyk, że tam jeszcze za jego czasu był grób tej Heligundy w Wiślicy na zamku.

XVII.

X. KASPER NIESIECKI,* S. J.

TOPOR HERB.—PRZODKOWIE TEGO DOMU.

WALCER Hrabia z Tyńca, o którym pisze Bielski fol: 109 y Andreas de Zarnow, Paprocki Okolski. Ten długo sié bawiác w postronnych kraiach, a osobliwie przyy dworze Króla Francuskiego, widzác ze sié nieiaki Arinaldus Xiáze Niemieckie o Krolewné Francuzká Heligundé staraĺ, a ta w przyiaźniey iego nie profitowała, tak sié dla urody y piéknych obyczaiow wkradĺ w iey serce, ze sié dała do Polski uprowadzić. Nie nadała mu sié iednak kradziona zdobycz, bo potym gdy owe amory ostygły, żyła nieprzystoynie z nieiakim Wiślimirem, y owszem Walcera w ciészkie péta okuła, luboć on potym z tey niewoli wyszedĺ, y tak Wiślimira iako y Heligundé zabiĺ, ta pogrzebiona w Wiślicy na zamku, którey tam twarz na ka mieniu wyciosaná widziano wroku 1242; obszerniey té historyá opisuie Paprocki o herbach do ktorego Czytelnika odsyłam,wprawdzieć o tey historyi żaden z Francuzkich historykow nie namienia. Przecież té samé historyá znaydziesz u Sommersberga de rebus Silesiacis Tomô Secundô fol: 37 w historyi y Kronice Bogufała Biskupa Poznańskiego szeroko rozwiedzioná, ale tamten historyk, Walcera nie do Familii Topor ale do popiela niegdy Xiáżécia Polskiego nadciága, którego tu słowa kładé: Erat temporibus illis Urbs famosissima, murorurum altitudine circumsepta, nomine Wislicia, cujus olim Princeps tempore Paganismi fuerat Wislaus decorus, qui ipse de stirpe Regis Popeli duxerat originem. Hunc quidam Comes, etiam stirpis ejusdem, ut fertur, fortis viribus, nomine Walterus robustus, qui in Polonico vocabatur: Wdały Walgers: huius Castrum Tyneg prope Cracoviam ubi nunc Abbatia Sti. Benedicti per Casimirum Monachum, Regem Polonorum seu Lechitarum, fundata consistit, in quodam seditioso conflictu captivave-

*Korona Polska prry złotej wolności starożytnemi rycerstwa polskiego y Wielkiego Xiéśtwa Litewskiego kleynotami, naywyższemi honorami, heroicznym méstwem y odwagá, wytworná nauka, a naypierwey cnotá, pobożnościá y świátobliwościá ozdobiona. Tom czwarty. 1743 Lwów. fol. p. 365-367.

rat, captumque in vincula conjecit, ac in profundo Turris
Tinecensis mirae custodiae deputaverat tenendum.

Ale i Baranowski dobrze uważa, że ieżeli ta o Heligundzie
powieść iest prawdziwa, tedy to musiało bydź ieszcze za Po-
gaństwa, poniewaz Tyniec w roku 1044, iuz był w réku królew-
skich, kiedy Król Kazimierz Mnich fundował tam klasztor, a
zatym musieli mieć Krolowie Polscy dawniey przed tym na
Tyńcu władzá.   Paprocki w te słowa o Tyńcu pisze z Jedrzeia
de Zarnow.

XVIII.

PROCOSIUS.*

CHRONICON SLAVO-SARMATICUM.

P. 109.

WALGIERZ cognomine Wdaly, frater major natu Zbiludi, dominus in Tyniec, qui postea profectus in Franciam Reginulam Heligundam inde abduxit, quae multarum discordiarum cum Wislomiro Chostek, Domino in Wislica, causa extitit. Tres item filii ipsius Paluca alias Wittosław in baptismo nominatus, Starža ex Heligunda et Pabian ex Rynga progeniti.

P. 128 f.

Walgerus Starżon de Panigrod Wdaly id est udatny alio dictus vocabulo. Smilae herois minor natus filius, in Preginia, Tenczyn, Tyneg, Czekarzewice, Tarlow etc. dominus a. 975. dėnatus: heros in Lechisis multis celebris historiis, qui vix non universas lustravit in Europa regiones. Consors fuit Heligunda alicujus ex regibus Galliae reguli filia, pro qua magnas habuit contentiones cum Vislimiro duce ex gente Popieli suo consanguineo.

---

* The text is reprinted from Heinzel, 'Walthersage,' S. 59.

XIX.

K. W. WÓJCICKI.*

The saga is introduced thus:

Przytoczyliśmy to podanie Serbów na dowód, że niebrakuje tego rodzaju powieści i w innych pokoleniach wielkiego szczepu Słowian. Trojan w mgle wieków tak odbija, jak nasze Waligóry i Madeje. Z wielkiej liczby klechdów starożytnych, kronikarze jedné nam przechowali ze Słowiańskich czasów. Słuchajmy powieści, którá nam Baszko, i zasłużony heraldyk Bartosz Paprocki opowiadają zgodnie. Zapomniał już o niéj lud dzisiaj; a jednakże dawniéj powszechnie w okolicach Tyńca i Wiślicy znaná była; przytoczyć já wiéc muszé jako ważny i ciekawy pomnik téj gałázki literatury.

WDALI Walgerz, albo Walter, hrabia, na Tyńcu i pan zamku Tynieckiego, bawiác sié w postronnych krainach, dla przejrzenia spraw rycerskich, zatrzymał sié na dworze króla Francuzkiego. Máż urodziwy, odwagi i zręczności niepośledniéj, w gonitwach i turniejach piérwszy dank odnosił, i oczy wszystkich zwrócił na siebie, szczególniéj córki królewskiéj imieniem Helgundy. Dla niéj przyjál urzád podczaszego; a gdy misy stawiał na stole, uważał z jakiém zajęciem wpatrywala sié w jego oblicze, jak oczyma ścigala każde poruszenie dorodnego dworzanina.

Był na tymże dworze Arinaldus, królewicz Niemiecki. Ten rozkochany w Helgundzie jakkolwiek wzgardy doznawał, ciągle gorzał namiétná miłościá. Walgerz dla ujécia sobie wiécéj nadobnéj królewnéj, przekupiwszy stróże zamkowe, codziennie podchodził pod jéj okna, i głosem miłym i dźwięcznym śpiéwal dumy smutne.

Helgunda zbudzona, zachwycona śpiéwem niewidomego trubadura, przywołać rozkazala strażników zamku, ażeby jéj wyjawili nocnego śpiewaka. Gdy ci przekupieni, niechcieli wyznać prawdy, tłumaczác sié, że z zakrytym obliczem przychodzi: królewna śmierciá im zagroziwszy, zmusila do wydania Wal-

---

* Klechdy starożytne Podania i Powieści Ludowe. Warszawa 1851, p. 32-42.

gerza. " *Poczéła go dopiéro zapalczywiéj milować, a potém i do siebie na pokój wzywać.*' * Tam postanowiła, widząc przeszkody od ojca, uciec z Walgerzem do Polski.

Ale zazdrośny Arinald wywiedział sié tajemnicy, śpieszy do swego królestwa, przez które musiał Walgerz powracać, i na Renie zakazawszy przewoźnikom, aby mniéj nie brali jak grzywné złota, starali sié przytém uciekającego zatrzymać.

Walgerz z Helgundá wkrótce nadbiega, rozkazuje surowo przewoźnikom, by go co prędzéj na drugi brzeg wysadzili; a gdy ci zatrwożeni, posłuszni Walgerzowi, zażądali zapłaty, ten rzuca złoto, wpław Ren przebywa, i ku Polszcze śpieszy.

Arinald dowiaduje sie, że Walgerz już Ren przebyl, uzbraja sié, co prędzej, dosiada bieguna i dopédza przeciwnika.

—" Stój zdrajco"! wołał nań zdaleka: przewozu niezapłaciłeś i królewská córé'ś ukradł"!

—" Kłamiesz"! odwróciwszy sié Walgerz odpowiedział: "przewóz zapłaciłem, a córa Królewska dobrowolnie ze mná jedzie.

Popédliwy Arinald wyzywa go na pojedynek, z warunkiem, że kto zostanie zwyciézcá, zostanie panem i Królewnéj, i łupu przeciwnika.

Rozpoczyna sié bójka. Helgunda, co stała za Walgerzem, życzác mu zwyciéztwa, była bodźcem Arinaldowi, stojác mu na oczach. Niemiec zagrzéwany jéj widokiem, parł silnie Walgerza, tak, że ten cofać sié przymuszony, ujrzał przed sobá kochanké, dla któréj bój zaciéty toczył. Widok jéj zapalił go mocniéj; uderza, obala wroga na ziemié i bez litości zabija.† Zdziéra zbroje, a ze zwyciézkim łupem i królewna powraca do zamku swojego, Tyńca.

Ale zaledwie przybył, poddani żałobliwie sié uskarżali na *Wisława piéknego*, Książécia Wiślickiego, z rodu *Popiela* jeszcze, o ciéżkie krzywdy, jakich doznawać musieli. Walgerz gdy napróżno żádał sprawiedliwości, rozgniewany zbiera swoje rycerstwo, i w jednéj bitwie rozbiwszy Wisława chorágwie, samego jak brańca okuć rozkazał, i do wieży wsadził na zamku Tynieckim.

W krótce na rozkaz Króla, Walgerz pośpieszył stanáć ze

---

* Własne słowa Bartosza Paprockiego z dzieła: " Herby Rycerstwa Polskiego."—1584 r. folio.

† Godisław Baszko, Kronikarz.

swoim zastępem do obrony granic. Helgunda rospaczała przy odjeździe męża. Gdy zajęty wyprawą rycerská długo nieprzybywał, Helgunda opływając we wszelkie dostatki poczéła téschnieć i zwierzyła sié wiernéj służebnice z uskarżeniem: " żem ani dziewka, ani żona, ani też wdowa."

Zrozumiała przywiazana, a przebiegła służka téschnicé swojéj Pani; radzi przeto, żew zamku jest wiézień dorodny, co já potrafi ukoić.

Wprowadzono *pięknego Wisława*, rozkutego z wiézów, do komnaty Helgundy: ta zapomniawszy poprzysięgłej wiary mężowi, nie tylko staje sé występná; ale z wiéźniem do Wiślicy ucieka.

Po skończonéj wyprawie wojennéj, przybywa na Tyniec Walgérz, okryty sławá rycerská. Lecz zaledwie wjechał na podwórzec zamkowy, zdziwiony, niewidzác Helgundy, co zwykle wybiegała za mury na powitanie méża, zapytuje służby, dworzan i czeladzi o powód, i odbiera okropná wiadomość, że uciekła z Wisławem.

Uniesiony zemstá i rozpaczá, sam jeden, w téj saméj zbroi okrytéj kurzawá, śpieszy do Wiślicy. Helgunda była samá, Wisław na łowy wyjechał. Chytra i zdradziecka niewiasta, wybiega przeciw Walgerza, a padajác na kolana, skarży Wisława, że já przemocá uprowadził z Tyńca; zaklina, by sié ukryl wskazanéj komorze, a wyda mu Wisława dla zaspokojenia słusznéj krzywdy.

Usłuchał Walgerz, lecz zapóźno poznał zdradé wiarołomnéj żony: napadniéty, przemocá okuty w kajdany. Wisław lékajác śié by wiézień nie uszedł, oddał go pod straż swojéj siostry Ryngi.

Dla wiékszéj méczarni Walgerza, posadzono go na zelaznym wole, a obróż z szyi przybito do ściany. Tak skuty miał za więzienie komnaté gdzie w poblizkości Wisław z Helgundá w oczach wiéźnia okazywali swojá miłość. Walgerz musiał patrzéć na wiarołomná żoné i okrutnego zwodziciela i wroga, lecz nic niemówil, ponure zachowujác milczenie.

Rynga majác dozór nad nim, szpetna aż do obrzydzenia, litujác Walgerza méczarni, a wiécéj w nim rozkochana, obiecuje z wiézów uwolnić z warunkiem, że já pojmie za małżonké, a życie uszanuje brata.

—"Przystajé, i przyrzekam wszystko"! odrzekł Walgerz

chciwy uwolnienia: "jeno rozkój mié z tych kajdan i podaj mój oréż niezlomny." Rynga otworzyła kłódki kajdan i miecz Walgerzowi oddała; wisiał on albowiem na osobnéj ścianie. Walgerz już wolny, oréż za plecyma ukrył, zachowując zwyczajná postać bolesná, milczácá, ponurá. Helgunda z Wisławem jak zwykle przyszli sié pieścić na zwyczajnem miejscu. Walgierz pierwszy raz do nich sié odezwał, przerwawszy uporne dotád milczenie. "Cóż rzekniecie, gydbym ja teraz nad wami pomścił krzywdy i cierpień moich"? Helgunda podziwem i trowgá przejéta, dostrzegając, że oréż Walgerza nie wisi na ścianie, rzekła do kochanka: —"Wislawie! ja sié go lékam; patrz, i miecza już niéma Walgerza." Ale Wisław ufając wierności swojéj siostry, odrzekł z pogardá spoglądając na wiéźnia. —"Gdybyś miał i sto mieczów, nielékam sié wcale, a nawet ci odpuszczé gdybyś mié i zabił." Walgerz zrzuca kajdany—z wyniesionym mieczem staje nad łożem: spuścił go z zamachem, i wycisnáł dwa jékliwe westchnienia, konajácéj Helgundy i Wislawa. Pomsciwszy sié krzywdy swojéj z Ryngá na Tyniec powrócił, zabrawszy wszystkie skarby, które tak zrécznie Rynga uwiezła i śmierć brata ukryła, że dworzanie i rycerze Wisława dopiéro sié o morderstwie dowiedzieli, kiedy Walgierz ze zbawczyniá Ryngá w warownym już stanéli Tyńcu. Zwłoki Helgundy pochowano w Wiślicy. Kronikarz Godzisław Baszko pisze, że w roku 1242 widział jeszcze na kamieniu grobowym twarz Helgundy wyrytá. Bartosz Paprocki za dowód podaje, żeWalgerz do rodziny Toporczyków należał, iż po wsiach, starodawnie, do Tyńca należácych, kiedy na gwałt wołają, tedy krzyczá: "Starza! Starza!" albo "Stary-koń! Stary-koń!" a te rodziny z dawnego wieku sá jednéj z Toporczykami dzielnicy.

APPENDIX I.

VON DEM ÜBELEN WÎBE.*

301   lanc, breit ist ir swinge
     und ist hagenbüschîn ;
     die sleht si durch daz houbet mîn.
     daz selbe tet si hiure.
     so getâne âventiure
306   wârn hêrren *Walthern* unkunt,
     dô er und mîn frou *Hildegunt*
     fuoren durch diu rîche
     also behagenlîche.

* Cf. *Zeitschrift* xii, 367-68.

APPENDIX II.

DIST l'Arcevesques : "Jo irai, par mun chief.
800 "—E jo od vus," ço dist li quens Gualtiers :
"Hum sui Rollant, jo ne le dei *laissier*."
Entre s'eslisent vint milie chevaliers.   AOI.

LXX.

Li quens Rollanz Gualtier de l'Hum apelet :
"Pernez mil Francs de France nostre tere,
805 "Si purpernez les destreiz e les tertres,
"Que l'Emperere nisun des soens n'i perdet."
Respunt Gualtiers : "Pur vus le die bien faire."
Od mil Franceis de France la lur tere,
Gualtiers desrenget les destreiz e les tertres.
810 N'en descendrat pur malvaises nuveles,
Enceis qu'en seient set cenz espées traites.
Reis Almaris, de l' regne de Belferne,
Une bataille lur livrat le jur, pesme.   AOI.

CLXXIX.

2035 Einz que Rollanz se seit aperceüz,
De pasmeisun guariz ne revenuz,
Mult grant damage li est apareüt :
Mort sunt Franceis, tuz les i ad perdut
Seinz l'Arcevesque e seinz Gualtier de l' Hum.
2040 Repairiez est de la muntaigne jus,
A cels d'Espaigne mult s'i est cumbatuz :
Mort sunt si hume, si's unt paien vencut ;
Voeillet o nun, desuz cez vals s'en fuit
E si recleimet Rollant qu'il li aïut :
2045 "Gentilz quens, sire, vaillant hum. ù ies tu ?
Unkes nen oi poür là ù tu fus.
Ço est Gaultiers ki cunquist Maëlgut,
Li niés Droün, à l' vieill e à l' canut.
Pur vasselage suleie estre tis druz.
As Sarrazins me sui tant cumbatuz

2050 Ma hanste est fraite e perciez mis escuz,
E mis osbercs desmailiez e rumpuz.
Par mi le cors de lances *sui* feruz:
Sempres murrai, mais chier me sui venduz."
A icel mot l'ad Rollanz *coneüt;*
2055 Le cheval brochet, si vient puignant vers lui.   Aoi.

CLXXX.

"Sire Gualtiers," ço dist li quens Rollanz,
Bataille oüstes od la paiene gent:
"Vus sulez estre vassals e cumbatant,
Mil chevaliers en menastes vaillanz.
Ierent à mei; pur ço vus les demant.
Rendez les mei, que bosuing en ai grant."
Respunt Gaultiers: "N'en verrez un vivant.
Laissiez les ai en cel dulurus camp.
De Sarrazins nus i truvasmes tanz,
Turcs e Ermines, Canelius e Jaianz,
Cels de Balise, des meillurs cumbatanz,
Sur lur chevals arrabiz e curanz;
Une bataille avum faite si grant
N'i ad paien devers altre s'en vant.
Seisante milie en i ad morz gisanz.
Vengiez nus sumes à noz acerins branz.
Avum iloec perdut trestuz noz Francs;
De mun osberc en sunt rumput li pan;
Mortels ai plaies es costez e es flancs
De tutes parz en ist fors li clers sancs;
Trestuz li cors m' en vait afiebliant:
Sempres murrai, par le mien esciant.
Jo sui vostre hùm e vus tien à guarant:
Ne me blasmez, se jo m'en vai fuiant.
—Ne l' ferai mie," ço dit li quens Rollanz;
"Mais or m'aidiez à tut vostre vivant."
D'ire e de doel en tressuet Rollanz.
De sun blialt ad trenchiez les dous pans:
Gualtier en bandet les costez e les flancs.   Aoi.

CLXXXI.

Rollanz ad doel, si fut maltalentifs:
En la grant presse cumencet à ferir;
De cels d'Espaigne en ad getet morz vint,
E Gualtiers sis, e l'Arcevesques cinc.
2060 Dient paien: "Feluns humes ad ci.
Guardez, seignurs, que il n'en algent vif.

Tant nus unt fait ne deivent estre prins.
Mais trestuit estre detrenchiet e ocis,
Tut par seit fel ki ne 's vait envaïr,
E recreant ki les lerrat guarir!"
Dunc recumencent e li hus e li cris:
2065 De tutes parz les revunt envaïr.
Deus les aïut qui unkes ne mentit !   Aoi.

――――――

CHARLEMAGNE APPROCHE

CLXXXII.

Li quens Rollanz fut *mult hardis e fiers,*
Gualtiers de l'Hum est bien bons chevaliers,
Li Arcevesques prozdum e essaiez:
Li uns ne voelt l'altre nient laissier.
2070 En la grant presse i fièrent as paiens.
Mil Sarrazin i descendent à pied,
E à cheval sunt quarante millier.
Mien escientre, ne 's osent aproismier.
Il lancent lur e lances e espiez,
2075 Wigres e darz, e museraz e atgiers.
As premiers colps i unt ocis Gualtier,

APPENDIX III.

ROLANDSLIED.*

OLIVIER unde Ruolant	1188
unde Walthere ther Wîgant,	1189
Gêhart unde Walther,	3217
Thô frowete sih ther helet Ruolant,	3369
thaz er there heithenen samenunge vant.	3370
er sprah zuo Walthêre:	
" nu île, thu helet mâre,	
wele thir tûsent manne	
unt ne sûme thih niht ze lange:	
vâh uns thie perge,	3375
ê sîn thie heithenen innen wērthen,	
thaz wir thie hôhe begrîfen,	
ê uns thie heithenen unterslîchen.	
thie andere thu warne	
(hie ist thes tiuveles geswarme),	3380
thaz sie sih wâfen sciere.	
sage Turpîn unt Oliviere,	
then helethen allen samt;	
seme mir thisiu zesewe mîn hant,	
ihne kume niemer vone therre herte,	3385
unz ih slahe mit mîneme swerte.	
sine hilvet nehein ire grôzer scal:	
ire wirthet hiute sô getân val,	
thaz man iz wole sagen mah	
unze ane then jungesten tah.	3390
mir ne swîche ther guote Durendart,	
si geriuwet al ire hôhvart."	
Unter thiu kom Walthêre.	6528
verwundet was er sêre,	

* From the text of Bartsch's Edition.

than ih iu ê gesaget hân.   6530
er was ther Ruolantes man.
er sprah : "jâ mîn lieber herre,
ih gesihe thih vile gerne,
ê ih sô ersterbe.
mahtu uns iht gehelven?   6535
heithenen thie gelfen
habent uns scathen getân."
"wâ sint nu mîne man,
thie ih bevalh ze thîner hant,"
sprah ther helet Ruolant,   6540
"tûsent mîner helethe?
nu gip sie mir withere :
ih betharf ire wole ze mîner nôt.
thise ligent alle hie tôt."
"semmir thîne hulde," sprah Walthêre,   6545
ire nelebet neheiner mêre
wane ih aleine.
thie wuotigen heithenen
ranten unsih allenthalben ane :
sie hâten mêre thenne sehzeh tûsent man.   6550
vile wole wir ire erbiten.
wir erkanten wole thîne site,
wâre wir entrunnen,
thaz wir niemer thîne hulde gewunnen.
jâ vâhten, herre, thîne man   6555
soz guoten knehten wole gezam.
thie thîne ligent tôt thâ nithere :
ouh sluogen wir sie thâ withere,
thaz ire neheiner genas.
niene zurne thu thaz,   6560
thaz ih thannen sî komen.
nu ih thîne stimme hân vernomen,
nune mah mir niht gewerren.
zwiscen Manbrât then pergen
unt then hôhen Jogeîn,   6565
thâ lie ih, herre, then scathen thîn,
ih sage thir ze wunder :
unser kom nie theheiner vone ein ander.
ih thurhreit thaz wal,

thaz ih uber al   6570
neheinen lebentigen vant."
" nu lôno thir got," sprah Ruolant,
"thîner nôte was vile.
iethoh was thaz kindes spil.
nu ist iz ane theme zît :   6575
hie ze stete sculen wir opheren then lîp
mit anderen unseren genôzen,
thaz wir iht werthen verstôzen
vone theme engele sange.
thu sûmest uns ze lange."   6580

    Thar huoben sih thô thie thrî
(ih wân iz alsô gescriben sî)
in then thrin naman unseres herren :
thô hâten sie helve niht mêre.
thie einmuotigen thegene   6585
sluogen thie urmâren menige,
thaz sie vore in muosen erbeizen.
sie umbestuonten sie mit spiezen,
mit scozzen unt mit gêren.
tha ersluogen sie Walthêren.   6590
harte rah in thô Ruolant.
sô waz er ire ûfrehter vant,
thie muosen Walthêren gelten.

ORIGIN AND DEVELOPMENT OF THE WALTHER SAGA.

I. ELEMENTS OF THE SAGA.

I. ANALYSIS OF THE SAGA.

WALDERE.	WALTHARIUS.
1. Ætla. A. 6.	Attila King of the Huns or Avars (in Pannonia) pushes his conquests westward. 11 ff.
2. Cf. Guðhere, friend of the Burgundians, (3).	Attila attacks in turn Gibicho, King of the Franks; Heriricus, King of the Burgundians; and Alphere, King of the Aquitanians. 12 ff.
3. Cf. Hagena B. 15; Guðhere, A, 25; Waldere, B, 11. Hagena and Waldere are old friends [as hostages at Ætla's court?] (20). Guðhere, friend of the Burgundians, is Waldere's foe (cf. 19, 24, 27).	All three kings give Attila hostages; Gibicho sends Hagano of noble blood, "veniens de germine Troiae," in place of his son Guntharius who was too young. 27 ff. Heriricus sends his daughter Hiltgunt. 72 ff. Alphere sends his son Waltharius. 90 ff.
4. Waldere is son of Alphere. A. 11.	Waltharius is the son of Alphere; he is yet a youth in "primevo flore," 78 ff.
5.	Hiltgunt is the only daughter of Heriricus; is noble born and fair. 36 ff.
6.	Waltharius and Hiltgunt are betrothed before leaving home. 80 ff.
7.	Waltharius, Hiltgunt and Hagano all reared carefully by Attila and Ospirin. 96 ff.
8. Waldere is called Ætla's vanwarrior. A, 6.	Waltharius and Hagano become the foremost of Attila's hosts. 105 ff.; Hiltgunt is made keeper of Ospirin's treasures 113.
9.	Hagano, hearing that Guntharius is occupying Gibicho's throne and refusing tribute to Attila, escapes to his royal master. Ospirin and Attila fearing Waltharius may follow Hagano, offer him a Hun to wife, but W. feigning loyalty to Attila, declines the offer. 119 ff.

NOVALICIAN CHRONICLE.	NIBELUNGENLIED:
1. Atila, lux Pannoniae, King of the Huns or Avars, scourge of God, makes conquests in the west. C. viii.	Ezele (Etzele, Ezel) King of the Huns (276, 6) has subdued twelve kingdoms (188, 6; 212, 4) and three dukedoms (188, 6; 212, 4) and is everywhere feared for his power (203, 6).
2. Atila attacks Alferius, King of Aquitania, Eriricus King of Burgundia, and Gibico, King of the Franks. C. viii.	
3. All three Kings give Atila hostages. Alferius sends his son, Waltarius; Eriricus his daughter Ildegunde; Gibico, Agano. C. viii.	Hagene, son of Adrian, and vassal of Gunther, together with Walther von Spâne, was hostage at Ezele's court (268, 3, 4). Hiltegunt is also at Ezele's court (268, 3).
4. Waltarius is the legitimate son of Alferius,sprung from noble lineage. C. viii.	Walther von Spâne (268, 3; 258, 2); der von Spâne (274, 4).
5. Ildegunde, the daughter of Eriricus, is fair. C. viii.	Hiltegunt (268, 3).
6. Waltarius and Ildegunde were betrothed before leaving home. C. viii.	
7. Waltarius, Ildegunde and Agano are all reared by Atila and Ospirin. C. ix.	Hagene and Walther grew up at Ezele's court (268, 3).
8. Waltarius and Agano become the foremost of Atila's hosts; Ildegunde,keeperofOspirin's treasure. C. ix.	Hagene and Walther fought many battles in honor of King Ezele (274, 4).
9. Agano hearing that Cundharius has succeeded to Gibico's throne and refused tribute to the Pannonians, makes his escape to his royal master. C. ix.	Hagene is sent back by Ezele (268, 3).

GRAZ FRAGMENT.	VIENNA FRAGMENT.
1. [Ezel the king and his] "wîp" [rule over the Huns] (2, 1, 1).	Ezele (Ezel) and Helche are King and Queen of the Huns. (1,b,12).
2. Pre-supposed in the situation. (cf. Nos. 3, 7).	
3. For Hagene, Walther and Hiltigunt (cf. No. 7).	Walther, Hildegunt and Hagne, probably as in *Waltharius.* Cf. 1, a, 10; 1 b, 12 ff.
4. Walther's noble lineage is doubtless implied in Hagene's praise of Hiltegunt. (cf. No. 6).	Walther is son of Alker and his queen, Hilde. (Cf. 2, 2 f.; 1, b, 18).
5. Hiltegunt's noble birth probably implied in the statement that she would grace an empress' crown (1, 1, 1).	
6. Hagene says he stood by when they [Walther and Hiltegunt] were betrothed [before they came to the Huns](1,2,1); cf. also Hiltegunt's waiting.	
7. Hagene, Walther and Hiltegunt are among the Huns [at Ezel's court?] (2, 1, 2).	
8. [Walther and Hiltgunt probably occupy situation of *Waltharius,* while] Hagen distributes gifts to the Huns. (2, 1, 2; cf. 1, 2, 2).	Walther was always at the front in Ezele's wars, and is to be the *'purgatòr'* of the Huns, (1,b,14).
9.	

BITEROLF UND DIETLEIB.	ALPHARTS TOD.
1. Etzel and Helche are king and queen of the Huns (cf. 284 ff.; 334 ff.).	
2.	
3. Walther (762 ff.), Hagen (4809 ff.); Hildegunt (767 ff.) are all at Etzel's court [as hostages]; W. and H., are knighted by Etzel. (cf. 770-1).	
4. Walther is son of Biterolf's sister (671, 2108); Alpkere's child (9904, 9952, 10112) is recognized as from Spanjelant from his shield (615 ff.) and is called king of Spanjelant (575 ff.) and 'der von Kärlingen' (2105, 5092); resides in Paris (694 ff.).	Walther, 'geborn ûz Diutschlant' (426), is called 'von Kerlingen' (77 ff.).
5.	
6.	
7.	
8.	
9.	

ROSENGARTEN.	DIETRICHS FLUCHT.	RABENSCHLACHT.
1.	Etzel and Helche are king and queen of Hunland (5008 ff.).	Etzel and Helche are king and queen of the Huns (26, 4).
2.		
3.		Walther is Etzels vassal (553, 3).
4. 'Walther von dem Wasgenstein,' one of the boldest knights (princes) by the Rhine (32 f., 235 f.) 'ein here von Wasgensteine' (1407) 'geborn von Kerlinc' (F. 1. 66).	'Walther von Lengers' (5902); 'von Kerlingen' (8638); 'der ellens rîch' (7360).	'Walther der Lengesaere' (47, 714); .cf. 'mit ellens hant' 715.
5. Di schône Hiltegunt claps her hands at Walther's victory (F. 2. 11).		
6.		
7.		
8.		
9.		

THIDREKSSAGE.	BOGUPHAL'S CHRONICLE.
1. Attila, King of Hunland, has his seat at Susat, his capital. c. 241.	
2.	
3.	
4. Valltari, the son of Ermenrikr's sister, is sent by Ermenrikr as hostage to Attila at the age of twelve years. c. 241.	Walterus Robustus is a count, having a castle, Tynecz, near Cracovia, and is of the stock of King Pompilius.
5. Hildigundr, the daughter of Jarl Ilias of Greece, is sent as hostage to Attila, at the age of seven winters. C. 241.	Helgunda is the daughter of a certain king of the Franks.
6.	
7. Valltari and Hildigundr remain at Attila's court. C. 241.	Waltharius, Helgunda, and the son of a certain king of Almania, are all at the court of Helgunda's father.
8. Valltari and Hlldigundr have positions, perhaps as in the Waltharius.	Walterus, is distinguished for his sweet singing, with which he wins the princess.
9.	

PAPROCKI.	BIELSKI.
1.	
2.	
3.	
4. Walcerus, Count of Tyniec, is young and fair.	Walcer, Count of Tynec, is of the family of Topór.
5. Heligunda is a French princess.	Heligunda is the daughter of a French king.
6.	
7. Walcerus, Heligunda, and Arinaldus, a German prince, are at the court of the French King.	Walcer, Heligunda (and probably a German) are at the court of the French king.
8. Walcerus serves at the king's table. Arinuldus sues for the hand of Heligunda.	
9.	

NIESIECKI.	PROCOSIUS.	WÓJCICKI.
1.		
2.		
3.		
4. Walcer, Count of Tyniecofthehouse of Topór.	Walgierz, the older brother of Zbiludi, is called Wdaly, and is lord of Tyniec, Preginia, etc.	Wdali Walgerz, count of Tyniec, is far, c o u r a g e o u s ard skillful.
5. H e l i g u n d e is a French [princess].	Heligunda, daughter of a certain king of Gaul.	Helgunde, daughter of a Frankish King, is fair.
6.		
7. Walcer, Heligunde, and Arinaldus, a german Prince, are at the French king's court.	Walgierz, Heligunda, are [at the King's court] in France.	Walgerz, Helgunde and Arinoldus, a German Prince, are at the court of the Frankish King.
8.		
9.		

WALDERE.	WALTHARIUS.
10. Waldere is not chided for cowardice in combat, but is called a far-famed warrior. A, 12 ff.	Waltharius wages new wars, returns victorious, 170 ff.; finds Hiltgunt in Attila's hall, and asks her to flee with him to his native land. 221 ff.
11.	Hiltgunt hesitates but finally assures herself of W.'s sincerity. 235 ff.
12.	Waltharius bids her be ready in a week with treasures for the journey. 260 ff.
13.	Waltharius after seven days prepares a great feast for Attila, administers the potion to the Huns and escapes with Hiltgunt. 287 ff.
14.	Waltharius' steed is called Leo. 327.
15.	Attila hearing of the escape offers rich reward for the capture of the fugitives; but no one ventures pursuit. 360 ff.
16.	In 40 (14) days Waltharius comes with Hiltgunt to the Rhine. 428 ff.
17.	Waltharius pays the ferryman with fish caught on the journey. 434.
18.	The next day Guntharius learns through the fish and the ferryman of Waltharius' return. Hagano recognizes in W. his old friend and Guntharius rejoices in the return of Gibicho's treasure. 440 ff.
19. Guðhere seeks combat unjustly. A, 26 f; (cf. 20).	Guntharius, with twelve knights, (among whom is Hagano) goes in pursuit of the treasure. 475 ff.
20. Guðhere expected in vain that Hagena's hand should have given Waldere battle and worsted him. B, 14 ff.	Hagano recalling Waltharius' valor and his own vow of friendship tries in vain to dissuade G. from the attack. 478 ff., also 518 ff. 617 ff.
21.	Waltharius and Hiltgunt seek shelter in a narrow pass (of the Vosagus); W. sleeps while H. watches. 489 ff.
22.	Hiltgunt sees Guntharius and his men approach and awakes Waltharius saying: "The Huns are upon us." 532 ff.

Novalician Chronicle.	Nibelungenlied.
10. Waltarius wages new wars for Atila, returns crowned with victory, finds Ildegunde in Atila's hall and asks her to escape with him. C. ix.	
11 Ildegunde hesitates ; but soon assures herself of Waltarius' sincerity. C. ix.	
12. Waltarius bids Ildegunde be ready in seven days with provisions for the journey. C. ix.	
13. Waltarius after seven days prepares a feast, administers the potion, and escapes with Ildegunde. C. ix.	Walther escapes with Hiltegunt from Ezele's court (268, 3).
14. Waltarius' steed is called Leo. C. ix.	
15. Atila hearing of the escape of W. and H., offers rich reward for their capture; but no one ventures pursuit. C. ix.	
16. In forty days, Waltarius comes with Ildegunde to the Rhine. C. ix.	
17. Waltarius pays the ferryman with fish he had caught on the journey. C. ix.	
18. Cundharius learns the next day through the fish and the ferryman of Waltarius'return. Agano recognizes his old companion at Atila's court, and Cundharius rejoices in the return of Gibico's treasure. C. ix.	
19. Cundharius with twelve knights (among whom is Agano) pursues the fugitives in quest of the treasure. C. ix.	
20. Agano, recalling his friendship and fate with Waltarius and the valor of W., tries in vain to dissuade Cundharius from the attack. C. ix.	Cf. Hagene's indifference in the combat (No. 25).
21. Waltarius and Ildegunde seek shelter in a pass ; the former then rests while the latter keeps watch. C. ix.	
22. Ildegunde sees Cundharius and his men approach and arouses Waltarius, saying "the Huns are upon us." C. ix.	

GRAZ FRAGMENT.	VIENNA FRAGMENT.
10.	
11.	
12.	
⚘	
13.	Walther so took leave of the Huns that they must lament, for he slew many of their kindred. (1, b, 12–13. Cf. 2, 13). Hildegunt recalls with gladness how Walther brought her from the Huns. (2, 4).
14.	
15.	
16.	
17.	
18.	
19.	
20.	
21.	
22.	

BITEROLF UND DIETLEIB.	ALPHARTS TOD.
10.	
11.	
12.	
13. Walther has returned [with Hildegunde] from the Huns (575 ff.; 620 ff.).	
14.	
15. Walther is attacked by Rüdigere because of the abduction of Hildegunde (7644 ff., etc.).	
16.	
17.	
18.	
19.	
20.	
21.	
22.	

ROSENGARTEN.	DIETRICHS FLUCHT.	RABENSCHLACHT.
10.		
11.		
12.		
13.		
14.		
15.		
16.		
17.		
18.		
19.		
20.		
21.		
22.		

THIDREKSSAGE.	BOGUPHAL'S CHRONICLE.
10. Valltari meets Hildigundr at a feast of Attila and asks her to flee with him. C. 242.	Walterus wins Helgunda's favor by nightly song, and persuades her to flee with him to his native land.
11. Hildigundr hesitates, but is at length assured of Valltari's sincerity. C. 242.	
12. Valltari bids Hildigundr come at sunrise, with treasures, to the city gate. C. 242.	
13.	Walterus seeing his opportunity, escapes with Helgunda.
14.	
15. Attila hears of the escape of Valltari and Hildigundr, and sends twelve of his men after the fugitives. One of the twelve is Hoegni, son of Aldrian. C. 243.	
16.	Walterus comes with Helgunda to the Rhine.
17.	Walterus pays the ferryman with a mark of gold.
18.	
19.	The Prince of Almania pursues Walterus. (Cf. No. 27).
20.	
21.	
22.	

PAPROCKI:	BIELSKI.
10. Walcerus wins Heligunda by his nightly song, and induces her to escape with him.	Walcer wins Heligunda, but her father objects because Walcer is a foreigner.
11.	
12.	
13. Walcerus and Heligunda escape to Poland.	Walcer and Heligunda escape at night, taking with them treasure.
14.	
15. Arinaldus pursues the fugitives. (Cf. No. 19).	The German, Walcer's rival, pursues the fugitives.
16. Walcerus comes with Heligunda to the Rhine.	
17. Walcerus pays the ferryman a mark of gold.	
18.	
19. Cf. No. 15.	
20.	
21.	
22.	

Niesiecki.	Procosius.	Wójcicki.
10. Walcer wins Heligunde by his beauty and attractive manner, and induces her to flee with him to Poland.		Walgerz wins Helgunda's favor by nightly song, and persuades her to flee with him to Poland, as the King objects to their union.
11.		
12.		
13. Walcer and Heligunda escape to Poland (cf. No. 10.)	Walgierz abducts Heligunda from France.	Walgerz escapes with Helgunde.
14.		
15.		Cf. 19.
16.		Walgerz comes with Helgunde to the Rhine.
17.		Walgerz pays the ferryman a mark of gold.
18.		
19.		Arinoldus pursues Walgerz.
20.		
21.		
22.		

WALDERE.	WALTHARIUS.
23.	Hiltgunt is fearful and beseeches Waltharius to kill her to save her from the foe. Waltharius reassures her of the fidelity of his sword, which has served him in many battles. 545 ff.
24. Guðhere refuses the sword and treasure. A, 28 f.	Guntharius refuses Waltharius' proffers of peace and orders the attack. 640 ff.
25.	Waltharius slays 11 knights; Guntharius and Hagano withdraw to the wood. 668 ff.
26.	Waltharius and Hiltgund rest during the night and continue their journey the next morning. 1151 ff.
27. Waldere challenges Guðhere. B, 14 ff.	Guntharius and Hagano leaping from ambush renew the attack; Waltharius encourages Hiltgunt and challenges his foes. 1210 ff. cf. No. 23.
28. Cf. Waldere's sword A. 24, and Mimming, Weland's work, A, 2-3.	Waltharius cleaves with his sword (long sword, cf. short sword v. 1390) Guntharius' thigh, cf. No. 8 and 23. 1364. Loses his own right arm at Hagen's stroke, 1381 ff.; thrusts out Hagano's eye, knocks out three of H.'s teeth. 1393 ff.
29.	The combatants are reconciled and Hiltgunt binds their wounds and administers wine. 1405 ff.
30.	The Franks return to Worms and Waltharius with Hiltgunt continues his journey to Aquitaine. 1446.
31.	Here the wedding of W. and H. is celebrated, and Waltharius reigns thirty years after Alphere's death. 1448 ff.
32.	Waltharius' subsequent battles and triumphs referred to. 1451 ff.

NOVALICIAN CHRONICLE.	NIBELUNGENLIED.
23. Ildegunde is fearful and be-seaches Waltarius to slay her to save her from the foe. W. reassures her. C. ix.	
24. Cundharius refuses Waltarius' proffers of peace and orders the attack. C. ix.	
25. Waltarius slays all of the knights except Cundharius and Agano, who dissemble flight. C. ix.	Walther slew many of Hagene's friends before the Waschsen-stein, while Hagene sat upon his shield (358, 2).
26. Waltarius continues his jour-ney. C. ix.	
27. Cundharius and Agano leap from their concealment and renew the attack. C. ix.	
28.	
29. The enemy, weary of combat and thirst, are unable to sub-due Waltarius. They see a flask of wine hanging from Waltarius saddle . . . . C. ix.	
30.	
31.	
32. Cf. Waltarius' career in the monastery. C. x.–xiii.	

GRAZ FRAGMENT.	VIENNA FRAGMENT.
23.	
24.	
25.	
26.	
27.	
28.	
29.	Walther [is reconciled with Gunther and] has safe escort at Volker's hand through Gunther's land (1, b, 16); but cannot pass through Metz, as Ortwin, the ruler is hostile to him. (1, a, 4).
30.	Walther announces his return to Alker who, with the queen Hilde, rejoices and sends summons to his men to go forth to welcome Walther and Hildegunt. (1, a, 8 ff).
31.	Walther and Hildegunt celebrate their wedding. (2, 6, ff). Alker will make Walther lord in his [Alker's] lands, and Walther is to become the Hun's '*purgetór.*' (1, b, 14).
32.	

Biterolf und Dietleib.	Alpharts Tod.
23.	
24.	
25.	
26.	
27.	
28. Walther bears Wasge, his weapon, far-famed (12286, 10-481, 642 ff.)	Walther's sword rings like a bell (373, 3).
29.	
30.	
31.	
32. Cf. Walther's encounter with Biterolf and his protection of Biterolf's land.	Cf. Walther's exploits in the various episodes of this epic.

ROSENGARTEN.	DIETRICHS FLUCHT.	RABENSCHLACHT.
23.		
24.		
25.		
26.		
27.		
28.		
29.		
30.		
31.		
32. Walther part in the Rosengarten episodes.	Walther's part in this epic.	Walther's deeds in this epic.

THIDREKSSAGE.	BOGUPHAL'S CHRONICLE.
23. Hildegundr is fearful at the approach of the Huns, but Valltari reassures her, saying that he has seen shields cleft before. C. 243.	
24.	
25. Valltari slays eleven of Attila's men and Hoegni escapes into the forest. C. 244.	
26. Valltari and Hildigundr refresh themselves with wild boar's flesh. C. 244.	
27. When Valltari and Hildigundr have eaten bare the boar's back, Hoegni renews the attack. C. 244.	
28. Valltari hits Hoegni with the boar's back-bone, tearing out his eye and rending his chin. C. 244.	Walterus slays the Prince of Almania in single combat.
29. Ermenrikr reconciles Attila by sending him rich gifts. C. 244.	
30. Hoegni returns to Attila; Valltari and Hildigundr continue southward over the mountains to King Ermenrikr. C. 244.	Walterus and Helgunda continue their journey to Tynecz.
31.	
32. Valltari has contest with Thetleifr C. 128–129; is set over the castle Gerimsheim C.151; is slain in combat with Villdifer C. 331.	Waltherus' combat with Wyslaus in second part of the saga.

PAPROCKI.	BIELSKI.
23.	
24.	
25.	
26.	
27.	
28. Walcerus slays Arinaldus in single combat.	Walcer slays the German in single combat.
29.	
30. Walcerus and Heligunda continue their journey to Tyniec.	Walcer and Heligunda continue their journey to Poland.
31.	
32. Walcerus' combat with Wislimier.	Walcer's combat with Wislaw.

Niesiecki.	Procosius.	Wójcicki.
23.		
24.		
25.		
26.		
27.		
28.		Walgerz slays Arinoldus in single combat.
29.		
30.		Walgerz and Helgunde come in safty to Tyniec.
31.		
32. Walcer's combat with Wislimer.	Walgierz's combat with Vislimirus.	Walgierz's combat with Wislaw.

From the parallel view of the contents of the versions of the Walther Saga the following conclusions may be drawn :—

1. That the chief episodes of the Saga are preserved in all three of the full texts : the Waltharius or Alemannic version ; the þidreks-Saga or Old Norse version ; Boguphali Chronicon or the Polish version. Correspondences in these three texts are as follows :—

a. Walther's sojourn at a foreign court ;
b. Walther's betrothal with Hildegunde at the court ;
c. Flight of Walther and Hildegunde ;
d. Pursuit of the fugitives ;
e. Wa'ther vanquishes his foes in single combat.
f. Walther and Hildegunda continue their journey homeward ;
g. Walther's exploits after his return home.

2. That each of these three versions presents a different grouping of Ethnical elements.

A.—*Alemannic Version* :

a. Attila, King of the Huns, marches against Gibicho, King of Franks ; Heriricus, King of the Burgundians ; and Alphere, King of the Aquitanians.
b. Walther, son of Alphere, is sent as hostage to Attila.
c. Hildegunde, daughter of Heriricus, is sent as hostage to Attila.
d. Hagen is sent by Gibicho as hostage to Attila.

B.—*Old Norse Version* :

a. Attila, King of the Huns, having his seat at Susat, forms an alliance with Ermenrick, King of Puli (Apulia ?).
b. Walther, son of Ermenrick's sister, is sent with twelve knights by Ermenrick as hostage to Attila.
c. Hildegunde, daughter of the Jarl of Greece, is hostage at Attila's court.
d. Hagen, son of King Aldrian, is at Attila's court, and is sent by Attila, with eleven other knights, to pursue Walther.

C.—*Polish Version* :

a. In place of Attila and his court (as represented in the other two versions) we have here a King of the Franks and his court.
b. Walther, the Robust, Count of Tynecz, in Cracovia, sojourns at the court of the King of the Franks, to learn the arts of chivalry.

c. Hildegunde, daughter of the King of the Franks, is at her father's court.

d. Instead of Hagen, we have here the son of the King of Alemannia who is at the court of Hildegunde's father. Wyslaus the Handsome, Chief of Wylicia, is in a sense the representative of Hagen, as Gunther's ally.

2. HISTORICAL ELEMENTS OF THE WALTHER SAGA.

The border land between saga and history is still enchanted ground. The old historians were fond of making forays into this magic realm to supply the missing chapters of their chronicles. Less chivalrous, though not less bold some adventurous scholars of the present generation have donned the veiling-cloak and dragged the facts of history back into the mists of saga and myth.

It seems time now, if ever, to base the investigation of the saga (and so far as possible the myth) upon a firm historical foundation. By this procedure alone will it ever be possible to separate the historical from the mythical element. Even this method may not enable us to arrive at well-established identification of many mythical and historical personages[1]; but it will clear the atmosphere and banish many fog-brewers from the domain of Heroic Saga and make possible the science of the Heroic Saga.

The essential germ of the historical method was recognized by the great pioneer investigators in this field, Jacob and Wilhelm Grimm. [2] Since the days of the Grimms and their successors, Lachmann and Müllenhoff, the mythical and poetical methods of saga interpretation have seemed at times to vie in no unequal contest with the historical. At present, however, the historical method is beginning to take firm hold upon the study both of myth and sage. [3] In determining the historical background of a saga two considerations must be kept in view:

First:—That there are various strata or channels of history along which events are transmitted, and that the most trustworthy of these is the written record. But the range of events recorded in the chronicles is as narrow as the events are sparse.

Secondly:—That behind or around the written records lies a vast unwritten chronicle which is transmitted through the memory of succeeding generations. In this latter medium of transmission facts assume the character of living forces, forming new combinations, taking on new proportions, acquiring new fervor and varied colors, according as the aims, the prejudices, the conditions, or the imagination of the narrator may dictate. It is this second medium of

---

1 Cf. Vigfusson and Powell, "Siegfried-Arminius" (in Grimm Centenary); Heinzel, "Hagen-Aetius" ('über die Walthersage,' s. 75 ff.)

2 J. Grimm, "Gedanken über Mythos, Epos und Geschichte" (Kl. SS. 4. 74 ff.); W. Grimm, "Zeugnisse über die deutsche Heldensage," D. Wälder, 1. 195 ff.

3 Cf. Beer, *Germania* xxxiii, 1 ff.; Bugge, "Über die Entsteh. d nord. Gotter-u. Heldensagen"; Heinzel, "Über die Walthersage"; and "Über die Ostgothische Heldensage" (*W. Stzber.* 119, iii); Symons (in Paul's *Grundriss*, ii, 1 ff.).

transmission, *tradition*, which constitutes the chief source of the saga ; and it is as much the duty of the investigator to keep in view the trend of tradition underlying the development of saga as it is his duty to hold fast to his historical moorings. In short, in the study of culture and belief in whatever form, it is quite as important to know what tradition says as to know what recorded history recounts of the great men and events of the past. But in order to separate the historical and mythical element of the saga, we must begin with history.

The Saga of Walther of Aquitaine contains clearly recognizable historical elements. Before proceeding to the treatment of the so-called mythical elements, it will be well to eliminate and examine the historical. The following characters have a well-authenticated historical record : Ermanric, Dietric, Attila, Helche (Erka), Gibico, Guntharius. It will be in place here to recall the essential facts of their career as transmitted by history, in order to secure a suitable point of departure.

Ermanric.—Ammianus Marcellinus, Ermanric's contemporary, gives the following account of him :

Igitur Hunni pervalis Alanorum regionibus, quos Greuthungis confines Tanaitas consuetudo nominavit, interfectisque multis et spoliatis, reliquos sibi concordandi fide pacta iunxerunt : eisque adiunctis, confidentius Ermenrichi late potentes et uberes pagos repentino impetu perruperunt, bellicossimi regis, et per multa variaque fortiter facta vicinis nationibus formidati. Qui vi subitae procellae perculsus, quamvis manere fundatus et stabilis diu conatus est, impendentium tamen diritatem augente vulgatius fama, magnorum discriminum metum voluntaria morte sedavit (31, 3.)

Jordanes' account of Ermanric is briefly as follows :

Some time after the death of Geberic, who was the King of the united Gothic peoples about 331, Ermanric (Ermanaricus) the noblest of the Amali, followed as King of the Goths. He subjugated many northern peoples to his rule, so that the old historians fittingly compared him to Alexander the Great. After having conquered the "Gothos, Scythias, Thuidos in Aunxis, Vasinabroncas Merens, Mordensimnis, Caris, Rocas, Tadzan, Athual Navego, Buhegentas, Coldas,"[4] he marched against the Heruli. Having subjugated these he vanquished in turn the Veneti, Antes (Entes), Sclavi (Sclaveni), the Aestes along the coast of the German Ocean, "so that he ruled over all the peoples of Scythia and Germania as over his own subjects."

The tragic end of Ermanric is thus related by him as follows :

Quod genus expeditissimum multarumque nationum grassatorem Getae ut viderunt, paviscunt suoque cum rege deliberant, qualiter tali se hoste subducant. Nam Ermanaricus, rex Gothorum, licet, ut superius retulimus, multarum gentium extiterat triumphator, de Hunnorum tamen adventu dum cogitat, Rosomonorum (Rasomonorum Rosomorum, Roxolanorum) gens infida quae tunc inter alios illi famulatum exhibebat, tali eum nanciscitur occasione decipere. Dum enim quandam mulierem Sunilda (Sunihil, Sunielh) nomine ex gente memorata pro mariti fraudulento discessu rex furore commotus equis ferocibus inligatam incitatisque cursibus per diversa divelli praecipisset,

4 Cf. Cap. 23.

fratres eius Sarus et Ammius (Iammius, Aminus, Ammus) Germanae obitum vindicantes, Ermanarici latus ferro petierunt ; quo vulnere sae-vius egram corporis imbecillitate contraxit. Quam adversam captans Balamber (Belamber, Balamir, Balamur) rex Hunnorum in Ostrogothorum parte movit procinctum, a quorum societate iam Vesegothae quadam inter se intentione seiuncti habebantur. Inter haec Ermanaricus tam vulneris dolore quam etiam Hunnorum incursionibus non ferens grandevus et plenus dierum centesimo decimo anno vitae suae defunctus est. Cuius mortis occasio dedit Hunnis praevalere, in Gothis illis quos dixeramus orientali plaga federe et Ostrogothas nuncupari. (Cap. 24.)

It is evident at a first glance that Jordanes has drawn his account, in part at least, from an already well-developed Ermanric saga, but a comparison of his account with that of Ammianus will show that certain trustworthy historical facts are common to both and constitute a firm historical basis for the Ermanric saga (cf. Ths. below). What the later chroniclers—Flodoardus (' Hist. Eccles. Remensis,' 4, 5) ; Chronicon Quedlinburgense (Menken, 'SS. Rer. Germ.,' iii, 170) ; Eckehardus (' Chronicon Urspergense,' p. 85ᵃ) ; Otto von Freisingen (Chronicon v, 3) ; Saxo Grammaticus (Stephan, L. viii, p. 154-157)— have to say of Ermanric, where not based upon Ammianus and Jordanes, must be regarded as history highly tinged with the color of mediæval tradition, and belongs rather to the Saga than to the history of Ermanric.

Herminericus, one of the two Roman Consuls in the year 465, may be mentioned here as having had some possible influence upon the traditional account of the great Gothic King Ermanric of the fourth century.[5] This Herminericus was the son of Aspar, a Goth or Alan, and survived Aspar, who was assasinated in 471, A. D.[6]

Hermeric, leader of the Suevi in 411, A. D., may possibly have been confused in the popular mind with the somewhat similar name of the Gothic Ermanric (Hermanaric). The record of Hermeric's career is brief. He appears as leader of the Suevi 411, A. D., when they, with the Asding Vandals under Gunderic occupied Gallicia.[7] Hermeric and his Suevi were attacked by Gunderic and the Asding Vandals in 419, A. D., and shut in among the Nervian mountains for a year.[8] Hermeric led the Suevi into the territory abandoned by the Vandals to Genseric ; but Hermeric was defeated by Genseric near Merida and, compelled to flee, perished in the waters of the Guadiana.[9]

Theoderic, the East Goth.—The account given of Theoderic the East Goth by Jordanes,[10] Procopius,[11] Anonymus Valesii,[12] briefly summarized, is as follows :

Theoderic born about 454, A. D., was the son of Theodemir, one of

---

5 Cf. K. Hofmann, *Anz. f. d. A*, xiv, 289.
6 ' Roncallius, Vetustiora Latinorum Scriptorum Chronica,' ii, 587. **Patavii,** 1787.
7 Dahn, ' Könige der Germanen,' i, 144.   8 *Ibid.*, i, 147.   9 *Ibid.*, i, 151.

the three brothers ruling the East Goths then settled in Pannonia. When seven years old Theoderic was sent as hostage to the court of Constantinople, where he remained three years. Having returned with a comitatus of ten thousand men, he surprised the Sarmatians and captured the city of Singidunum (Belgrade). In 473 he aided Theodemir in settling the East Goths near Thessalonica as allies (foederati) of the empire. After Theodemir's death, about 474, Theoderic waged wars fourteen years against Emperor Zeno and his rival, the Gothic chieftain Theoderic, son of Triarius. In 488 Theoderic began his four years invasion and conquest of Italy. Passing around the Venitian Gulf he encountered the Gepidae, and at Sontius (Isonzo) was met by Odoacer. He gained two victories over Odoacer, one at Sontius (Aug. 28, 489), another at Verona (Sept. 30, 489) ; when Odoacer fled to Ravenna. Then came the three years of treachery by Tufa, a deserter from Odoacer, and by Frederic the Rugian, companion of Theoderic. The Burgundians came to Odoacer's relief, but he was defeated by Theoderic at the Pine Wood. The siege of Ravenna was raised Feb. 30, 493, by capitulation ; Theoderic violated the treaty and slew Odoacer with his own hand March 15, 493. Then followed the thirty years of Theoderic's peaceful rule in Italy. During this period he had marshes drained, harbours built, and agriculture improved, Burdened by remorse for the execution of Boetius and Symmachus he died Aug. 30, 526.

Theoderic I, the West Goth, who is sometimes confused with the Ostrogoth, was chosen successor to Wallia (419, or 420, A. D.), attempted (426) to gain possession of Arles, the center of Roman authority in Gaul, but was prevented in his attempt by Aëtius. In 436 Theoderic, seeing the Romans engaged in war with the Burgundians, laid siege to Narbonne, but was baffled by the crafty strategem of Count Litorius. Unwilling to withdraw at the request of Avitus, and beaten by Litorius, Thederic retreated behind the walls of Toulouse, whence he again sallied forth against the Romans, as opportunity offered, and attempted to plant his standard on the banks of the Rhone, but through Orientius' intervention he finally made peace with Aëtius.

Theoderic next prepared to attack Genseric, King of the Vandals, but the latter encouraged Attila to essay the conquest of Gaul. Theoderic, deceived by Attila's promises and encouraged by Avitus, joined the Romans against the Huns, and fell in battle on the Catalaunian plains, in 451.

Cf. also *Theoderic II* who became the King of the West Goths in 453 by the assassination of his brother, Thorismund. Allied with the Romans, he tried to have Avitus elected Emperor as successor to Maximus. Theoderic soon afterward crossed the Pyrenees and won a signal victory over the King of the Suevi near the river Urbicus. After the death of Avitus he was compelled to return home to defend his

---

10 ' De Rebus Getecis,' Cap. lv–lix.   11 ' De Bello Gothico,' Lib. i, cap. 1.
12 Wagner's Ed. I, pp. 609 ff.

own land against Agiulf. He allied himself with Genseric against Majorian, but was obliged at length to unite with Majorian against the Vandals. Theoderic II was assassinated by his brother Euric in 466.

Attila.—Of all the characters of Germanic Saga, none has left a deeper and more distinct impress upon tradition than Attila, (the son Mundzuc, or Mundiuch), King of the Huns, Scourge of God. The career of this meteor of history is recorded with much detail by Priscus,[13] Cassiodorus,[14] Jordanes[15] and others. Briefly summarized it runs thus:

First period, Conquests in the East. After the death of their uncle, Rua, (433) the brothers Bleda and Attila succeeded to the rule of the Huns. Having made a treaty with the Romans they set out to subdue the Scythian peoples. Attila put his brother Bleda out of the way (445) and thus became sole ruler of the Huns. Having found the old "sword of Mars," which was sacred to the Scythians and had not been seen for ages, he renewed his wars with fresh vigor and at length forced Rome to an ignominious treaty.

Attila's second great movement, initiated by his conflicts with the Romans, was the campaign against the Germanic peoples of the west. While his eyes were thus turned westward, encouragements came from two directions: one from Geneseric "the fearful Vandal,"[16] the other from one of the Frankish princes, who sought Attila's aid against the united force of Aëtius and the other Frankish prince. Attila accordingly advanced westward with five hundred thousand[17] men, feigning to the Romans (Valentinian) that he intended to attack the West Goths, and to Theoderic, the West Goth, that he wished to free Gaul from the Roman yoke. In the year 451 Attila's army appeared in two main divisions: one moving along the right bank of the Danube via Augst to the Upper Rhine, the other coming around the Odenwald toward Mainz. The southern division probably passed via Strassburg toward Paris, though it seems not to have reached this city.[18] Attila was with the former division at Metz. Having plundered and burned Scarpona and Rheims, he marched on via Châlons, Troyes and Sens toward Orleans. Aëtius meanwhile had crossed the Alps, united with the forces of Gaul—

"Franci, Sarmatae, Armoriciani, Liticiani, Burgundiones, Saxones, Ripuarioli, Briones, quondam milites Romani, tunc vero jam in numero auxiliorum exquisiti, aliique nonnulli Celticae vel Germanicae nationes—"[19]

and secured through Avitus the co-operation of Theoderic, the West Goth. Aëtius with his vast army of united Romans, Germans

---

[13] Ἰατρεία Γοτθιχή I, ff. [Mullerus (Didot), vol. iv, 72.]
[14] Ad. M. A. Cassiodori, Op. Appendix 412 ff.   [15] ' De Rebus Getecis,' cap. 35 ff.
[16] Dahn, K. d. G., i, 150.   [17] Seven hundred thousand according to other accounts.
[18] Wietersheim, ' Gesch. d. Volkerwanderung,' v, 355.   [19] Jordanes, Cap. 36.

and Celts surprised Attila at Orleans and caused him to retreat to thé plain of Champagne between Châlons and Verdun or, accordiug to Jordanes and his authority Cassiodorus, to the Catalaunian plains. Here the armies met and in that world-renowned battle which turned the tide of Hunish conquests from the West and banished the "Scourge of God" from the banks of the Rhine. The following year (452-53) Attila advanced into Italy and plundered Aquileja, the Venetian territory, the plain of Lombardy even to the Po. Soon after this (453), Attila died of hemorrhage on the bridal night with his new wife Ildico.

Erca, Helche.—Before attempting any discussion of the three different names given to Attila's queen in the Walther Saga, let us see if traces of them are to be found in history. Here mention is made of two of Attila's numerous wives, Kreka (Lat. Cerca) and Ildico, whose names are not unlike Erca and Helche of our Saga.

Kreka. Priscus[20] gives the following account of Kreka, Attila's queen:

Ἐγὼ δὲ τῇ ὑστεραίᾳ εἰς τὸν Ἀττήλα περίβολν ἀφικνοῦμαι, δῶρα τῇ αὐτοῦ κομίζων γαμετῇ· Κρέκα δὲ ὄνομα αὐτῇ, ἐξ ἧς αὐτῷ παῖδες ἐγεγόνεσαν τρεῖς, ὧν ὁ πρεσβύτερος ἦρχε τῶν Ἀκατίρων καὶ τῶν λοιπῶν ἐθνῶν νεμομένων τὴν πρὸς τὸν Πόντον Σκυθικήν. Ἔνδον δὲ τοῦ περιβόλου πλεῖστα ἐτύγχανεν οἰκήματα, τὰ μὲν ἐκ σανίδων ἐγγλύφων καὶ ἡρμοσμένων εἰς εὐπρέπειαν, τὰ δὲ ἐκ δοκῶν κεκαθαρμένων καὶ πρὸς εὐθύτητα ἐπεξεσμένων, ἐμβεβλημένων δὲ ξύλοις [κύκλους] ἀποτελοῦσιν· οἱ δὲ κύκλοι ἐκ τοῦ ἐδάφους ἀρχόμενοι ἐς ὕψος ἀνέβαινον μετρίως. Ἐνταῦθα τῆς Ἀττήλα ἐνδιαιτωμένης γαμετῆς, διὰ τῶν πρὸς τῇ θύρᾳ βαρβάρων ἔτυχον εἰσόδου, καὶ αὐτὴν ἐπὶ στρώματος μαλακοῦ κειμένην κατέλαβον, τοῖς ἐκ τῆς ἐρέας πιλωτοῖς τοῦ ἐδάφους σκεπομένου, ὥστε ἐπ' αὐτῶν βαδίζειν. Περιεῖπε δὲ αὐτὴν θεραπόντων πλῆθος κύκλῳ· καὶ θεράπαιναι ἐπὶ τοῦ ἐδάφους ἀντικρὺ αὐτῆς καθήμεναι ὀθόνας χρώμασι διεποίκιλλον, ἐπβληθησομένας πρὸς κόσμον ἐσθημάτων βαρβαρικῶν. Προσελθὼν τοίνυν καὶ τὰ δῶρα μετὰ τὸν ἀσπασμὸν δοὺς ὑπεξῄειν, καὶ ἐπὶ τὰ ἕτερα ἐβάδιζον οἰκήματα, ἐν οἷς διατρίβειν τὸν Ἀττήλαν ἐτύγχανεν, ἀπεκδεχόμενος ὁπότε ἐπεξέλθοι Ὀνηγήσιος· ἤδη γὰρ ἀπὸ τῶν αὐτοῦ οἰκημάτων ἐξεληλύθει και ἔνδον ἦν. Μεταξὺ δὲ τοῦ παντὸς ἱστάμενος πλήθους (γνώριμός τε γὰρ ὢν τοτς Ἀττήλα φρουροῖς καὶ τοῖς παρεπομένοις αὐτῷ βαρβάροις ὑπ' οὐδενὸς διεκωλυόμην), εἶδον πλῆθος πορευόμενον καὶ θροῦν καὶ θόρυβον περὶ τὸν τόπου γινόμενον, ὡς τοῦ Ἀττήλα ὑπεξιόντος. Προῄει δὲ τοῦ οἰκήματος βαδίζων σοβαρῶς, τῇδε κἀκεῖ περιβλεπόμενος. Ὡς δὲ ὑπεξελθὼν σὺν τῷ Ὀνηγησίῳ ἔστη πρὸ τοῦ οἰκήματος, πολλοὶ (δὲ) τῶν ἀμφισβητήσεις πρὸς ἀλλήλους ἐχόντων προσῄεσαν καὶ τὴν αὐτοῦ κρίσιν ἐδέχοντο. Εἶτα ἐπανῄει ὡς τὸ οἴκημα, καὶ πρέσβεις παρ' αὐτὸν ἥκοντας βαρβάρους ἐδέχετο. Ἐν τούτῳ δὲ καὶ ἡ Ῥέκαν (leg. καὶ Κρέκα, ut supra) ἡ τοῦ Ἀττήλα

---

20 Mullerus' 'Fragmenta' (Didot's Ed.), iv, 89, 93.

ƒαμετὴ παρὰ Ἀδάμει τῶν αὐτῆς πραγμάτων τὴν ἐπιτροπὴν ἔχοντι δειπνεῖν ἡμᾶς παρεκάλει. Καὶ παῤ αὐτὸν ἐλθόντες ἅμα τίϭι τῶν ἐκ τοῦ ἔθνους λογάδων φιλοφροϭύνης ἐτύχομεν. Ἐδεξιοῦτο δὲ ἡμᾶς μειλιχίοις τε λόγοις καὶ τῇ τῶν ἐδωδίμων παραϭκευῇ. Καὶ ἕκαϭτος τῶν παρόντων Ϭκυθικῇ φιλοτιμίᾳ κύλικα ἡμῖν πλήρη διανιϭτάμενος ἐδίδου, καὶ τὸν ἐκπιόντα περιβαλὼν καὶ φιλήϭας ταύτην ἐδέχετο. Μετὰ δὲ τὸ δεῖπον ἐπὶ τὴν ϭκηνὴν ἐλθόντες ἐς ὕπνον ἐτράπημεν.[21]

The account of Kreka given by Priscus is, then, briefly this : As Attila's queen (*par excellence*, it would seem) she bears him three sons, the eldest of whom was made King of the Acatiri, the others becoming *reguli* of other tribes or nations ; she is presented with gifts by the Roman legate, Maximus ; she invites the Romans to a feast and has domestic treasures of which Adamis is the custodian. While Kreka was doubtless the historical original of Erca (Herkia, Herche, Helche), the last of Attila's wives, Ildico, can scarcely have been forgotten by the saga-tellers.

Ildico. Jordanes gives the following account of Ildico, Attila's last wife, and of the fatal bridal night :

Qui [Attila], ut Priscus historicus refert, extinctionis suae tempore puellam, Ildico nomine, decoram valde, sibi in matrimoniam post innumerabiles uxores, ut mos erat gentis illius, socians, eiusque in nuptis nimia hilaritate resolutus vino somnoque gravatus resupinus jacebat redundansque sanguis, qui ei solite de naribus effluebat, dum consuetis meatibus impeditur, itinere ferali faucibus illapsus cum extinxit. Sequente vero luce, quum magna pars diei fuisse exempta, ministri regii, triste aliquid suspicantes, post clamores maximos fores effringunt inveniuntque Attilae sine vulnere necem sanguinis effusione peractam, puellamque demisso vultu sub velamine lacrimantem."[22]

This account of Jordanes seems to be based upon a lost chapter of Priscus, hence the interpretation of a part of Jordanes' cap. 49 as cap. 23 of Priscus.[23]

Gibica.—Gibica appears among the names of the Burgundian Kings of worthy memory, mentioned in the ' Lex Burgundionum,' iii :

"Si quos apud Regiae memoriae auctores nostros, id est Gibicam, Godomarem, Gislaharium, patrem quoque nostrum et patruos, liberos fuisse constiterit, in eadem libertate permaneant: quicunque sub eisdem fuerint obnoxii servitute, in nostro dominio perseverunt." (Bouquet, iv, 257, E).

Gundioarius, King of the Burgundians, is mentioned as a contemporary of Aëtius and Attila. His compact with Aëtius, who had worsted him in war in the year 435, A. D., is thus recorded in the Chronicle of Prosperus Aquitanus :

" Eodem tempore [about 435, A. D.] Gundicarium Burgundionum Regem intra Gallias habitantem Aëtius bello obtinuit, pacemque ei

---

supplicanti dedit; qua non potitus est, siquidem illum Chuni cum
populo suo ac stirpe deleverunt.'' [24]

Gundicarius' defeat by Attila in the following year (436) is mentioned by Paulus Diaconus in his ' Libello de Episcopis Mettensibus '
as follows :

"Eo igitur tempore [436 A. D.], cum reverendus his Praesul vitam
cunctis virtutibus decoratum duceret, Attila Rex Hunnorum omnibus
belluis crudelior, habens multas barbaras nationes suo subjectas
dominio, postquam Gundigarium Burgundionum Regem sibi occurrentem protriverat ad universas deprimendas Gallias suae saevitiae
relaxavit habenas.'' [25]

The same event is referred to in the ' Historia Miscella ' by Paulus
Diaconus :

"Attila itaque primo impetu, mox ut Gallias ingressus est Gundicarium regem Burgundiorum sibi occurrentem protrivit, pacemque ei
supplicanti dedit.''

In this account of Attila's subjugation of the Burgundians (436),
there is doubtless confusion of the overthrow of Gundicarius by the
Huns, serving as Roman mercenaries (436), with the expedition of
Attila (451). [26]   May not the two divisions of Attila's army in 451 have
further confused the account?

Guntiarius.—Olympiodorus of Thebes, states [27] that Guntiarius
(Greek form Guntiarios) praefect ($\varphi\acute{v}\lambda\alpha\rho\chi o\varsigma$) of the Burgundians, and
Goar, praefect of the Alans, proclaimed Jovinus Emperor at Mainz 411,
or 412.   That this Guntiarius is the same as Gundicarius mentioned
above, seems probable.   In the minds of later generations at any rate
they would naturally have become identical.

It is possible, also, that traces of other famous characters of the
same, or similar names, have been added to some of the traditional
accounts of Gundicarius ; as, for example, of Gundericus, the king of
the Vandals.

Gundericus, King of the Vandals, from 406-428.   The main facts of
Gundericus' career are the following : In the year 419 at the head of
the Asdings, he attacked Hermericus, the leader of the Suevi, and
held them shut in for a year among the Nerva Mountains.   Having
united the Alans to his kingdom, he formed a host superior to the
Suevi, Goths and Romans.   In the year 422 his Vandals and Alans
defeated Castinus, the Roman *magister militum*, together with his
West Gothic mercenaries, compelling them to flee, with the loss of
twenty thousand men, to Tarragona.   In the year 425 Gundericus
made conquest of the cities of Carthagena and Sevilla.   About two
years later, 427 or 428, Gundericus perished in battle, probably while
fighting against the Suevi.   According to tradition, he was visited by
God's chastisment for plundering the churches in Sevilla. [28]

24 Bouquet, i, 631, B.   25 *Ibid.*, i, 631 ; Pertz, ii, 262.
26 Cf. Wietersheim, G. d. V., iv, 353 ff.   27 Mullerus, ' Fragmenta ' (Didot, iv).
28 Cf. Dahn, ' Könige der Germanen,' i, 143-151, 182, 210, 215, 241.

The foregoing historical account furnishes an ample historical background for the Walther Saga. It requires no forced reasoning to identify in the characters of the Saga, Attila, King of the Huns; Kreka, his queen; Ermanric, King of the Goths; Theoderic, the Ostrogoth; Gibica, the King of the Burgundians; Gundicarius, also King of the Burgundians at the time of their overthrow by the Huns, while they dwelt along the Rhine—the epical period of their history. Thus a compairison will show that Attila corresponds to Attila and Etzel of the Saga; Kreka to Erca, Herche, Helche (cf. Müllenhoff *Zeitschrift,* 10, 170 ff.; Grimm Hs3. 76, 393); Ermanric to Ærminrikr; Theoderic to Deodric, Dietrich, Thiðrekr; Gibica to Gibico and Gibicho; Gundicarius to Guðhere, Guntharius (cf. Jahn, Gesch. d. Burg. i, 303). The name Ospirin given to Attila's queen in the Waltharius seems to be peculiar to this version of the Saga (cf. Zeitschrift, 10, 171 ff.).

3. LEGENDARY ELEMENTS.

In addition to the historical elements, which are readily identified, the Walther Saga contains a class of characters which, doubtless, reflect actual history, but which can only be indistinctly traced in the historical records handed down to us. To regard these characters as purely legendary is to ignore the relation of history to tradition, and to misconceive the processes by which the historical Saga is developed. On the other hand, to begin the interpretation of such characters by tracing them in the Eddic Lays is to complicate the problem and vitiate the conclusions; because these Lays, though in many cases containing very early forms of the Sagas, present these characters in combination with distinctively Northern legendary and mythical elements.

Thus the characters which we designate as Legendary: Hagen, Heriricus, Hildegunde, Alphere, Walther; and the knights, who attack Walther in single combat at the Wasgenstein: Camelo, Ekevrid, Eleuter (Helmnod), Gerwicus, Hadawart, Kimo (Scaramundus), Patavrid, Randolf, Tanastus, Trogus, Wurhardus—if not traceable in historical record, are at least the outgrowth of a historical past and not inventions, pure and simple. This is clear from the faint historical traces of the names, which may be briefly stated here.

Hagen. Heinzel [29] has made a skillful attempt to identify Hagen with Aetius, and the coincidences between the two he sums up briefly as follows:

1. The name Hagathiau for Hagen's father in the Waltharius;
2. The repeated sojourns of Aëtius among the Huns, as hostage and fugitive, and the sojourn of his son there as hostage;
3. The historical position of Aëtius; first as friend, and then as foe of the Huns; consequently as friend of the Germanic foes of the Huns, the Burgundians;
4. The Burgundians fighting on the side of Aëtius against Attila, in the year 451;
5. The Germanizing of Aëtius by his marriage with a Gothic princess;
6. The diplomacy of Aëtius, which might appear as the cowardice of Hagathiu;
7. The accusation of Aëtius as the assassin of Attila through Hildico;
8. The avenging of Attila's murder by his subjects.

---

29 'Walther Saga,' S. 63 ff.; 75 ff. 'Nibelungen Saga,' W. S. B. 109, 672, 114, 495.

Besides these, the general accord that both were great warriors and commanders, and that in the 'Nibelungenlied' Hagen is *Scharmeister*, as Aëtius was *magister militum.*

Other considerations in Heinzel's argument are perhaps even more weighty than some of the coincidences noted above. Such are:

1. Identification of Aldrian, Hagen's father, with Alaric I, the West Gothic king, at whose court Aëtius lived from about his tenth to his fourteenth year, Alaric's affection for Aëtius thus giving rise to the popular tradition that he was Aëtius' father.

2. The possible confusion in Epic tradition of this Alaric with Alaric II, who ruled in Gaul and fell at Vouglé while fighting against the Franks, in the year 507.

Whether Heinzel's identification of Hagen with Aëtius be accepted or rejected, it must remain a masterly attempt at historical interpretation of obscure legendary elements.—Scherer's identification of Walther with Aëtius will be discussed below in connection with Walther.

If we turn, now, to find the name of Hagen in history, our eye falls first upon one closely resembling Hagen, Aigyna (Aighyna, Aiginus) the principle events of whose career, so far as they are recorded, are the following:[30]

In 626 A. D. Aigyna guarded, as duke, the Frankish frontier along the banks of the Garonne, against the inroads of the Wascons. In the same year he effected the banishment of Palladius, and his son Seducus, Bishop of Toloso, for having been accomplices in the uprising of the Wascons. The following year he allowed his rival, Ermenar, to be assassinated at Clichy, thus giving rise to a seditious outbreak. In the year 635 he led a corps of the Burgundian-Frankish army (probably his own retainers) against Wasconia, and afterward conducted the humiliated Wascons to the palace of Clichy to obtain their pardon of Dagobert.

This Aigyna, whom Fredegar calls "a noble Saxon," seems to be the nearest approach in these early historical records to the Hagano (Haganus, Agano: 'Chron. Noval.') of the Walther Saga. It is not impossible that some of the situations in this Saga find their explanation in the career of Aigyna. The following considerations may be suggested here:

1. Aigyna is a noble Saxon;[31]

2. Aigyna takes part in the Burgundian-Frankish attack upon the Wascons;[32]

3. Aigyna, as duke under Frankish authority, would explain Hagen's coming from Troja (Tronje);[33]

---

[30] 'Fredegarii Chronicum,' Cap. 54.   [31] Cf. "Nobilis hoc Hagano," etc. W. 27.
[32] Cf. Hagano's relation, as vassal of Gibicho and Guntharius. W. 29, 116 ff.
[33] Cf. Hagen von Tronege, Nibelungenlied (Zarncke) 267, 7; Hagano . . . . Indolis egregiae ueniens de germine Troiae. W. 28; Hagen aff Trönia, O. S. D. 365, 2; aff Tröya 340, 5; 367, 7.

4. Aigyna's position as protector of the Aquitainian border might explain Hagen's being witness at the betrothal of Walther and Hildegeunde.[34]

5. Aigyna's conquest of the Wascons might have given rise to the conception of Hagen as the father of Hilde, of Portegal ; [35]

6. The cruel character of Aigyna would serve as the parallel for the grim-visaged Hagen of the Nibelungenlied.

7. Aigyna was also a contemporary of the furious Brunhilde (whose character is reflected in the Nibelungenlied ?).[36]

What, then, is the value of this parallel between Aigyna, the Saxon, and Hagen, as compared with Heinzel's identification of Hagen and Aëtius ? The situation at present with regard to these, as to many other legendary characters, is this : such identifications rest upon too bare a basis of detail to amount to positive proof. In the case of unmistakable historical characters like Ermanric, Theoderic, and Attila, whose deeds belong to the political history of the world, and have come down in written record, it is not difficult to follow the thread of history through mazes of myth and saga. But in the case of characters whose deeds have appeared in history either in desultory jottings, or where recorded more in detail, appear under names different from those handed down by legendary tradition, historical identification is peculiarly difficult, and is long in finding general acceptance. This is seen in the cases of the master attempts of Vigfusson-Powell, (Siegfried-Arminiuos) and Heinzel (Hagen-Aëtius).

The Hagen-Aëtius identification of Heinzel and the Hagen-Aigyna parallels given above, though in themselves not conclusive in every particular, do show this : that the historical back-ground furnished ample material for the development of such legendary characters, and that there is a strong presumption that the historical saga has combined in such legendary personages, as we know it has in the case of historical personages, the epic elements of characters widely separated in point of time and even locality. Hence there would be no inconsistency in supposing that certain traits of the character of Aigyna served to fortify the conception of Hagen-Aëtius the contemporary of Attila ; particularly inasmuch as the grouping of events in the Walther Saga points to a period considerably later than the time of Attila. Heinzel [37] himself concedes the possibility of such anachronism :

"Die Erben der römmanischen Generale Aëtius, Aegidius und Syagrius in Gallien waren die fränkischen Könige. Es wäre dem nach nicht auffällig, wenn die Sagengestalt Hagens Eigenschaften zeigte, welche auf die Merovinger wiesen. Das scheint bei dem Namen Hagen von Tronje der Fall zu sein."

This much seems clear concerning the legendary character, Hagen, as portrayed in the Walther saga :

---

34 Cf. G. F. 1, 2, 1.   35 Cf. Gudrun, 1936 ; Prose Edda ; Grimm, Hs. 373 ff.
36 Cf. Fregedar, C. 19 ff.   37 'Walthersaga,' s. 79.

1. The historical background contained the essential elements found in the character of Hagen;

2. The geographical localization of the character as Hagen von Tronege (Tronje, Troia) is justified by the actual existence of Trhonia, the modern Kircheim in Alsatia, the identity of which has been clearly shown by Heinzel.[38]

The form Troia in the 'Waltharius' might be explained as poetic confusion with the ancient Troja of his model Virgil ; or as following up the tradition, that the Franks were sprung from Trojan origin,[39] or as coming directly from Nova Troja (Kircheim).

3. The later appearance of the name Hagen in the documents of the eighth century point to the earlier existence and localisation of the name, and thus to the early development of the saga.

Heriricus.—Gregorius Turonensis [40] gives the folllowing acconnt of King Chararicus which is probably the Frankish form of Heriricus :

"Posthac ad Chararicum regem dirigit. Quando autem cum Siagrio pugnavit, hic Chararicus evocatus ad solatium Chlodovechi cuimus stetit, eventum rei expectans, ut cui eveniret victoria cum illo et hic amicitiam colligaret. Ob hanc causam contra eum indignans Chlodovechus abiit, quem circumventum dolis cepit cum filio, vinctosque totondit et Chararicum quidem presbyterum, filium vero ejus diaconem ordinari jubet. Cumque Chararicus de humilitate sua conquereretur et fleret, filius ejus dixisse fertur : In viridi, inquit, ligno hae frondes suecisae sunt, nec omnino arescunt sed velociter emergent ut crescere queant ; utinam tam velociter qui haec fecit, intereat. Quod verbum sonuit in aures Chlodovechi quod scilicet minarentur sibi caesariem ad crescendem laxare, ipsumque interficere. At ille jussit eos pariter capite plecti. Quibus mortuis regnum eorum cum thesauris et populo acquisivit."

Chararicus is lauded by Malbrancus [41] as *Rex Morinorum.* The Morini are mentioned by Virgil,[42] Cæsar,[43] and in Cæsar's time occupied the country along the English Channel extending inland. Ptolemy [44] mentions two cities of the Morini, Gesoriacum or Bononia (Boulogne) and Taruenna (Thérouenne). D'Anville [45] says of their territory :

" En y joignant le Castellum Morinorum, on voit qu'outre le diocèse de Bologne le territoire des Morini embrasse les nouveaux diocèses de St. Omer et D'Ifre, qui ont succédé a celui de Terouenne."

If the territory of the Morini at this early period extended to Cassel, we may reasonably suppose that with the Frankish conquest of Gaul, they were pushed even farther inland and that in the traditional terminology of the fifth and sixth centuries the name still survived to designate the ethnical successors of this nation. Hence, there would be no incongruity in calling Chararicus the Frankish king *Rex Morinorum,* to indicate some political or ethnical relation of this king to that people.

38 'Walthersaga,' s. 80 ff.   39 cf. Gregorious Turonensis.   40 Lib. ii, c. 41.
41 Lib. iv, c. 38.   42 Aen., viii, 727.   43 B. G., iv., 21.   44 ii, 9 § 8.
45 'Notice de l'Ancienne Gaule,' p. 466.

Further we have mention in Gregorius Turonensis [46] of Chararicus king of the Suevi in Spanish Gallicia, and father of Theodemirus. It was in the time of Theodemirus, who was made king about 559, that the Suevi were converted to the Catholic Faith.[47] There may have been some confusion in the popular mind between Chararicus king of the Morini and Chararicus king of Gallicia. The geographcal position of the latter would suggest such confusion.

It seems not at all improbable that Chararicus, as Frankish King ruling over the Burgundian territory after its subjection to Frankish authority, should have come to be regarded as King of the Burgundians. This is the more plausible, as the confusion of Frankish and Burgundian relations is already evident in the Walther Saga, where the Burgundian Gundicarius is represented as King of the Franks. If, then, we have succeeded in identifying the Heriricus of the saga with the Chararicus of Gregorius Turonesis we shall have established another bond of the close relationship of our saga with its historical background.

Hildegunde.—In the case of Hildegunde, whom the Saga calls the daughter of Heriricus, the actual historical background is not so clear. The name itself, however, together with the name of Hilde, Alker's queen, and presumably Walther's mother, points unmistakably to Burgundian-Frankish origin. The name Hilde is an almost constant quantity in Burgundian-Frankish history of the Merovingian period, as indeed of the Sagas connected with the period. We need but recall some of the most prominent Chlotchilde, Brunhilde, Balthilde, not to mention the names of men, Childebert, Childerich. So, too, the second part of the name occurs in Fredegunde and the ethnic name itself Burgunde.

The coincidence of the first part of the name Hildegunde with Hilde, the presumable mother of Walther, suggests the close ethnical and political relationship of Burgundians and Aquitanians at the time when the Alemannic version of the Saga developed. Compare the fact that Heriricus and Alphere had betrothed their children in early childhood. This may indicate also a family relationship existing between the two Kings.

One other point remains to be noted here : that the form Hildegunde contains the stem element of the name Hildico [48] (Ildico) Attila's last spouse. It is not unlikely that this may have given rise to the name of this royal hostage, Hildegunde, who held such a responsible position at Attila's court. Then, too, the last fatal feast of Attila on the night of his nuptials with Ildico, may have left its traces in the feast which Walther and Hildegunde prepare—note in particular the potion, the long sleep.

---

46 ' De Virtutibus ' S. Martini, Lib. i, c. 11.   47 ' De Reg. Gothorum,' Cap. 90.
48 The masculine form corresponding to Hildico is borne by one of the two Vandals, *Praepositae* Heldicus and Cubadus. Cf. Dahn, ' Könige der Germanen,' i, 217, 232, 236.

The name of *Childechinda*, the daughter of Chilpericus I occurs in early Frankish history.[49] While this form can scarcely be identified with that of Hildegunde, it indicates together with those mentioned above, that the name Hildegunde belongs to Frankish-Burgundian soil; and hence need not be a poetic creation, pure and simple (as Heinzel would seem to suggest,) in imitation of the forms Hilde, Hildeburg, Hildeswidh, Helisant, in similar tales ("in den ähnlichen Erzählungen nachgebildet ");[50] but like these is doubtless traceable to Burgundian-Frankish tradition of the sixth century. This, at least, is evident: that the Hildegunde of the Walther Saga harmonizes with the historical elements and conditions out of which the Saga grew, and is not in any version of the Saga a vague, mythical character, but a genuine, legendary personage of flesh and blood, reflecting actual history.

Alphere.—The name of Alphere, father of Walther, and king of the Aquitanians, (according to the Waltharius) seems to have escaped the old chroniclers. San-Marte[51] recognizes the name in Alf or Half, son of Hialprek and spouse of Hiordisa, Sigurd's mother. This Alf is not to be confounded with Alf the Old, son of Ulfr, mentioned in Helga-Kvida i, 215, and Hyndluliod.[52] The Nornagest Saga[53] gives us more reliable information concerning Hialprek. It calls him king in Frankland, and this evidently refers to the historical Hilpericus (Chilpericus, 561–581). Compare also Hilpericus who ruled contemporaneously with his brother Gundiocus as king of the Burgundians, from about 437 to 470.[54] Here again we find ourselves in the midst of Burgundian-Frankish events, as in the case of the names Hagen, Heriricus and Hildegunde discussed above.

Whether there be a family connection between this Alf of the Edda and Alphere must remain a matter of conjecture. Jacob Grimm[55] cites names of similar ending (Folchere, Gunthere)—which, by the way, belong to the Burgundian-Frankish region—and suggests that M. H. G. form Alphêr, instead of the regular form Alphere (=Goth. Albharis) may be due to confusion with Alpkêr (=Goth. Albgáis).

There remains, however, another point to consider: whether the name Alpheré is to be connected with the Lombard heroic cycle of which Alboin (Ælfwine, Elfwine) is the central figure. A number of considerations make it quite probable that there was some connection between the two:

1. The similarity of the first element of the names Alphere (<Albhari) and Alboin (Alb-wine).

2. The frequent intercourse between the Lombards, Burgundians and Franks.

49 Cf. Bouquet, iii, 68 D, 209 C.   50 ' Walthersage,' S. 82.
51 ' Walther von Aquitanien,' S. 36 ff.   52 Cf. Simrock, ' Edda,' S. 119–120.
53 Chap. 3 and 4.
54 Cf. Binding, ' Gesch. d. burgundisch-romanischen Königreichs,' S. 38 ff.
55 Haupt, *Zeitschrift*, 5, 3.

3. The fact that the first element (see below) in the name of Alphere's son, Waldhere (Waltharius), and even the full name Waltari itself appear in Lombard Chronicles ; compare Waldrada,[56] the second daughter of Wacho and Austrigusa, and wife of Scusuald, King of the Franks ; and *Waltari*, son of Wacho and Sigelenda, and Wacho's successor as King of the Lombards. Note also the name of the Lombard Justinian, Rothari, in this connection. If then this connection be established, we have Alphere related to the great saga-cycle of the Lombard kings.

We have already seen family intercourse between the Lombard and Frankish royal houses in the marriage of Waldrada and Scusuald. If we turn again to Frankish-Aquitanian history [57] we find about six generations after Alboin or Ælfwine, the name Waifarius on Aquitanian soil. This Waifarius appears as Aquitanian *Princeps* between 758-68, A. D., and has under his command the Wascons of the little Wasco-Toulousan State (or Kingdom ?) founded by Felix 660-70, A. D. The name Waifarius looks like a near relative when placed by the side of Alpharius (Alphere), and Waltharius. May we not have here a lost link in the Lombard-Aquitanian (or Lombard-Frankish) relationship ?

It would seem from this that J. Grimm [58] was not so far wrong in suggesting that there may have been a saga of Alphere as well as of Walthere :

"Aber auch die Saga von Alphere, seinem [Walthere's] vater, ist uns nicht verschollen, und ich zweifle kaum dass es davon epische lieder gab."

As evidence of such an Alphere Saga he cites from the Kolocz Codex, S. 189-240.

"ich bin *Alpharius* genannt
und hân ouch bürge und lant
enhalbe (enenthalben) über Rin."

Waltharius.—In this part of the treatise are given the occurrences of the name Waltharius in Lombard and Franco-Gallic history before 1000, A. D. Perhaps the earliest considerable account of the name is that given by Paulus Diaconus :[59]

I, 21. "Habuit autem Wacho uxores tres, hoc est, primam Ranicundam, filiam regis Thuringorum. Deinde duxit Austrigosam, filiam regis Gepidorum, de qua habuit filias duas. Nomen uni Wisegarda, quam tradidit in matrimonium Theodeberto, regi Francorum. Secunda autem dicta est Walderada, quae sociata est Cusupaldo, alio regi Francorum, quam ipse odio habens uni ex suis, qui dicebatur Garipald, in conjugium tradidit. Tertiam vero Wacho uxorem habuit Herulorum regis filiam nomine Saligam. Ex ipsa natus est filius, quem Walthari appellavit, quique Wachone mortuo super Langobar-

---

56 Cf. Introduction to the ' Edictus Rothari '; Paulus Diaconis ' De Gestis Langobardorum," lib. vi ; Meyer, Sprach u. Sprachdm. der Langobarden,' S. 120-121.

57 Cf. Fredegar ' Chr. Contin.' P. iv., c. 124-135 ; Perroud ' Des Origines du Premier Duché D'Aquitaine,' 115 ff.

58 Haupt *Zeitschrift*, 5, 4 ff.   59 ' De Gestis Langobardorum,' Lib. vi.

dos jam octavus regnavit. Hi omnes Latingi fuerunt; sic enim apud eos quaedam nobilis prosapia vocabatur. I, 22. Walthari ergo cum per septem annos regnum tenuisset, ab hac luce subtractus est. Post quem nonus Audwini regnum adeptus est, qui non multó post tempore Langobardos in Pannoniam adduxit.''

Essentially the same account is found also in the "Origo Gentis Langobardorum,'[60] 'Chronicon Gothanum.'[61] The name of Walthari occurs also in the introduction of the 'Edictus Rothari,'[62] where he is called the ninth king of the Lombards instead of the eighth, as he is called in the passage quoted above.

Having thus traced the name '' Waltharius '' in Lombard history, we find it appearing next in Frankish-Galic records as follows :

1. Waltharius mentioned in "Diploma Pippini Regis pro Nundinis S. Dionysii," Anno 753.

2, Waltharius is mentioned as one of the signers in '' Pippini Praeceptum pro constructione et dotatione Monasterii Prumiensis," Anno 762. (August thirteenth of the ninth year of Pippin's reign.)

3. Waltharius chorepiscopus, mentioned among those present at the synod *in ecclesia noviomensi*, Anno 814.

4. Waltharius vir nobilis (uxor Suanahilda, filia uxor Odalrici) circa anno 825, is attacked by Purchardus, leader of the Alamanni (ex 'Translatione Sanguinis Domini ').[63]

5. Waltharius abbas Augensis, circa 850.[64]

6. Waltarius, '' Regi Lothario a secretis," Anno 866.[65]

7. Waltarius is mentioned in the document 'Ad Episcopus Regni Lotharii,' Anno 867.

8. Waltharius together with Gauslenus Fulco and Lautwinus executes the capitularies sent by King Charles to Burgundy.[66]

9. Waltharius Walerus juvenis episcopus senonensis, nepos Waltherii Aurelianensis episcopi.[67]

10. Walterus Aurelianiensium episcopus, sent by Hugo to King Ludovicus, Anno 879.[68]

11. Walterius vir illustris in biturica civitate, Anno 917.[69]

12. Walterius fidelis Richardi, Anno 918.[70]

13. Walterius praefectus victuriaci castri, mentioned in Flodoardi Annales.[71]

14. Gualterius, sacerdos et monachus, mentioned in "Chr. Mon. Casinensis," as having the church or the monastery S. Mariae in Luco, Circa anno 950.[72]

15. Valterus exchanges his possession in Villa de Losa for a part of S. Michaelis in Villa Torralias, circa 959.[73]

16. Walterus (Gualterus) Augustudunensis episcopus, anno 991.[74]

17. Walterus episcopus spirensis, anno 1004.[75]

---

60 Meyer ' Sprache u. Sprachdenk. d. Langobarden,' S. 110.   61 *Ibid.*, S. 115.
62 *Ibid.*, S. 16.   63 Pertz, iv, 448.   64 Pertz, ii, 38.   65 Pertz, i, 458, 472.
66 Bouquet, vii, p. 667 D.   67 Pertz i, 524, 525, 599.   68 'Annales Vedastini,' Pertz, ii, 197.
69 Bouquet, ix, 715 D.   70 Bouquet, ix, 717 C.   71 Pertz, iii, 401.   72 Pertz, vii, 634.
73 Chr. St. Michaeli's in Pago Virdunensi, Pertz, iv, 81.
74 Pertz, iii, 644, 646, 647, 658, 659, 663, 665, 689.   75 Pertz, iii, 70.

Besides the name Waltharius, may be added here others closely resembling this in form, but of apparently very different etymological origin : Walcherius, Walgarius (Waldgarius), Waldericus, Walaricus (Walericus), Walaërius.

1. Walcherius, vir illustris, recorded "una cum fidelibus nostris " : "id est Hagione, Theodberto, Remedio, Gerehardo Fulcario, Bovilone, Walcherio, Rauchingo, et Ermenaldo Comite palatii nostro." [76]

2. Walgarius father of Gervoldus, Episcopus Ebroicensis abbatis coenobii Fontanellensis, mentioned anno 787.[77]

3. Waldgarius, Episcopus Ferdensis, mentioned in Vita S. Anskarii, circa a. 848.[78]

4. Waltgarius "comes, nepos Odonis regis" mentioned in the " Regionis Chronicon," anno 892.[79]

5. Waltgarius Fresno, filius Guelfi, anno 898.[80]

1. Waldericus, Dux Francus, is mentioned by Fredegarius anno 636 :

Anno xiv, regni Dagoberti, cum Wascones fortiter rebellarent, et multas praedas in regno Francorum, quod Charibertus tenuerat, facerent, Dagobertus de universo regno Burgundiae exercitum promovera jubet, statuens eis caput exercitus, nomine Chadoindum, Referendarium, qui temporibus Theuderici quondam regis multis proeliis probatur strenuus : qui cum decem Ducibus cum exercitibus ; id est : Arimbertus, Amalgarius, Leudebertus, Wandalmarus, Waldericus, Ermenus, Barontus, Chairaadus, ex genere Francorum, Chramnelenus, ex genere Romano, Wilibadus Patricius ex genere Burgundionum, Aigyna ex genere Saxonum, exceptis comitibus plurimus, qui Ducem super se non habebant, in Wasconia cum exercitu perexissent, et tota Wasconiae patria ab exercitu Burgundiae fuisset repleta, Wascones de inter montium rupibus egressi ad bellum properant.[81]

2. Walaricus (Walericus), Dux Francus, anno 711.
"Anno dccxi Walaricus duxit exercitum Francorum in Suavis."[82]
" Quand Walaricus duxit exercitum Francorum in Suavis contra Vilaris." [83]

3. Walaricus (Gualaricus) Leuconaënsis abbas.[84]

4. Walaeruis, comes Burgundionum, mentioned as one of the signers of the compact with Gundebaldus, King of the Burgundians.[85]

From the occurrences of the name of Walther, here cited, it may be possible to arrive at some conclusion as to the origin and nationality of our hero who is to be discussed more at length toward the close of this treatise. The facts are collected here with the other material setting forth the historical elements of the Saga. It is not meant that all the occurrences of the appellation Walther, as presented, have a connection with that of our hero, but that this enumeration shall serve

76 Bouquet, iv, 714.   77 Pertz, ii, 291 ; Bouquet, v, 315 A.   78 Pertz, ii, 706, 707.
79 Pertz, i, 604.   80 Pertz, i, 608.   81 Clar. Codex, lxxviii.
82 ' Ex alliis Franc. Annal,' Bouquet, ii, 642, D.   83 Bouquet, ii, 644.
84 Ex Vita S. Walarici Abbatis Leuconaënsis ; Bouquet, iii, 496.   85 Bouquet, iv, 256.
86 Chron. cap. 78.

as a record of the designation in history, and thus furnish some indication as to where the name, or group of names, left the most lasting impress on the historical record.

Walther's Opponents. Of the eleven knights, or warriors of Guntharius, who meet Waltharius in single combat, we have but vague information. As W. Müller[87] has pointed out, there are seven who belong doubtless to Frankish or Frankish-Burgundian territory : Camelo of Metz (581); Kîmo, son of Camelo's brother, called also Scaramund (686) ; Hadawart of Worms (782, 831) ; Patavrid, son Hagen's sister (846) ; Gerwitus (or Gerwicus), formerly count "in Wormatiae campis"; Trogunt (or Trogus) of Strassburg (1009); Tanastus of Speier.

Attempts have been made to identify some of these warriors more closely. The name Camelo, is generally admitted to signify 'der Alte,' and its bearer was also called Ortwîn according to J. Grimm,[88] Müllenhoff[89] and Scheffel-Holder.[90] Thus Ortwîn, 'der Junge' of the Nibelungenlied, would correspond to Camelo's nephew Kîmo (=Keim, 'der Jung ' ?) San-Marte thinks that Kîmo's additional designation, Scaramund, points to other legendary accounts, and refers to the termination *-mund* in such names as Sigmund (who is a Frank in the Edda) and Faramund, the first Frankish King.[91] To Tanastus is assigned by San-Marte[92] a Frankish, or Celtic-Frankish origin, as is seen in Windegast, Wisogast, Arogast, Salegast. Some of the remaining names have been tentatively located : Ekevrid, the Saxon, refers according to W. Müller[93] to the war between the West Goths and Saxons in the time of Euric. This author bases his view upon the account of Sidonius Appolinaris (8, 6, 9), who reports that Euric, the West Goth, vanquished the Saxons, who had come in ships to Aquitania. Lachmann would assign Randolf and Helmnod (or Eleutherj to Worms. J. Grimm and W. Müller, with better reason, would identify Randolf with Randolf of Milan (vassal of Ermenrich, according to 'Biterolf') and Randolf of Ancona (one of the Berner's men, according to 'Dietrichs Flucht'); and Helmnod with Helmnot ("Helmnot von Tuscan,' cf. 'Alphart ') who, in the 'Nibelungenlied ' and in 'Alpharts Tod,' is a vassal of Dietrich. W. Müller concludes that they were Romans, or East Goths :

"Da nun beide durch ihre Herkunft nach Italien weisen, so darf man in ihnen Römer oder Ostgothen sehen, mit welchen beiden Völkern die Westgothen Kriege führten. Der 'contus ferratus' deutet bei Randolf auf die Ostgothen, der griechische name Eleuther ('Ελευθερος) bei Helmnod auf einen Angehörigen des römischen Reichs.[94]

W. Müller's[95] attempt to make the last warrior *Ewurhardus* a Hun is not so successful.

---

87 'Mythol., d. d. Hs.,' 24.   88 ' Lat. Ged.,' 116.   89 *Zs. f. d. A.*, vi, 440.
90 ' Waltharius,' 3,178; but cf. W. Müller, "Mythol. d. d. Hs.,' 24
91 San-Marte, ' Walther v. Aquitanien,' 40.   92 *Ibid.*, 40.   93 ' Mythol. d. d. Hs.,'24 ff.
94 ' Mythol. d. d. Hs.,' 25-6   95 *Ibid.*, 26.

2. RELATION OF THE VERSIONS.

The first step in determining the original form of the Saga, is to ascertain what elements, or episodes, are common to all the versions; or, if none are constant throughout all the texts, to find what episodes are most permanent. A glance at the analysis of the texts will show that certain incidents are uniform almost without exception, and others with but few variations. ⟨There are at least four episodes which recur consistently in all of the complete and most of the fragmentary versions of this Saga :⟩

1. The sojourn at a foreign court. Walther and Hildegunde are together at court outside of Walther's land. (W, N C, Nl, probably G F and V F, BD, Ths, BC, P, B, N, PC, Woj.)

2. The escape. Walther flees with Hildegunde [and takes treasure with him] (W, NC, Nl, VF, BD, Ths, BC, P, B, N. PC, Woj.) The taking of treasure is a natural accompaniment of such escape and doubtless belongs to this episode, though it is not equally emphasized in all the versions.

3. Pursuit and combat. Walther fights with his pursuers in single combat. (WF, W, NC, doubtless in Nl, VF, BD, Ths, BC. P, B, probably N and P, Woj.) In BD the combat is between Walther and Rüdigere because of the abduction of Hildegude ; but this is doubtless a reminiscence of the same motive as that of the combat with the Huns in the Ths and VF.

4. Triumphant return home. Walther, victorious over his pursuers, continues his journey homeward with Hildegunde (W, wanting in NC doubtless by accident, VF, Ths, BC, P, B, implied in N and PC, Woj.) The NC account seems to break off abruptly before reaching the return of Walther and Hildegund.

There is also another episode or group of episodes, which many of the versions contain in some form or other. This is the account of Walther's exploits after his return. (W, NC, implied in VF, BD, Ths, BC, Woj.)

The fact that these general outlines are so consistently preserved in the great majority of the texts, and are contradicted by nothing in the fragmentary accounts of the Saga, furnishes a strong presumption that these episodes, the first four at least, belong to the original form from which the extant versions developed. It is to be noted, however, that while the general sketch of the Saga remains essentially the same, the details of the separate incidents vary greatly in the versions ; for example, according to the first episode, the foreign court is

that of Attila in the Waltharius, Novalician Chronicle, Nibelungenlied, Vienna Fragment, Biterolf und Dietleib, Thidreksaga and, probably, in the Waldere and Graz Fragments, while in the Polish version it is the court of the king of the Franks. Again, the pursuit and
combat in the Waltharius take place at the hands of Gunther and his
men ; while in Thidreksaga it is Attila's men who pursue and attack
Walther ; and in the Polish version, the Prince of Alamannia. Thus,
in the German version of the Saga we have two combats mentioned;
one with the Huns, the other with the Franks* (Burgundians). The
question then arises whether one, or both, or neither, of these contests
belonged to the original form of the Saga. The account of the combat
with the Huns occurs in the Vienna Fragment, Biterolf und Dietleib
and the Thidreksaga ; while the contest with the Burgundians is mentioned in the Waldere, Waltharius, Novalicien Chronicle, Nibelungenlied, 'von dem übelen Wibe.' The fact that the notice of the
battle with the Burgundians is found in the Waldere and Waltharius,
shows that it had a place in the Saga as early as the ninth century.
If, however, we allow time for the development of the essential differences between the Waldere and the Waltharius and assume with
Symons,[96] that the Waldere is as early as the middle of the eighth
century, we may reasonably date the separation of the Waldere and
Waltharius forms at the beginning of the eighth century, If this be
correct, it precludes the possibility of the very late development of
the story of this combat. It is not improbable that the original form
of the Saga from which the Low German and Alemannic versions
(Waldere and Waltharius) developed, contained also the account of
the contest with the Huns. That there was a faint reminiscence of
such a struggle may possibly be inferred from the reference in Waltharius[97] to the vengeful rage of Attila, and his promise of rich
reward for Walther's capture. Whether the combat with the Huns is
"nur eine variation der ersten [der alemannischen gestalt] und gewis
fränkisches ursprungs" as Mullenhoff[98] maintains, or is the more
original, as Heinzel[99] thinks probable, is not yet clear. It seems
more likely that both combat-episodes developed about the same time
and were afterwards separated in the growth of the Saga. This
much, however, seems certain from the almost constant occurrence
of the battle incident in the versions, that the story of the combat was
contained in the original form from which the extant texts have developed. Thus, the primitive setting of the narrative consisted not
simply of an account of the escape home without notice of either
contest (' Flucht in die Heimat '), as Heinzel[100] supposes ; but of the
sojourn at a foreign court (that of Attila) ; the escape with the maiden
(Hildegunde) ; the pursuit and combat (with the Burgundians and,
possibly, with the Huns), and the triumphant return. The story of
the exploits of Walther after his return may have been added later to

---

96 Pauls 'Grundriss,' ii, 10.   97 v, 372 ff.   98 *Zeitschrift*, xii, 273.   99 ' Walthersage,' 62.
100 ' Walthersage,' 62.   *' Franci Nebulones ' in W.

these first four; but it must be remembered that these exploits, too, are implied, and in fact referred to, in the close of the Waltharius: [101]

> "Omnibus et carus post mortem obitumque parentis
> Ter denis populum rexit feliciter annis,
> Qualia bella dehinc vel quantos saepe triumphos
> Ceperit, ecce stilus renuit signare retusus."

Having determined approximately the essential episodes of the form of the Saga which constituted the original of the extant versions, it remains to follow the development of this germ and thus trace the relation of the various versions to this original form and to one another.

In order to fix a point of departure, it will be necessary, first, to ascertain which text is the oldest. The analysis given above has shown conclusively, that the Walther Saga is based upon unmistakable historical events and is to be regarded accordingly as a historical product. Hence we are justified in applying historical criteria in ascertaining the age of the versions of the Saga.

Waltharius.—Referring again to the analysis of contents, the following may be deduced as a third generalization in the series of conclusions arrived at above: [102]

Of all the versions, Waltharius represents most faithfully the historical events contained in the saga, and is, therefore, apparently the oldest.[103]

1. Alemannic Version. Attila, King of the Huns, pushes his conquests westward, and attacks the nations beyond the Rhine: Franks, Burgundians, Aquitanians. All of this is essentially historical as recorded by the early chroniclers.

2. Old Norse Version. Attila, King of the Huns with his residence at Susat (or Susa), forms a league with Ermanric. Anachronism and confounding of the persons and plans are apparent, whatever explanation be given of the Ermanric and Susat here mentioned;[104] such confusion indeed as we are accustomed to see in the epics of the thirteenth century.

3. Polish Version. Attila, Ermanric, the Burgundians and Aquitanians are all omitted; in their place appear Franks, Alemania (Arinaldus) and Polonia (Wyslaus and Rynga). Here we lose all the details of the historical setting of the Saga and have a new ethnic element (the Polish) to account for.

It is evident from this summary that only in the Latin poem, Waltharius, is a strictly consistent grouping of historical events and characters preserved: the sharp outlines of Attila's conquest of western Europe; the participation of Burgundians, Franks, and Aquitanians in the struggle with the Huns; the relation with the Burgundians and Franks; the ultimate victory over the Huns; the historical

---

101 V., 1449-52.   102 Page 155-6.   103 Cf. Müllenhoff, *Zeitschrift*, x, 163 ff.; xii, 274.
104 Cf. Holthausen, 'Soest in der Thiðrekssaga.' *PBB,* ix, 452 ff.

characters, Attila, Gibicho, Guntharius, Hagano (if we accept Heinzel's identification of Hagen with Aëtius); the unusually faithful representation of the geographical situation, as Attila's campaign westward beyond the Rhine; the position of Franks, Burgundians and Aquitanians; the localities west of the Rhine: Worms, Châlons, Metz.

So, too, the hero's career receives the most consistent treatment in the Latin poem. All the principle episodes of his activity are in keeping with the trend of actual events underlying the Saga. Nor is the hero called upon to play rôles which lie without the sphere of his skill as seems to be the case in the contest with Thetleifr in the Thidrekssaga. Moreover, in the Latin poem there is a clearer discrimination in the treatment of Saga cycles; a conspicuous absence of that indiscriminate jumble which permits Ermanric, Attila, and Theoderic of Verona, to appear as contemporaries in the Thidrekssaga. All these points combined, would lead us to look to the Latin poem as the clearest and earliest extant form of the Saga; and as an evidence of the great age, and excellent preservation of the original elements, which belong to the fifth century.[105]

Waldere.—The MS. of the Waldere Fragments dates from the ninth century, which gives this version of the Saga the appearance of a greater age than that which can be claimed for the Waltharius. The question then is: which is older, the Waldere or the Waltharius form of the Saga? If we now compare the Waldere with the corresponding episode of the Waltharius we shall find that, while there is essential agreement, there are important differences between them. The situation of the Waldere is apparently this: Walther returning with treasure from the Huns is attacked by Gunther (unjustly, because Walther has made generous terms of peace); one after another of Gunther's men has fallen in single combat with Walther; at length comes Hagen's turn to fight with Walther. Here we begin to encounter difficulties; two different points of view regarding the speaker in A, are presented. The one which has most general acceptance is, that Hildigunde addresses Walther.[106] If this be assumed, the speech would seem to have reference to the moment in the combat when Hagen has attacked Walther (W., 1287 ff.) and shivered the latter's sword (W., 1374-5); whereupon Hildigunde inspires Walther with fresh courage, reminding him that the choicest of gifts lent him for his and her aid yet remains, referring probably to the sword which Gunther had refused.

According to the other view of the situation as represented by Heinzel, the speaker is a companion warrior of Walther and not Hildigunde, since the references in the speech to Walther's former combats do not fittingly come from a women. If the speaker is not

105 Cf. Heinzel, ' Walthersage,' S. 62 ff.
106 Haigh, ' The Anglo-Saxon Sagas,' 130; Scheffel-Holder, ' Waltharius,' 171; Fischer, Zu den Waldere-Fragmenten,' 13.

Hildegunde, there would seem to be but one probable alternative, as Heinzel [107] believes; namely, it is Hagen who speaks. If this be assumed, the references to the virtue of Mimming, Weland's work, to Walther's valor in the sword-play, to Walther as *wine min*, would be quite in place; the words *gifede to eoce unc* (A 25) would refer possibly to the sword given when Walther and Hagen were knighted by Etzel (BD, 770-71); the situation would represent the moment when Hagen has utterly refused to fight with Walther and given him the Sword Mimming, leaving him and Gunther to end the combat. This explanation would preclude the necessity of reconciling the references and courageous words in A with Hildegunde's timidity which is so prominent in the Waltharius. This explanation would make Hagen remain true to his old companion as the latter evidently had expected him to do (W, 1239 ff.). The passage contains real difficulties, but such as are of minor importance, and the general agreement in situation between WF. and W. is placed beyond question. In any case Stephens' order of the Fragments must be retained.

The Waldere Fragments contain, however, besides these variations of motive mentioned above, some references not found in the Waltharius: Gunther is called "wine Burgenda" (B. 14) not king of the Franks, as in W.; and reference is made to Theoderic or Deodric (B. 4), which shows a connection at this early period between the Saga of Walther and that of Theoderic; while in W. no trace exists of any such connection. This reference to Gunther as friend or lord of the Burgundians accords more closely with history and would seem to indicate a clearer, and hence earlier, conception of Gunther. The same point of view is found in Widsið, who represents Gifica as ruling the Burgends. With this conception of Gunther as a Burgundian, it is not easy to locate Hildegunde. We are left to conjecture, that she may have represented some province of Gothic or Frankish Gaul.[108]

If we now turn to the Waltharius, we shall find that there is already clear recognition of the Saga of Weland in the reference to Waltharius' coat of mail as "Welandia fabrica" (965), which is a parallel to "Welandes geworc" in Waldere (A, 2). The question here is twofold: was the original given to Ekkehard I. by his master Geraldus,[109] a different version from that of the Waldere; or, did Ekkehard I. and his successors change their original by adapting it to Frankish conditions of a later time (tenth century [110])? The following seems to be the most likely: The original of Ekkehard I. was an alliterative poem in German speech. The arguments for this are:—

1. Traces of such alliteration in the Latin Waltharius. Jacob Grimm [111] suggested such traces by translating the Latin back into German; as, for example, *Waltharius vocor ex Aquitanus sum generatus* (597)=*Walthari fona Wascôm*; *Hagano spinosus*=*Hagano*

107 'Walther Saga,' S. 11.   108 Cf. *infra*.   109 Scheffel-Holder, 'Waltharius,' 130.
110 Heinzel, 'Walther Saga,' 23-24.   111 'Lat. Gedichte d. x u. xi Jh.,' 99 ff.

*H*agan*î*n, and others. Since Grimm's time, this view has gained ground. The results of Schweitzer [112] fortify afresh this theory by the addition of other examples ; as, for example, *Caput attolens scrutatur* ⟨535⟩=*H*ebet das *h*aupt und *h*orcht ; *Absit quod rogitas mentis depone pauorem* (551)=*F*erne sei . . . . *f*orderest . . . . *f*orcht. So, too, verses which correspond to lines in the Waldere and Nibelungenlied :

*S*vâtf.·g and *s*veordvund *s*ecg äfter ôdhrum=
Cruentus et laesus vir alter post alterum (cecidit).

*L*if for*l*e·'san odhdhe *l*ange dôm . . . .
Vitam linquere vel longam gloriam . . . .

Das *l*iebe mit *l*eide ze jungiste *l*one
Amoris dolorem novissimam mercedem esse;

2. The actual existence of such alliterative fragment of the Saga as preserved in the Waldere ;
3. The survival of the Saga in the heroic form of the M. H. G. epic ; as, in the Graz and Vienna Fragments ;
4. The indirect evidence derived from the association of this Saga with other M. H. G. epics.

It seems probable that Ekkehard I. chose for his Latin poem the central episodes of his original (chief among which was the combat), and omitted such as did not harmonize with his conception of epic treatment. This is clearly indicated at the close of the poem ; for example, where he sums up all of Walther's subsequent exploits of thirty years in half a dozen verses. In like manner, he may have omitted such references to the Theoderic and Weland Sagas as the Waldere contains. But that he essentially changed, or invented, episodes is the less likely as his main purpose seems to have been skillful translation into epic form rather than literary creation. That he should clothe the Saga with the classical adornment of Virgil or Prudentius as Peiper [113] has shown, and give it the coloring of Monastic life of his time, as Geyder [114] has presented, and invest it with the geographical and historical setting of a later period, is what we should naturally expect. But when due allowance has been made for such accretions and modifications, we shall have left what may be regarded as the essential kernel of the original German version of the Saga. This original was probably the Upper German (Alemannic) form, while the Waldere represents the Low German (Saxon ?) form. Heinzel's [115] objection that the primitive type of the 'Waltharius' cannot be of Alemannic origin because the poet represents Attila as passing the Araris and Rhodanus on his way from Worms to Châlons is, as the critic himself admits, only one evidence of the author's unfamiliarity with the geography of the region. Thus, we have in the 'Waltharius' a tenth century adaptation of an original German version, either contemporary with that of the Waldere, or slightly later.

---

112 ' De Poemate Latino Walthario,' p. 50.
113 ' Ekkehardi Primi, Waltharius,' p. 80; W. Meyer, MSB (1873) 385 ff.
114 *Zeitschrift*, 9, 145 ff.   115 ' Walthersage,' 25.

2. LATER VERSIONS OF THE SAGA.

The *Novalician Chronicle* in Lib. ii, written before 1027,[116] represents the form of the Saga as found in the Waltharius, but connects it with the life, or local tradition, of an old warrior who entered the cloister in Novalese. The first part of the Novalician account follows closely the St. Gall version, which had migrated thither evidently through monastic intercourse. The career of Walther in the cloister of Novalese has a parallel in the Legend of St. William, or in the *Chanson de Geste* of 'Guillaume au court nez.' The latter was like Walther an Aquitanian and, like him, abducted a princess from a heathen land. Heinzel[117] suggests, that the germ of the account of the monks Walther and William, is possibly to be found in the life of King, or Duke, Hunwald of Aquitaine the son of Eudo, Waifhari's father, and King Pippin's opponent, who abdicated in the year 745 in favor of Waifhari and entered a cloister; but, after the death of his son, left the cloister, as an old man, and renewed his opposition to Pippin; and finally fled to Italy and fought on the side of Desiderius againts Charles the Great. This and other similar legends may have given color and even episodes to the account of Waltharius, the Monk; but we doubtless have in the second part of the Novalician Saga the local tradition of a monk Waltharius whose early life was that of a warrior, and which local tradition was associated later by the Novalician Chronicler with the account of Waltharius *manu fortis*,[118] of the St. Gall version. It is not impossible, too, that we have in the Novalician Walther echoes, or associations, of the Lombard King Walthari; or even of a Lombard variation of the Walther Saga. If such be the case, it would explain the chronicler's presumably unjustifiable[119] excerpts from the Waltharius. We have already referred to the possible, even probable, connection of the names Alpharius and Waltharius with the Lombard Walthari.

Graz and Vienna Fragments.—In these two M. H. G. Fragments, we have doubtless, the remains of a M.H.G. Epic of Walther and Hildegunde. The situation in GF, according to Heinzel's order of the leaves (which is evidently the correct one), is this : Hagen, having taken leave of Etzel and his Queen, distributes gifts to the Huns, and overhears Hildegunde making complaint to Walther, who is on the point of leaving her, and declaring her willingness to follow him.

---

116 Cf. Peiper, 'Ek. Prim. Walth.,' xliv, et. seq. 117 'Walthersage,' 26–7.
118 'Casus St. Galli,' Cap. 9 (*Mon. Germ*, ii, 117.) 119 Heinzel, 'Walthersaga,' 27 ;
Anz. f. d. A., xi, 67 ff.

Hagen interrupts the conversation and counsels Walther to marry her, saying that he (Hagen) was present when they two were betrothed. Whereupon Walther, sorry that Hildegunde has so long been without his attentions, assures her of his fidelity.

The narrative in VF, is as follows: Walther and Hildegunde are returning from the Huns, and come to Gunther's land (situated along the Rhine, with Worms, presumably, as capital), where they are received by Volker. The latter has come with sixty of his thanes from the Rhine, probably after the hostile encounter and the reconciliation with Gunther mentioned in W (though nothing is said of such encounter in the Fragment), to conduct them through the *Wasechen Walt* to Lengers; thither messengers are already sent in advance to announce Walther's arrival to Alker, his father. As they approach the city, they are welcomed by Alker and his retinue, whereupon preparations are made for the wedding of Walther and Hildegunde.

I cannot agree with Heinzel [120] that 1, 13 is a superfluous interpolation in the poem. The reference is clearly to the combat with the Huns, which is mentioned in the Thidrekssaga. Indeed, the correctness of the situation is clearly shown by Walther's hesitation (2, 16) to invite Etzel and Helche to the wedding feast. In the invitation to Etzel and Helche we may find an echo of the reconciliation between Attila and Ermanric, after the combat (Ths 244); and in the escort of Volker, that between Gunther (and Hagen) and Walther at the Wasgenstein (W, 1405 ff.).

Thus we have in the fragments, episodes of the earlier and later parts of the epic: in GF, preliminaries to the flight from the Huns; in VF, the return through Gunther's land to Lengers, and the reception by Alphere and Hilde preparatory to Walther's wedding and coronation. Thus, I would be inclined to regard these Fragments as parts of one and the same M. H. G. poem. The only argument against this is the apparent difference in strophic structure. The strophic forms, however, of these two Fragments have so close a resemblance to one another that the strophes of the separate poems differ scarcely more than single strophes in each fragment, hence they might belong to the same epic. Indeed, we have here what would seem to be a transition strophic form between that of the Nibelungenlied and that of the Gudrun, characterized by the cæsural and final rhyme of the former, and the closing long line of the latter. If the entire poem had been preserved, we should have found in it, perhaps, a third strophic form of the popular epic. It is likely that we have here the disconnected remnants of the great German epic of Walther, or Walther un l Hildegunde, which is so familiarly referred to in 'Walther von der Vogelweide,' 'Nibelungenlied,' 'Biterolf und Dietleib,' and other epics of the 'Heldenbuch.'

If we now look for the relation to WF, and W of the form of the Walther Saga preserved in this original M. H. G. poem, we shall find

---

120 'Walthersage,' 17.

that the ethnical situation agrees essentially with that of WF. In VF, Gunther is called "vogt von Rine" (1, 19), and his land is "der Burgönde lant," as in WF, B 14, he is called "wine Burgenda," while in W he is "King of the Franks." Thus, VF corresponds in situation to Nl, BD, DF, and Rs, and belongs, doubtless, to the older form of the Saga. It is scarcely probable that the M. H. G. poem descended directly from the form of the Saga as contained in the Waltharius. The former would rather seem to be a more direct successor of the original popular form of the Saga, of which the Waldere poem was the Low German (Saxon) version.

Thidrekssaga.—The Old Norse Thidrekssaga belongs, doubtless, to the first half of the thirteenth century, to the reign of King Haakon Haakonson. The language and style clearly indicate that it cannot be later than this period.[121] From the mode of treatment and order of the tales, it is evident that the Old Norse narrator drew from different versions of the Saga. No particular written form is mentioned as the source of the Old Norse version, but it appears from the prologue, which has been regarded as the work of the author of the Old Norse recension,[122] that at least two different sources furnished material for the saga :

1. Sagas or accounts of German men ;
2. Old poems, or songs ;

both of which sources are mentioned in the prologue as follows :[123]

"Thessi saga er samansett eptir sogn þyðeskra manna, en sumt af þeirra kvæðum er skemta skal rikum monnum ok fornort voru þegar eptir tiðindum sem segir i þessari sogu. Ok þo at þu takir einn mann or hverri borg um allt Saxland. Tha munu þessa sogu allir a eina leið segia. en þui vallda þeirra hin fornu kvæði."

This period represents the high-water mark of saga telling. As another passage from the prologue indicates, the fame of this Saga traversed almost all the lands of Europe :

"Saga þessi hefzt ut a Pul ok ferr norðr um Lungbardi ok Fenidi. i Svava. i Ungaria. i Pulina land. i Ruzia. i Vindland. i Danmork ok Sviþiod. um allt Saxoniam ok Frakland ok vestr um Valland. ok Hispaniam."

The Thidrekssaga contains some peculiar and striking divergences : Walther is the son of Ermanric's sister, and not of Alphere, as in WF, W, VF. Hildegunde is the daughter of Iarl Ilias of Greece. Ermanric, Attila and Theoderic are regarded as contemporaries. All this harmonizes in the main with the anachronisms of the German Theoderic epics of the thirteenth century.

If we now look for the relation of the Thidrekssaga to the Waldere, we shall find a possible connection in the references to the Weland and Theoderic stories. The probable relation may be stated somewhat as follows : the Low German version, the Saxon form of which is found

---

121 Unger, p. iv ; Müller, *Sagabibliothek*, ii, 276 ff., places it in the fourteenth century.
122 Müller, *Sagabibl.* ii, 278.   123 Unger, p. 2.

in the Waldere, connected the sagas of Walther, Weland, and Theoderic, and lived on in the German songs referred to in the prologue of the Thidrekssaga. In the thirteenth century, particularly from the time of Haakon Haakonson forward, the intercourse between Scandinavia and Southern Europe resulted in a new importation of German sagas to the north. On the other hand, the intercourse with Novgorod, through the commerce of the Hanseatic League, brought the north of Europe into touch with Russia and Byzantium. Hence we find, as might be expected, in the Thidrekssaga, a thirteenth century fusion of all these sources into the prose narrative of Theoderic. The Old Swedish version is evidently very closely related to the Old Norse Thidrekssaga. According to Hyltén-Cavallius,[124] it is an abbreviated translation of the Old Norse text or MS. ("en förkortad öfversättning af den fornnorska sagan, märkligt nog, utarbetad effer just samma skinbok") worked out between 1449 and 1476, probably soon after the former date.

Polish Versions.—The so-called Chronicle of Boguphal, or Great Polish Chronicle as it has been called since Warmski, has been found by the researches of Warmski [125] and Kętrzyński [126] to be a compilation of the fourteenth century. For the earlier periods, this compilation drew from Vincentius Kadlubek, or sources derived from him ; and for the period between 1217 and 1272, from the Great Polish Annals; in the composition of which Boguphal, Bishop of Posen (d. 1253), seems to have had a smaller share than Godyslaw Baszko, the *Custos* of Posen, who lived till the end of the thirteenth century. Though Vincentius served as a source of chapter twenty-nine of the Chronicle, it must be remembered that the section of this chapter containing the Walther saga is one of a large number of accounts for which no source has as yet been agreed upon. There is some probability that the account of Walther and Hildegunde was interpolated at a later period, as it is related with events of the twelfth century, and not with the legendary accounts of the early heathen period,[127] to which the chronicle refers this saga. Heinzel [128] is, perhaps, not far from the truth in supposing that the chronicler drew, in part at least, from oral sources—a prose tradition, or even a lay after the order of the Danish "Kæmpeviser."

But when we examine the later Polish accounts of Walther and Hildegunde, we find reference to other sources. Paprocki mentions as his authorities an Anonymus (thought by Semkovicz,[129] to be the same as the Great Polish Chronicle, but considered by Heinzel, with better reasons, to be one of the originals of the Chronicle) and Andreas of Zarnow, to whom are to be ascribed variations found in

124 'Didrik af Bern,' p. iv; Ungér, 'Saga Thidriks Konungs af Bern,' p. viii.
125 ' Die Grosspolnische Chronik.' Krakau, 1879.
126 *Przewodnik Naukowy i Literacki*, 1880, 269-280; 1882, 863.
127 Cf. Röpell, 'Geschichte Polens,' i, 51 ff.   128 'Walthersaga,' 36
129 Cf. Antóniewicz, *Anz. f. d. A.*, iv, 111.

Paprocki, but not in the Chronicle; such, for example, as the name
Arinaldus for Walther's rival; and Rynga for Wislaw's sister; and
Wislimier for Wislaw; and other matters of detail.[130]

Bielski, in the first part of his account, may have made use of either
Paprocki or the Chronicle; but in the second part he agrees with the
Chronicle rather than with Paprocki, particularly in mentioning
Wislaw as Prince of Wislica, and in the details of the encounter with
Wislaw. Another item of Bielski's account, that Walther and Hildegunde take treasure with them, would seem to indicate a third source
connecting Bielski's account more directly with the Waltharius
version. The further touches peculiar to Bielski; as, the unwillingness
of the Frankish King to allow Walther to have Hildegunde because
he was a foreigner, could find a ready explanation in the animosity
existing between Poles and Germans. Niesiecki, Wójcicki, and the
later Polish chroniclers, drew their materials doubtless, from the Great
Polish Chronicle, Paprocki, and Bielski.

A comparison of the Polish with the German versions shows:

1. That the general outlines of the Saga are preserved in the Polish,
though the episodes and ethnical grouping are materially changed;

2. That the Polish version is a fusion of two evidently heterogeneous
parts, a foreign, and a native; the first containing episodes of the
Walther Saga; the second, a union of this Saga with that of Wislaw,
or (as Paprocki, and presumably, Andreas of Zarnow, have it) of
Wislimier;

3. That Walther combats against one foe, not many (twelve), as in
W, Ths.

That the Polish form of the Saga connot have been derived from
Ekkehard's Waltharius, is evident from the fact that most of the
characteristic details of the St. Gall version are wanting in the
Polish.[131] How, then, did the original, or originals, of the Polish
versions come to Tyniec? Passing over Rischka's argument for the
existence of the Saga in Poland before the *Folkwandering* as untena-
ble (see below), we find no evidence that the Saga migrated to Poland
before the second half of the tenth century (962) when Poland, under
Prince Misaca, or Mscislaw, became tributary to the German Emperor,
Otto I. Mscislaw married Dubrawka, the Christian daughter of
Boleslaw I; and in 966 accepted Christianity, thus bringing Poland
under Christian influence. Otto I. encouraged all efforts to missionize
among the Poles. Thus the German sagas may have found their way
to Poland in the time of Mscislaw, "the first historical Piast, the actual
founder of Poland."[132]

As to the founding of the Monastary at Tyniec there are two views:
Dlugosz states that it was founded in 1044 by Kazimierz, who,
according to tradition had been a monk at Clugny before he came to

---
130 Cf. Heinzel, 'Walthersage.' 42–3.   131 Rischka, 22 ff.
132 Schiemann (Onken), 'Gesch. Polens,' 390.

power, and established in the Monastery at Tyniec some Bendictine Monks from Clugny, placing over them as abbot a certain Frenchman, called Aaron. Röpell[133] claims, however, that the Monastery at Tyniec was founded earlier, by Boleslaw the Great. Here is possibly a second avenue, leading directly from France, by which German sagas may have reached Poland in the tenth century, a generation after Ekkehard wrote his Waltharius. The term *Wdaly* applied in the Polish version to Walther, has been shown to be Russian.[134] This would suggest a migration of the Saga *via* Novgorod.[135] Nehring explains the transference of the Saga to Poland from chap. 241 of the Thidrekssaga as due to the confusion of Púl, Púli (Apulia), with Pulle (Poland). Thus he finds in the Polish version a combination of Walther's relationship to Ermanric, as in the Thidrekssaga, with the crossing of the Rhine, as in Waltharius. Of the parallel between the song of Walterus and of Horand in Gudrun, too much, perhaps, has already been made. It is at best an incidental touch in the saga.

To sum up, then: the Walther Saga may have come into Poland through Hanseatic intercourse between Germany and Novgorod, and from Germany or France, directly, through German intercourse with Poland. The form of the Saga thus introduced may have combined elements found in the original of Ekkehard's Waltharius, and in one or more of the originals of the Thidrekssaga, and may have had a separate existence in Poland until it was at length united with the saga of Wyslaus (or perhaps in another form with Wislimierz), and finally localized at Tyniec. The immediate occasion of this localization may have been, as Nehring and Heinzel think, the epitaph of a certain Helgunda, which was seen there by Andreas of Zarnow, as late at 1242. This, however, does not necessarily preclude the earlier existence of the Polish saga in this region, as Heinzel and Knoop maintain. Indeed, it seems not improbable that in the second part of the Polish saga, we have traces of the version found in the Middle High German poem ' Von dem übelen Wibe.' This would furnish the reason, in the two parts of the Polish version, for an earlier connection, than Knoop[136] is inclined to admit when he refers the Polish saga to the period of the Polish reaction against the Germans in the fourteenth and fifteenth centuries.

Wislaw, of the Polish saga, has been correctly identified with Wizlan of Greece (Russia), in Dietrichs Flucht;[137] with Wizlan King of Bohemia, in Biterolf;[138] and Wenezlan King of Poland, in Dietrich and Wenezlan.[139]

133 'Gesch. Polens,' i, 639 ff.
134 Cf. Karlowicz and Nehring, *Atheneum*, 1881, 233; 1883, 393.
135 Cf. Müllenhoff, *Zs. f. d. A.*, xii, 344.   136 ' Die deutsche Walthersage,' etc., 12 ff.
137 Heinzel, ' Walthersage,' 91.   138 Nehring, *Atheneum*, 1883, 360.
139 Zupitza, ' D. Heldenbuch,' 5, liv.

3. WALTHER OF AQUITAINE.

Before attempting any interpretation of Walther, it may be well to review briefly previous attempts in this direction.

Mythical interpretation of Walther.—At the outset, let us clear away the mists which have collected around the Saga by the work of Rischka and Rydberg. Rischka's [140] argument that the Polish saga of Walther is the primitive form, developed from the German myth found in the sagas of Odhur and of Hothar and Baldur—Waldgierz being Odin, and Hildegunde, Freyja—rests upon the following assumptions:

1. That the Heroic Saga is developed out of a myth or divinity ("und so entsteht aus einer Göttergestalt eine Heldensage," S. 32. Here he follows Simrock);

2. That coincidence of episodes is a sufficient criterion of identification of mythical and heroic characters;

3. That the *Folkwandering* was the occasion of the migration of this saga to the most widely separated regions;

4. That the Polish form of the Saga was probably developed among a part of some Germanic people remaining in the territory afterwards occupied by the Slavs (Poles), and having united with Slavic elements, was localized.

The futility of Rischka's attempt as regards both method and matter, has been demonstrated by Bugge [141] and by Heinzel. [142] This might seem in itself sufficient refutation of Rischka's argument. But this method of saga-treatment, which confuses heroic saga with myth, and brings all saga material into an interminable jumble with remote mythical cycles, is so serious in its results, that it must be summarily disposed of at the outset. The following considerations may serve to show the weakness of Rischka's treatment: unproved assumptions, as we have seen above, form the basis of the argument. Rischka magnifies unduly the pre-migratory German element surviving on Polish soil, and ignores the more important subsequent German influences from the end of the tenth century forward. The disparity between the first and second parts of the Polish saga, he fails sufficiently to recognize. The most characteristic features of the saga found in the German versions are wanting in the Polish. The spirit and character of the Baldur and Necklace myths are too far removed from the Walther Saga. The supposable similarity between

140 Rischka, 34 ff.   141 'Stud. ü. d. Entst. d. Nord. Götter- und Heldensagen,' 176.
142 'Walthersaga,' 97 ff.

the Saga of Walther, and that of Hotherus rests upon a misunderstanding of the name Mimming.[143] Much that has been said against Rischka's method applies with equal weight to Rydberg's [144] mythical interpretation, which makes Walther represent Ivaldi in Grimnismal and Snorra Edda, with the following coincidences: the names Walther and Ivaldi; Walther's skill as a spearman; the abduction of Hildegunde; the combat with Gunther. This interpretation, like that of Rischka, rests upon the assumption that the Heroic saga developes out of myth; or, as Heinzel [145] puts it:

"auf der meiner Meinung nach unbeweisbaren und nach aller Erfahrung höchst unwahrscheinlichen Voraussetzung, dass es in weit entfernten Urzeiten ein festes System germanischer Mythologie oder eigentlich Theologie gegeben habe, in der es keine Analogiewirkungen in den Vorstellungen, keine Unklarheiten und Widersprüche gegeben habe."

Apart from Heinzel's refutation of Rydberg's argument, suffice it to say that the fact that two Northern myths furnish sufficient coincidences for the basis of such superficial identifications is in itself a strong argument against both Rischka and Rydberg.

Müllenhoff's interpretation of the Saga of Walther as a recasting of the mythical Saga of Hilde('Zs. f. d. A.' 12, 274; 30, 235 ff.) rests upon accidental coincidences, and has in reality no real claim upon our consideration here. Heinzel (Walthersage 93) has demonstrated the weakness of the argument by showing that these coincidences are to be explained by the influence of a mythical upon a historical Saga.

Historical Identification.—Fortunately, the tendency now toward the historical method of saga-treatment is gaining ground. All the more prominent interpretations of the Walther Saga have rested, more or less firmly, upon a historical basis. The eyes of most investigators have turned toward Aquitaine for the home of Walther. The most trustworthy traces of the Saga certainly point toward the West or South, not toward the East or North. Fauriel's [146] view that Walther was a Gallo-Roman, was opposed by Geyder [147] on the ground that the Germans would not likely have celebrated a hostile hero, which Walther must have been, if he had been a Gallo-Roman. Müllenhoff's [148] modification of Fauriel's view—that Walther was originally the ruler of Gaul in the epic age—is, if anything, less definite than Fauriel's original explanation. It might be objected to both of these views, that none of the versions of the Saga make any specific reference to Gallo-Roman, or Gallic, personages or events as having importance in the issues treated in the Saga.

---

143 Bugge, *ibid.*, 176.   144 'Undersökningar i germanisk mythologi,' i, 742 ff.
145 'Walthersaga,' 100.   146 'Histoire de la Poésie Provençale,' i, 408.
147 *Zs. f. d. A.* ix, 145, 153.   148 *Zs. f. d. A.* x, 163 ff; xii, 274.

Scherer's [149] attempt to identify Walther with Aëtius, seems to have been suggested by Fauriel. In the light which Heinzel has thrown upon the subject by his attempted identification of Hagen with Aëtius, Scherer's view must fall, whether Heinzel's Hagen-Aëtius theory be accepted or not.

The view that Walther was a West Goth has found strong defenders. J. Grimm [150] expressed this as follows :

"Walthere muss als ein ursprünglich westgothischer held betrachtet werden, der sich von burgundischen und fränkischen unterscheidet."

This view has been further supported more recently by W. Müller [151] who differs from Scherer and Heinzel, however, in that he does not see in Walther "nur enstellte Geschichte," but rather an ideal figure "da Walther keine nachgewiesene historische Person, sondern nur eine ideelle Figur ist." The supreme objection to this view is, that the German heroic saga is intensely real in its origins, as the historical element of the Saga has shown. The ideal figures are a later invention of an idealizing age.

Heinzel's [152] view of the shifting nationality of Walther in the development of the Saga is expressed thus :

"Vielleicht galt Walther bis zum 7. Jahrhundert, wo die Basken, aus Spanien kommend, in einem Theil von Aquitanien Fuss fassten und ein *Wascôno lant* bekannt wurde, noch für einen Boisken,—dann als durch das Auftreten der Basken in Frankreich dieses Volk dem deutschen Gesichtskreis näher rückte, für einen solchen. . . . Später galt er ebenso für einen alten französisch-burgundischen König in Langres, wo allerdings die burgundischen Könige und Herzoge ebensowenig residirten als die merovingischen. . . . Die Auffassung Walthers als eines Burgunden ist wohl durch seine Verbindung mit Hildegund veranlasst, wenn diese erst als Urugundin, dann nach 451 als Burgundin galt."

We have seen in the course of the discussion that there were probably two well-defined versions of the Walther Saga as early as the eighth century ; hence we are to look for the date of the origin of the saga at a still earlier period. A fully developed literary form, such as that actually found in the Waldere, and implied in the original of the Waltharius, presupposes a considerable period of growth. Allowing time for such growth, we may safely assume that the saga originated between the middle of the fifth and the end of the seventh century. If we turn to the Waltharius, which, as was shown above, has preserved the saga in its clearest historical outlines, we find that the essential elements belong to the second half of the fifth century, and hence point to this period as the time in which the Saga originated. Thus the earliest form of the Saga belonged to the end of the fifth, or beginning of the sixth century. The fact that the Waltharius, so faithful in its general historical outlines, calls Walther an Aquitanian, draws our attention to Aquitania as his native land.

149 Mittheilungen des Vogesenclubs, 1874, N. 2.
150 *Zs.f. d. A.* v, 3. Cf. also 'Lat. Ged. d. x. xi. Jhs.' 121, 125.
151 'Dietrichsage,' 172; 'Mythol. d. deutsch. Heldensage,' 11 ff. ; 'Zur Mythol. d. griech. u. deutsch. Heldensage,' 124 ff.   152 'Walthersage,' 71-2.

Let us trace, then, the conception of Aquitania during this early period.

Aquitania[153] of Cæsar's time, Aquitania Propria, or Novempopulana (of Diocletian's provincial division), occupied the country between the Atlantic, the Garonne, and the Pyrenees, and extended eastward nearly to Tolosa. Aquitania north of the Garonne, in Diocletian's time, extended northward and eastward nearly to the Liger, and southward almost to the Tarnis, and was divided by Diocletian into two provinces: Aquitania I, in the east, and Aquitania II, in the west. The West Goths, having pushed their way from Rome to Aquitania Propria (Burdigala), about 413, occupied, from 419 to 475, the three Aquitanias mentioned above, extending their domain eastward to the borders of Burgundia. Thus Aquitania and Burgundia were border provinces or kingdoms at the time of Attila's campaign to the West (451), and Aquitania Propria of earlier times was now Novempopulana; while Vasconia lay between Novempopulana and the Iberus, with Pampilona as its chief city. In 507 West Gothic Aquitania (I and II) came by the defeat of Alaric II, into the hands of the Franks under Chlodovech. At the death of Theoderic (526) Burgundia was fast coming under Frankish control, and after 534 was a part of the Frankish realm. At the death of Justinian (565), Burgundia formed the western border of the Lombard kingdom in Italy, and extended to the Mediterranean. Thus, we see that the general historical conception of Aquitania from the second quarter of the fifth century through the Merovingian and Carlovingian periods, was that of a province (country, hence, kingdom) lying immediately west of Burgundia. Such, too, is the conception in Waltharius, the earliest complete, and historically most faithful, full extant version of the saga.

The popular tradition of Walther, as transmitted by the epics, is, that he was of Germanic origin, and there seems to be no reason for questioning this belief. If he was of Germanic descent, and an Aquitanian, to what Germanic nationality did he belong? As an Aquitanian, he would have belonged, *politically*, to the West Goths before 507, and after that date to the Franks, if he was from Aquitania north of the Garonne; but, if he was from Aquitania Propria, to the West Goths until Chlothar II, who united this province to the Frankish realm. This does not mean that Walther must have been of West Gothic origin; indeed, he may just as likely have been a representative of some other Germanic race which passed into, or through, Aquitania at this period. This much may be claimed, however: *that Walther, in the oldest form of the saga, was a Germanic-Aquitanian under West Gothic supremacy.* The conception of Aquitania as a kingdom, does not, even in this early period, interfere with this point of view, inasmuch as the idea of kingship was one of

---

153 Cf. Droysen, ' Historischer Atlas.'

shifting significance, and the West Gothic rule a general territorial supremacy. That Alphere's kingdom, at this early period, was included, or even centered, in Aquitania Propria is quite possible; but the general notion of Aquitania extended over the province north of the Garonne, as we have seen. The designation of Alphere's realm as " Regna Aquitanorum," in the Waltharius (v. 77), evidently applies to Aquitania in the larger sense, and not to Aquitania Propria alone.

Whether Walther, in the earliest form of the Saga, had the same political importance as that given to him in the Waltharius, we have no means of determining ; it is natural to surmise that he had. Neither can we say with certainty whether he was a West Goth or belonged to some Germanic people closely allied with the Burgundians. That he was a Boisk, as Heinzel maintains, seems an unfounded hypothesis. It would be more reasonable to connect him with some branch related to the Lombard line whose king, Walthari, bears the same name a generation later. This would give us another link in the chain of evidence for the existence of the Lombard saga of Walthari and Alphari. The name Alpher occurs in Rabenschlact, 265-267, where Alpher is sent by Friederich of Ravenna as messenger to Dietrich of Bern. But perhaps it is enough to have ascertained the political relations of Walther at the time of the origin of the saga. It will now be in order to review, briefly, the different conceptions of Walther.

Walther as a Wascon.—The conception of Walther as a Wascon, an epithet which may have been applied to him in the original of the Waltharius, cannot be earlier than the seventh century, when the Wascons broke forth from their mountain retreat in ancient Wasconia, in Spain, into Aquitania Propria and formed what the Geographer of Ravenna [154] calls "Wasconum patria, quae antiquitus Aquitania dicebatur." The establishment of these mountaineers in Aquitania Propria was practically completed by 626 A. D.,[155] though the troubles between the Wascons and the Aquitanians continued till a much later period. Thus there is no reason for regarding Walther as a Wascon, except in so far that all Aquitanians were regarded as Wascons after their country had come to bear the name of the latter.

Walther as the son of Alphere (King of the Aquitanians). Turning to the versions of the Saga, we find three of them calling Walther the son of Alphere,—WF, W, NC ; this title still distinguishes him in the M. H. G. Versions,—VF, BD, and presumably GF. Here we have, doubtless, the early conception of our hero as an Aquitanian, and a distinct reminiscence of his royal line. But with the M. H. G. versions other titles appear.

Walther of Spain.—The conception of Walther as " von Spâne," " von Spanjelant," is preserved in Nl, VF, BD. This idea of Walther

154 Cf. Heinzel, ' Walthersaga,' 70.
155 Perroud, ' Des Orig. du prem. Duché d'Aquitaine,' 21 ff.

grew up, doubtless, after the establishment of the Spanish Mark by Charles the Great, 801. The confusion of Spain with the Spanish Mark, is one that could easily be made by the popular mind. It is to be noted, too, that he is called both 'der künec von Spanjelant' (BD, 576) and 'der vogt von Spanyge' (VF, 1, 10, 1); thus preserving reminiscences of his early rank as 'Künec' brought out in the Waltharius.

Walther of Kerlingen.—Walther is designated by the title 'von Kerlingen' in BD, AT, 'geborn von Kerlinc' RF1, and DF. This conception developed, doubtless, in the time of the Carlovingians and was perfectly consistent with that of Walther as 'von Spâne,' when the latter was regarded as identical with the Spanish Mark. But just here there seems to have come in a serious confusion; for in BD Walther is called 'Alpkêres Kint,' 'Künec von Spanjelant,' and 'der von Kärlingen,' but resides at Paris (see Analysis). It is plain that the hero's royal titles were all before the BD poet and that to him Kärlingen meant France, whose capital was Paris. Thus the confusion of Spain, a part of Kerlingen, with the whole Frankish realm is easy and natural.

Walther of Lengers.—It is worthy of note that the designation of Walther as 'von Lengers' and 'der Lengesaere,' occurs only in VF, DF and Rs respectively. Heinzel [156] suggests two possible explanations of the choice of Lengers as Walther's residence: it may have been due to the fact that this city became prominent through its Bishop Walther, son of Duke Hugo II. of Burgundy, and a possible confusion of Bassiniacum with Wasconia ; or the saga may have been attached to Lengers through the Sarmatae who settled there in the fourth century and were regarded, like Walther, as fugitives of the Huns. It seems more likely, however, that Lengers came to be regarded as the home of Walther at the period when it formed the most prominent border city of Carolingia (Kerlingen) on the old time-worn route through the Vosges, when Carolingia, the realm of Charles, bordered Lotharingia, that of Lothar (cf. Droysen, Hist. Atlas). That Lengers was a Burgundian city of the Vosges may have favored its choice as Walther's home (cf. Heinzel, 'Walthersage,' 70).

Walther of the Wasgenstein.—This designation is found in R, Ths, and doubtless came from the scene of Walther's combat with Gunther's men. Vosagus, as the pass is called in W, is traceable to to the Vosegus [157] and Vogesus of Roman times. Compare Lucan, Pharsalia I. 397–8 :

"Castraque quae Vogesi curvam super
ardua rupem
Pugnaces pictis cohibebant Lingones
armis "

---

156 ' Walthersage,' 73.

157 Cf. 'Vosego,' 'Mons Vosegus,' Bouguet, i, 142; 'Nec non Argentoratum vicinum castellum ad Vosegi radices ' (A.D. 356) Bouquet, i, 725. For the location of the Wasgenstein near the village Niedersteinbach on the border of Alsace-Lorraine, cf. Scheffel-Holder, S. 158 ff.

with the description in W (490 ff). The defile seems to have come to be regarded later as extending over the whole *mons Vosegus* as a district. Hence Wasgenstein as Walther's land in Ths is only natural and consistent with the later confusion, of which Ths affords many examples. With the Wasgenstein as Walther's land is connected, doubtless, the name of W's sword 'Wasge'; the account of his being set over Gerimsheim (Gernsheim in Hassen?) by Ermanric (Ths c. 151); of his presence (as guest?) in Breisach (AT, 307); of his German origin (AT, 426); and of his relation as vassal of Theoderic (AT, 11). This last conception of Walther is to be traced probably to Upper Germany, particularly to Alemannia, where Theoderic was regarded as the protector of the Upper Germans against the Franks.

Walther as Ermanric's Nephew.—The conception of Walther as the son of Ermanric's sister in Ths, and that of Hildegunde as the daughter of Iarl Ilías of Greece is due to the later confusion of Saga elements by the combination of different cycles into a great composite narrative such as we have in the Thidrekssaga.[158] Walther came to be regarded as Ermanric's kinsman, doubtless after the latter appeared in the Saga as Theoderic's foe, that is, from the tenth century on.[159] The view that Walther was connected with the Lombard cycle is consistent with this, inasmuch as Lombard heroes were regarded as being at Ermanric's Court.[160] Indeed, the Lombard conquest of Italy, united in the popular mind with the East Roman overthrow of the East Goths by Justinian, is doubtless reflected in the conception of Ermanric as Roman Emperor and Theoderic's foe.

Walther as a Pole.—The general characteristics of the Walther Saga which have passed over into the Polish versions, have preserved reminiscences of Walther's origin from Kerlingen, and of his companion, the fair Hildegunde, at the court of a Frankish (—Burgundian) king, and of the hero's great prowess in combat.

Walther the Hun.—In the 'Chanson de Roland' (cf. App. ii.) mention is made of 'Gualtiers de l'Hum,'* as one of the faithful defenders of the cause of Charlemagne. Heinzel makes use of this as an argument for the conception of Walther as of Hunish origin. But it is rather to be interpreted as meaning 'Walther from or of the Hun (or Huns),' and thus designating the most characteristic fact of his career; namely, his exile among the Huns. That this Walther from the Huns should fight, as king of Aquitania, upon the side of Charlemagne against the Infidels, is perfectly intellegible. Compare Hadubraht's scornful words to Hildebrant, 'alter Hún' ('Hildebrantslied,' v. 38). So, in 'Rolandslied,' 'Walthere the Wigant,' who

158 For the French elements in Ths, cf. Heinzel, ' Über d. Ostgoth. Heldensage,' W. S. B. cxix, 83.   159 *Ibid.*, 55.   160 *Ibid.*, 9.   *Or de Hums.

is slain in combat and avenged by Roland (6590 ff.), has a parallel in 'Walther der wîgant' (BD, 6423, etc.); in 'Walthêr der degen' (AT, 317, etc.); in 'Walther der ellensrîch' (DF, 7360, etc.). Compare also, 'Manu fortis' of Ekkehard, and 'Robustus,' 'Wdaly,' and 'Udatny' (Procosius) in the Polish versions.

In the course of the discussion based upon a score of clearly defined literary survivals of the Walther saga, we have shown that the elements of the Saga are essentially historical, belonging, for the most part, to the period of heroic struggle of the Germanic peoples of the West with the Huns ; that the original form of the Saga probably developed as early as the fifth century ; assumed a strongly Frankish-Burgundian color of the Merovingian period in the Waltharius version ; became itself the theme of a M. H. G. epic ; was connected with the great heroic cycles of the 'Nibelungenlied,' of the epic accounts of Ermanric, Theoderic, and Charlemagne. Thus we have justified the view that Walther of Aquitaine belongs to the historical group of heroic characters with whom all mediæval tradition associated him, and not to the realm of myth and fable.

BIBLIOGRAPHY.*

†ALTHOF, H.—Kritische Bemerkungen zum Waltharius. Germania 37, 1 ff. 1892.

AMPÈRE, J. J.—Histoire littéraire de la France. ii. 154 ff. 2 ed. Paris, 1867.

BAEHR, J.—Geschichte der römischen Litteratur im karolingischen Zeitalter. pp. 133–138. Carlsruhe, 1840.

BACMEISTER.—Die Geschichte von Walther und Hildegund, wie Walther durch die Nagelprobe seine Braut gewinnt und aus Hunnenland entführt, nebst dem groszen Kampf im Wasichenwald. Reutlingen, 1864.

BARTSCH, K.—Kleine Mittheilungen. Germania, xii, p. 88. Wien, 1867.

BAECHTOLD.—Geschichte der deutschen Literatur in der Schweiz, i, 40 ff. Frauenfeld, 1887.

BECKER, AUG.—Der Schauplatz des Walthariliedes. Westermanns Monatshefte, n. 344, 345. 1885.

BUGGE, S.—Tidskrift for Philologie og Pedagogik. viii, 72 ff.; 305 ff.

———, Studien über die Entstehung der nordischen Götter- und Heldensagen. 168 ff. München, 1889.

Cox and JONES.—Popular Romances of the Middle Ages. Am. Ed., New York, 1880.

DELFFS, S.—Ekkehard, a tale of the tenth century. Collection of German authors. Vol. xxi. Chap. xxiv: "The Song of Waltari." Leipzig, 1872.

DIETER, F.—Die Walderefragmente und die ursprüngliche Gestalt der Walthersage. Anglia, x, p. 227 ff. Halle, 1888.

FALCKENHEINER, C. P. G.—De Walthario Aquitano, latino illo decimi saeculi carmine et de natura variaque specie fabulae in hoc poemate nobis exhibitae dissertatio inauguralis .... Marburgi Hassorum, 1846.

FAURIEL.—Histoire de la poésie provençale, i, 269. Leipzig and Paris, 1847.

FISCHER, FR. CHR. J.--Sitten und Gebräuche der Europäer in v und vi Jahrhundert. Aus einem alten Denkmale beschrieben. Frankfurt an der Oder, 1784. Lips., 1792.

*In the arrangement of the works on the Walther saga, the alphabetical order has been chosen in order to avoid repetition of titles. †Came too late to be used.

Fischer, Fr. Chr. J.—De prima expeditione Attilae . . ac de rebus gestis Waltharii. Lips., 1780.

——, Continuatio ex manuscripto. Lips., 1797.

Fischer, Jos.—Zu den Waldere-Fragmenten. Diss. Breslau, 1886.

Gautier, L.—Les Épopées françaises, i, p. 104. Paris, 1878.

Genthe.—Deutsche Dichtungen des Mittelalters. B. iii. Eisleben, 1846.

Gervinus.—Geschichte der deutschen Dichtung. pp. 82–85. 1871.

Geyder, A.—Walther von Aquitanien. Eine altdeutsche Heldensage im Versmasze des Nibelungenliedes. Breslau, 1854.

——, Anmerkungen zum Waltharius. *Zs. f. d. A.* ix, pp. 145–166. 1853.

Goedeke, K.—Grundriss zur Geschichte der deutschen Dichtung. 2. Aufl. i, 11. Dresden 1884.

Grein, Ch. W. M.—Beovulf nebst den Fragmenten Finnsburg und Valdere. p. 76 ff. Cassel & Göttingen, 1867.

Grimm, J.—Ospirin, die Herchen und Hagano. Altd. Wäld. ii, 42 ff. Frankfurt, 1815. Cf. Kl. SS. v, 286–8; *Altd. Blätter*, ii, 324.

——, und Schmeller, Andr.—Lateinische Gedichte des x und xi Jahrhunderts, 1–126, 383–5. Göttingen, 1838.

Grimm, J.—Die Heldensage von Alphere und Walthere. *Zs. f. d. A.* v, p. 2 ff. Leipzig, 1845.

——, W.—Deutsche Heldensage. 1829. pp. 29, 302, 367. 3 Aufl.,1889.

——, Zur Geschichte des Reims. p. 148.

——, Graf Rudolf. 1te Aufl. 1828; 2te Aufl. 1844.

Haigh, D. H.—The Anglo-Saxon Sagas, 125 ff. London, 1861.

Havet, L.—Cours élémentaire de métrique grecque et latine. Paris, 1886.

Heinrich.—Hist. de la litt. allemande, i, p. 30.

Heinzel, Vigfusson and Powell—Corpus Poeticum Boreale. *Anz. f. d. A.* xi, p. 67 ff. Berlin, 1885.

Heinzel.—Ueber die Walthersage. *Wiener Sitzungsberichte* cxvii. (Sep., Wien, 1888).

d'Héricault, Ch.—Essai sur l'origine de l'épopée française et sur son hist. au moyen âge. Paris, 1860.

Hyltén-Cavallius, G. O.—Sagan om Didrik af Bern. Stockholm, 1850–54.

Jordan.—Der epische Vers der Germanen. Frankfurt a. M. u. Leipzig. 1868.

v. KARAJAN, TH. GR.—Ueber die Bruchstücke eines deutschen Walther in Strophenform aus dem 13. Jahrh. Der Schatzgraeber. Leipzig, 1842. Cf. *Zs.f. d. A.*, ii, 216 ff.; Hagens *Germ.*, v, 114.

KLEMM.—Attila nach der Geschichte, Saga und Legende dargestellt durch G. Fr. Klemm. Leipzig, 1827.

KNOOP, O.—Die deutsche Walthersage und die polnische Sage von Walther und Helgunde. 1887. (Cf. also v. Antoniewicz, *Afd. A.* xiv, 112 ff.)

KOBERSTEIN, A.—Grundriss der Geschichte der deutschen Nationallitteratur, i, § 34, p. 49. 5te Aufl. 1872.

KÖGEL, R.—Waltharius Manu Fortis. Paul's *Grundriss* ii, 181 ff. Strassburg, 1890.

KÖLBING, E.—Die Waldere-fragmente. *Englishe Studien*, v, 240, 292-3. Heilbronn, 1882.

LACHMANN, K.—Kritik der Sage von den Nibelungen. *Rh. Mus. f. Ph.*, iii, 435-64. Kl. SS. i.

LEYSER, H. J.—Bericht an d. Mitgl. d. dtsch. Gesellsch. S. 41 ff. Leipzig, 1837.

LIEBRECHT.—Zur slav. Waltharisage. *G.* xi, 172 f.

LINNIG.—Walther von Aquitanien. Heldengedicht in zwölf Gesängen, mit Erläuterungen uud Beitragen zur Heldensage und Mythologie. Paderborn, 1869. 2. Aufl. 1884.

MANSSEN, W. J,—Ekkehard, een verhaal uit de tiende eeuw. Tweede deel, tiende hoofdstuk : het Waltarilied. Rotterdam, 1870.

MASSMANN, H. F.—Walther und Hildegunde. *Zs. f. d. A.* ii, p. 216 ff. Leipzig, 1842.

DU MÉRIL, E.—Poésies populaires. pp. 313 ff., 428. Paris, 1843.

MEYER v. KRONAU.—Casus S. Galli. 285. No. 959.

MEYER, W.—Philologische Bemerkungen zum Waltharius. *Sitzber. d. bair. Ak.* S. 358 ff. München, 1873.

MEYER, P.—*Bibl. de l'École des Chartes.* 5, ii, 1884-89.

MOLTER, F.—Beyträge zur Gesch. und Liter. aus einigen Hss. der Markgräfl. Badischen Bibliothek, pp. 212-268. Frankfurt, 1798.

——, Prinz Walther von Aquitainen.—Ein Heldengedicht aus dem sechsten Jahrhundert. Aus einem lateinischen Codex der Markgräfl. Badischen Bibliothek metrisch übersetzt. Carlsruhe, 1782 (u. 1818). Cf. also Meusel's 'Hist. Lit. f. d. Jahr 1782,' 370-4.

MONE, F. J.—*Quellen u. Forschungen.* S. 182 ff. Aachen, 1830. *Anz.* v, (1836), 415. *Frankf. Archiv* ii, 92 ff.

200   WALTHER OF AQUITAINE.

MÜLLENHOFF, K.—Zur Geschichte der Nibelungensage. *Zs. f. d. A.* x, 163 ff. Berlin, 1856.

———, Zeugnisse und Excurse, vii, xxviii, xxxi. *Zs. f. d. A.* xii, 264 ff.; 367 ff.; 383. Berlin, 1865. Cf. *Zs.f.d.A.* xxx, 232 ff.

MÜLLER, W.—Mythologie der Deutschen Heldensage. Heilbronn, 1886.

———, Zur Mythologie der Grechischen und Deutschen Heldensage. Heilbronn, 1889.

MÜLLER, E.—Zum Waltharius. *Zs. f. d. Ph.* ix, p. 161 ff. Halle, 1878.

MUELLER, L.—De Re Metrica. Leipzig, 1861.

NEIGEBAUR.—Waltharius poema saeculi decimi . . . Monachii, 1853.

NAPIONE, G. F. G.—Opera de Piemontesi illustri., t. iv, p. 165. Torino, 1784.

NEHRING, W.—Ueber Walther u. Hildegunde. *Archiv f. slav. Phil.* viii, S. 352.

NÖSSELT.—*Hallische Anz.* 1780. St. 61, S. 484.

ORELLIUS.—Epistola critica ad Madvigium. 1830.

OSTERWALD.—Erzählungen aus der alten deutschen Welt. Th. iii Halle, Waisenhaus, 1850.

PANNENBORG, A.—*Göttting. Gel. Anzeigen,* 1873. Stück 29. S. 1121–1141.

PARIS, GASTON.—Histoire poétique de Charlemange. p. 50.

PEIPER, R.—Ekkehardi I. Waltharius. Berolini, 1873.

———, *Jenaer Litt. Z.,* No. 36., 1875.

PIPER.—Die älteste deutsche Litteratur bis um das Jahr 1050. 272, 274, 317. Berlin und Stuttgart, 1884.

PROVANA, L. G.—Waltharius (in Mon. Hist. Patr,, SS. iii). 1848.

DE REIFFENBERG.—Des Légendes poétiques relatives aux invasions des Huns dans les Gaules, et du poème de Waltharius. *Bulletin de l' Académie royale des sciences et belles-lettres de Bruxelles,* v (1838), Nos. 597–613. *Revue de Bruxelles,* 1838, Dec. pp. 1–33; 1839, Mars, pp. 28–49; Août, pp. 35–64.

———, Waltharius manu fortis ou Walther d'Aquitaine. *Annuaire de la bibl. roy. de Belgique,* ii, 1841, pp. 45–106; iii, 1842, pp. 39–174; v, 1844, pp. 35–152.

RICHTER, A.—Walther und Hildegunda. Holt & Co., N. Y.

RIEGER.—Alt- und angelsächsisches Lesebuch (Waldere text) 1861.

Rischka, R.—Verhältniss der poln. Saga v. Walgiers Wdaly zu den deutschen Sagen von Walther von Aquitanien. Brody, 1880.

San-Marte.—Die polnische Königssage. Berlin, 1848.

——, Walther von Aquitanien. Magdeburg, 1853.

——, Zarncke's Literar-Ctrbl. Nr. 25 Sp. 790–2, 1873.

Scheffel.—Ekkehard. Eine Geschichte aus dem zehnten Jahrhundert. Cap. 24. Das Waltarilied. Frankfurt, Meidinger. 1855.

Scheffel und Holder.—Waltharius. Stuttgart, 1874.

Scherer, W.—Der Wasgenstein in der Sage. Vortrag gehalten in der Versammlung des Vogesenclubs der Section Strassburg den 6. Dec. 1873. Mittheilungen aus dem Vogesenclub. Nr. 2. 1 Apr., 1874, Strassburg.

Schönbach, A.—Zu Walther und Hildegunde. Zs. f. d. A. xxv, 81. Berlin, 1881.

——, Waltharius. Zs. f. d. A. xxxiii, 340 ff. 1889.

Schoepflin.—Alsatia illustrata. i.

Schwab, Gustav.—Walther und Hiltgunt, epische Dichtung. Nach dem Lateinischen des Ekkehard. ii Band. Stuttgart und Tübingen, 1829.

Schweitzer, C.—De Poemate Latino Walthario. Lutetiae, 1889.

Simrock, K.—Das Heldenbuch. iii Band. Das kleine Heldenbuch. i Walther u. Hildegunde. 3 Aufl. Stuttgart und Augsburg, 1874.

Stephens, G.—Two Leaves of King Walderes Lay. London, 1860.

Stöber.—Walther von Wasgenstein und Hildegunde, eine altdeutsche Heldendichtung. (Alsatia, 51–73). 1852.

Symons, B.—Waltharisage. Paul's Grundriss ii, 57 ff. Strassburg, 1889.

Uhland.—Walther und Hildegund. (Schriften, i. 428 ff. Stuttgart, 1865.) Cf. Elsäss. Samstagsbl., xi, No. 29. 21. Juli, 1866.

Vogt, F.—Zur Salman- Morolfsage. Beiträge· zur Geschichte der deutschen Sprache und Literature, viii, 321 ff. Halle, 1882.

Wackernagel.—Geschichte der deutschen Litteratur. § 35, p. 71. 1848.

Wülcker.—Kleine angelsächs. Dichtungen, 8–10. 1879.

——, Grundriss zur Geschichte der angelsächs. Litteratur. i, 123; iii, 296–9. Leipzig, 1885.

Wülcker-Grein.—Bibliothek der Angel-Sächsischen Poesie. i, p. 7 ff. Kassel, 1881.*

* For editions of the 'Chronicon Novaliciense' cf. Muratori, 'Rev. Ital. Script.' II. p. ii, 704–6 and 'Antiq. Ital. Med. Aevi,' iii, 964 ff.; Pertz, 'Mon. Germ. Hist.' vii, 73–133. For the 'Thidrekssaga,' cf. Unger, Peringskiold, Müller (Sagabibliothek), and v. d. Hagen's 'Wilkina- und Niflunga Saga.' For the Polish, cf. texts above.

INDEX.

Adrian, 132.
Ælfhere, 3-4.
Ælfwine (Alboin) 171-2.
Ærminrikr, 165.
Aëtius, 161-2, 166-8, 179, 190.
Ætla, 3, 131.
Agano, 46, 132, 140.
Aigyna, 167-8.
Aktilia (Aktilius) 100.
Alf (Half) 171.
Alferius, 45, 132.
Alker, 68, 149, 170, 183.
Alldrian (Aldrian) 94, 144, 167.
Alphari, 192.
Alpharius, 172, 182.
Alpharides, 27, 29, 31-3, 37, 39, 41-2.
Alpharts Tod, 2, 83, 134, 142, 150, 175, 193-5.
Alphere, 7-8, 135, 155, 166, 171-2, 183-4, 192.
Alpher, 192.
Alpker, 78-9, 134.
Arinaldus, 119-20, 137, 145, 154, 178, 186.
Asinarius, 57.
Attila, 6-8, 15-16, 46, 50, 53, (in Susat cf. 178) 93-4, 98, 131-2, 136, 139-40, 144, 152, 155, 158, 161-6, 168, 170, 177-9, 183-4, 190-1.

Baldur, 188-9.
Bielski, 2, 114, 116, 137, 145, 153, 186.
Biterolf, 73-6, 86, 150, 187.
Biterolf und Dietleib, 2, 73, 134, 142, 150, 175, 183-4, 192-3.
Biterwulf, 102.
Bleda, 161.
Blœdelin, 79.
Boguphal (Chronicon) 2, 105, 116, 136, 144, 152, 155, 185.

Camelo, 20-3, 166, 175.
Chaerlingen, 72.
Chararicus, 169-70.
Childechinda, 171.
Cundharius, 46, 52-5, 132, 140, 148.

Deodric, 4, 165, 180.
Desiderius, 59.
Detzleff, 101-2.
Didrik, 102-4.
Dietleip, 78, 85.
Dietric, 158.
Dietrich, 78, 81-2, 84, 88, 165, 175, 187.
Dietrichs Flucht, 2, 89, 135, 143, 151, 175, 184, 187, 193, 195.

Eckwart, 88.
Eleuter, 31-2, 166.
Ekeurid, 25, 166.
Ekkehard I., 180-1, 186-7, 195.
Erca, 162-3, 165.
Ercha, 104.
Erchamboldus, 5.
Eriricus, 45, 132.
Erka, 98, 158.
Ermanric, 158-9, 165, 168, 178-9, 183-4, 187, 194-5.
Ermenrich, 175.
Ermentrik, 100-4.
Erminrikr, 93, 95-6, 98, 136, 152, 155.
Ermrich, 91.
Erpr, 99.
Etzel (Ezel) 64, 68-9, 72, 75, 77-80, 85, 91, 132-5, 165, 180, 182-3.

Freyja, 188.

Geraldus, 5, 180.
Gerimshem, 102, 194.
Gerwicus, 29, 166, 175.
Gibiche, 85, 87.
Gibica, 162, 165.
Gibicho, 6, 8, 18, 131, 139, 155, 165, 179.
Gibico, 46, 132, 158, 165 (Gybichus 46, 53).
Gifica, 180.
Gotelinde, 80.
Graz Fragment, 2, 65, 133, 141, 149, 177, 181-3, 192.
Gualtarius, 5.
Gualterius, 173.
Gualtiers de l'Hum, 124-6, 194.

Gudrun, 183.
Guillaume au court nez, 182.
Gunderic, 159.
Gundericus, 164.
Gundicarius, 163-5, 170.
Gunlaug Saga, 2.
Guntharius, 6, 17, 19, 21-2, 24, 26,
     39, 42, 131, 139, 147, 158, 165,
     175, 179.
Gunthere, 36, 139, 147.
Gunther, 69, 72, 76, 78, 80-1, 90, 132,
     149, 156, 177, 180, 183-4, 189.
Guntiarius, 164.
Guðhere, 3, 131, 165.

Hadawart, 26, 116, 175.
Hagano, 6, 8-9, 18-21, 27, 31, 33-5,
     38-42, 46, 52-5, 131, 139, 147-8,
     179-80.
Haganus, 46.
Hagathien, 22. (Hagathiu 166).
Hagen, 89, 100-1, 155-6, 166-9, 171,
     175, 179-80, 182-3, 190.
Hagena, 4, 131, 139.
Hagene, 64-6, 72, 75, 87, 132-3,
     140, 148.
Hagen von Tronege, 169.
Hoegni (Haugni) 94, 95, 144, 152.
Helche, 68, 72, 75, 77, 89, 91, 133-5,
     158, 162, 165, 183.
Helgunda, 105-9, 119-22, 136, 138,
     144, 146, 152, 154, 187.
Heligunda, 110-18, 137-8, 145-6, 153.
Helmnod, 31, 166, 175 (von Tuscân)
     83, 175.
Herbort, 82.
Herche, 165.
Heriricus, 6-8, 42, 131, 165, 169-71.
Hermeric, 159.
Hermericus, 164.
Herminericus, 159.
Hilde, 69, 133, 168, 170-1, 183, 189.
Hildebrant, 64, 77, 80, 83-7, 194.
Hildegulla, 100.
Hildegunde, 1, 51, 53-4, 60, 62-3,
     67, 70, 75-6, 81-2, 142, 155-6, 166,
     168, 170-1, 176, 179-80, 182-6,
     188-9, 194.
Hildegunna, 100.
Hildegunt, 123, 140-1, 149.
Hildico, 166, 170.
Hilgunda, 46, 48.
Hilldibrandr, 98-9.
Hilldigundr, 93-4, 136, 144, 152.
Hiltegunt, 65, 68-9, 71, 77, 80, 88,
     132-4.
Hiltgunt, 6, 8, 11-12, 15, 18-20, 43,
     131, 139, 147.
Hlod and Augantheow, (Lay) 2,
     104.

Horand, 187,
Hotherus (Hothar) 188-9.
Huc von Tenemarc, 83-4.
Hunwald, 182.
Hyllebrandh, 103-4.

Ildegunda, 45, 132, 140, 148.
Ildico, 162-3, 170.
Iarl Ilias (of Greece) 93, 136, 184,
     194.
Ilsam, 83.
Isunger, 97.
Ivaldi, 189.

Kimo, 23, 166, 175.
Kreka, 162-3, 165.
Krîmhilt, 87-8.

Mimming, 3, 102, 180, 189.

Nagelring, 102.
Nauðung, 98.
Nebulones (Franci) 54, 177.
Nibelungenlied, 1, 6, 4, 132, 140,
     148, 167-8, 175, 177, 181, 183-4,
     192, 195.
Niesiecki, 2, 116, 138, 146, 154, 186,
Niðhad, 4.
Nordungh, 104.
Novalician Chronicle, 1, 44, 132,
     140, 148, 177, 182, 192.

Odhur, 188.
Odin, 188.
Odoacer, 160.
Old Swedish Version, 100, 185.
Ortwin (of Metz) 68, 99, 149, 175.
Ospirin, 9, 51, 131, 165.

Pandarides, 24.
Paprocki, 2, 110, 117, 119, 137, 145.
     153, 185-6.
Pataurid, 27, 29, 166, 175.
Procosius, 2, 118, 138, 146, 154, 195.

Rabenschlacht, 2, 91, 135, 143, 151,
     184, 192-3.
Ramunc, 80.
Randolf, 30, 166, 175.
Rathaldus, 60.
Ratherius, 60.
Reinalld, 98.
Renaldh, 103.
Rôdgher, 103-4.
Rosengarten, 2, 85, 135, 143, 151,
     193.
Rosengarten Fragments, 87, 193.
Roðingaeir, 98.
Ruedegêr, 75, 77-82, 176.
Runga, 98.

Rynga, 112-13, 18, 121-2, 178, 186.

Scaramundus, 23-4, 166, 175.
Seveka, 103-4.
Sifka, 98-9.
Sifrit, 81, 87.
St. William, 182.

Tanastus, 31-3, 166, 175.
Theoderic (the East Goth) 159-60, 165, 168, 179, 181, 184-5, 191, 194-5.
Theoderic (the West Goth) 160-1.
Theoderic II., 160-1.
Thetleifer, 95-7, 152, 179.
Thidrekssaga, 2, 93, 136, 144, 152, 155, 177, 179, 183-94.
Thiðrecr, 93, 97-100, 165.
Tidrik, 103.
Trogus, 31-3, 166, 175.

Valdar, 104.
Valltari (af Uaskasteini) 93-100, 136, 144, 152,
Valterus, 173.
Vienna Fragment, 2, 67, 133, 141, 149, 177, 181-4, 192-3.
Vildefer, 104, 152.
Volkere, 67-9, 72, 183.
Von dem übelen Wîbe, 123, 177, 187.

Waifarius, 172, 182.
Walaricus, 174.
Walcer, 114-16, 137-8, 145-6, 153.
Walcerus, 110-13, 137, 145, 153.
Walcherius, 174.
Walderada, 172.
Waldere, 1, 3-4, 131, 139, 147, 177, 179-81, 183-5. 190, 192.
Waldericus, 174.
Walaërius, 174.
Waldgierz, 188.
Waldhere, 172.
Walgarius, 174.
Walgerz (Wdaly) 116, 118-22, 138, 146, 154, (Udatny) 195.
Waltari, 172.

Walterius, 173.
Walterus, 173.
Walterus (Robustus) 105-9, 136, 144, 152, 155, 187, 195.
Walter aff Waldsken, 100.
" af Wasekensten, 100-4.
" (Wdaƚy) 105, 119, 187, 195, Walthari, 38, 180, 182, 192.
Waltharius (Waltarius) 1, 5, 8-21, 23-9, 33-41, 43-52, 54-61, 131-2, 139-48, 155, 165, 169, 172-5, 177-84, 186-7, 190-5.
Walther (Walthêr) 62, 65, 67, 70, 72-6, 78-82, 123, 127-9, 133-4, 140-51, 155, 165-8, 170-1, 174-6, 182-94.
Walthere, 172.
Walther von Kerlingen, 83-4, 87, 90, 134-5, 193.
Walther der Lengesaere, 91-2, 135, 193.
Walther von Lengers, 89, 90, 135, 193.
Walther von Spâne, 64, 68, 132, 192-3.
Walther von der Vogelweide, 1, 183.
Walther von dem Wasgenstein, 85-6, 135, 193.
Walther und Hildegunde, 1, 62.
Weland, 3-4, 30, 147, 180-1, 184-5.
Welsung, 74.
Wenezlan, 187.
Widia, 4.
Widike, 102-4.
Willdifer, 99.
Wilkinasaga, 2.
Wisƚaw, 114-15, 121-2, 153-4, 186-7.
Wislimierz, 111-13, 116, 154, 186-7.
Wislomirus, 118, 154.
Witige, 88, 90.
Wizlan, 187.
Wójcicki, 2, 119, 138, 146, 154, 186, Wolter, 101.
Wurhardus (Ewurhardus) 24, 166, 175.
Wyslaus, 105, 107-9, 116, 152, 156, 178, 187.

ERRATA.

Page 1 read *Nibelungenlied,*—p. 3 (v. 20) *ðu to,*—p. 4 (v. 23) *þonne yfle* W,—p. 5 (note) *incipit,*—p. 9 (128) *magna,* (141) *cepitque,*—p. 12 (251) *exilii,* (266) *Panno-,*—p. 13 (299) *auram* for aurum P,—p. 14 (318) *bacchica* for bachica P,—p. 15 (381) *merentia* for maerentia P, (384) *harena* for arena P,—p. 16 (416) *strages,* (421) *accersitas,* (429) *Pannonica,*—p. 18 (481) *tardate,* (490) *tum* for tunc P,—p. 20 (585) *uolat rapidoque,*—p. 21 (615) *recepto,*—p. 22 (631) *praelia* for proelia P, (634) *consistant,* (638) *propinqum* for -quum P,—p. 24 (710) *pre-* for prae- P,— p. 25 (756) *Sax-,*—p. 27 (821) *Hec* for Haec P,—p. 29 (924) *tela,* (931) *cuspis* for cuspes P,—p. 35 (1130) *Phebus* for Phoebus P, (1141) *conpexibus,* (1160) *hac* for ac,—p. 36 (1165) *ad* for at, (1188) *Olimpo* for Olympo P,—p. 37 (1204) *pre-* for prae- P, (1231) *Protinus* for Protenus P,—p. 38 (1257) *Quippe,*—p. 40 (1328) *citius,* (1330) *saeui,* (1350) *Ilico,*— p. 41 (1386) *leuis* for laeuis P,—p. 42 (1404) *Auarenses,* (1406) *tergentes* for tergentis P.

Read *con-* for com- P in W vv. 140, 141, 144, 274, 287, 1126; and *in-* for im- P vv. 178, 1336.

Page 44 read *stegmate, perpulcrum, monacorum,* variants,—p. 45 *scole, monacorum, extenditque, vero,*—p. 50 *horreret,*—p. 52 *reliquorum, Vespere,*—p. 53 *oculos, Ilico,*—p. 54 *nunciare,*—p. 56 *monasterio, oportunis, skillia,*—p. 57 *sumptui, invasionem, ut celerius,*—p. 58 *ferens, Waltharius, inquid, summens, predatores, iniuriam, calciamenta,*—p. 59 *inportunis, calciamenta, ilico, penetentiam, leto, evo, vultu,*—p. 60 *discipline, que, in* summitate, *prenominata* for premonita, *teporem* for temporem,—p. 61 *ante* for aute, *pretaxata,*—p. 64 *unt, trâten,* caesura before *sô* in 358. 2. 3.—p. 66 omit) after *swíchen,*—p. 68 (6. 3) *gŭte,* (7. 3) *gesehen,*—p. 69 (19. 4) *öch,*—p. 70 (1. 4) *mŭlich,* (2. 3) *kvene,* (2. 4) *krône,* (3. 2) *gŭter,* (4. 4) *vö,*—p. 71 (9. 3) verren vnde n*ahen* man der vog*ele vie,*—72 (16. 4) *vn̄,*—p. 73 *der* for de,—p. 74 hiubel an *der hant, sâzen* for szâen,—p. 75 *fridemeister,*—p. 76 *die sint,*—p. 77 mir *die* tohter,—p. 78 *alsô gemuot,*—p. 80 müezens *uns* die, *getân,*— p. 81 *Walthêres, drizic,*—p. 82 *Dietrichen,*—p. 83 *münech, hin,*—p. 84 *münich,*—p. 86 *grôzer, Wasgensteine,*—p. 87 *mit,*—p. 88 cf. *Graff Wallther von Waxenstein* (*Zeitschrift* 11. 243ff.); and *Walthr ein helt võ Kerling* (*Zeitschrift* 11. 552). *Eckwart,*—p. 93 *Thidrekssaga,*—p. 96 U. for N., *vil* for vill, *herra* havuð,—p. 97 *Nv* for Ov, *þiðricr* for þiðicr, *rið* for riþ,—p. 99 *oc* for ok,—p. 106 *fluminis,*— p. 107 *anxiata,*—p. 108 *amasio,*—p. 110 *Paprocki, pisaná, ono szczéście,* Tam *mu,*—p. 111 *Niemiec, królewicowi, dodawała,*—p. 112 Walcerowéj żałując schronił do *komory, także,*—p. 113 *ale, uczynił, zraki,*—p. 115 *poimawszy,* nad *nim,*—p. 116 comma after Paprocki, *przy* for przyy and prry, na *kamieniu, w roku* 1242, *St.*

Benedicti, nauká (in note),—p. 123 hagen*büechin,*—p. 124 add note: Reprinted from Gautier, 'La Chanson de Roland,' Douzième Edition, —p. 125 *Respunt* for Rcspunt,—p. 127, 3271 for 3217, (3376) *werthen,*— p. 131 (3) who *is* too young,—p. 158 *patentes* for potentes(?),—p. 160 *Theoderic,*—p. 161 for variant dates of Attila's rule; cf. Jahn, 'Gesch. d. Burg.,' i, 340 ff.,—p. 162 περίβολον, εὐθύτητα, γαμετῆς, Θεράπαιναι, ἀντικρὺ, ὑπεξῇειν, οἰκήματα, ὧν τοῖς, φρουροῖς, τόπον, Ἀττήλα,—p. 163 ἡμᾶς, δὲ τὸ, δεῖπνον,—p. 166 cf. the names *Agano* of St. Maurice anno 523 (Pardessus 103, 104 (genuineness of document questioned) and *Agione.* P. Diac., D.G. L., vi, 1. 3,—p. 168 *römischen* Generale,—p. 169 cf. *Hereric* (Beowulf, 2207),—p. 171 *Ælfhere* (Beowulf, 2605),—p. 173 *Frankish-Gallic,*—p. 174 *promovere,*—p. 175 'der Junge,' Ἐλεύθερος.

DATE DUE

5/27			
GAYLORD			PRINTED IN U.S.A.